Andy Hinds

ACTING SHAKESPEARE'S LANGUAGE

T0321549

OBERON BOOKS
LONDON
WWW.OBERONBOOKS.COM

First published in 2015 by Oberon Books Ltd
521 Caledonian Road, London N7 9RH
Tel: +44 (0) 20 7607 3637 / Fax: +44 (0) 20 7607 3629
e-mail: info@oberonbooks.com
www.oberonbooks.com

A catalogue record for this book is available from the British
Library.

PB ISBN: 978-1-78319-008-9
E ISBN: 978-1-78319-507-7

Cover design by James Illman

'Andy Hinds offers a rich and detailed path towards a precise contact with the challenge of speaking and inhabiting Shakespeare's language. This book is an immensely useful resource for anyone teaching, speaking and acting Shakespeare.' **Ralph Fiennes, Actor**

'Brilliantly practical and precise in exploring the ways students/actors (young and old) can get to grips with the extraordinary language of Shakespeare in a real way.' **Ciarán Hinds, Actor**

'The complete "Acting Shakespeare" toolkit. Takes you firmly by the hand, and guides you expertly (and enjoyably) through every aspect of bringing life to Shakespeare's lines. Ideal for any actor or student preparing speeches for auditions.' **Joely Richardson, Actor**

'At last! *Acting Shakespeare's Language* is having your own personal acting coach at your fingertips. Each chapter is a compelling acting class; every page is a tantalizing lesson. Mr. Hinds provides a wide range of options, skills, and participatory exercises about how to make dynamic choices to unlock the humanity of Shakespeare's words. This book is an essential.'
Kenneth Noel Mitchell, Associate Chair of External Outreach at Tisch School of the Arts at NYU, Head of Acting at New Studio on Broadway

'This is an immensely useful book, and I feel impelled to rhapsodise a little! It is crammed with common sense and so beneficial to the actor. It is thorough, methodical, and an excellent gateway to many of the plays, providing an island of secure knowledge from which the student is encouraged to venture outward. Andy's voice is authoritative, warm, encouraging and clear: never condescending, rigorously demanding and sometimes rising to a captivating eloquence.'
Geoff Bullen, Associate Director at RADA

'A very direct, clear, lively and logical method of speaking Shakespeare. Practical and user friendly, this book opens wide the door for anyone bold enough to step through and speak Shakespeare's words out loud and with conviction, be it in a classroom or a rehearsal room.'
Cathal Quinn, Director of Voice and Speech at National Academy of Dramatic Art, Ireland

'Refreshingly direct, clear and passionate. This insightful and practical workbook guides you through the challenges and delights of verse and prose speaking. *Acting Shakespeare's Language* will be of particular help to the actor or student actor encountering Shakespeare for the first time.'
Andrea Ainsworth, Director of Voice and Text at National Theatre of Ireland (The Abbey)

'*Acting Shakespeare's Language* is written in a clear, practical and supportive manner. Mr. Hinds excels at helping young actors avoid many of the pitfalls of performing Shakespeare. His gentle but firm reminders that *doing* always trumps *emoting* will go a long way in ensuring exciting rather than indulgent future productions of Shakespeare's plays.'

Joseph Olivieri, Head of Acting, School of Theater, Film and Television, UCLA

'A book full of insight and wisdom. It provides readers with practical step-by-step instructions on how to engage with the language. It is full of useful tips and exercises, but Hinds is sensitive enough to present them in such a way as to allow room for discovery. His exercises engage the mind, voice and body but are simple to follow and can be applied to any character or speech.'

Paul Meade, Teacher of Acting and Classical Text at National Academy of Dramatic Art, Ireland

'*Acting Shakespeare's Language* makes for compelling reading for teachers, directors, actors alike. It is so accessible, so comprehensive – a book written and structured in such a way that the reader is drawn into a fascinating and hugely rewarding journey. For drama teachers, both experienced and new, and their students, this book takes away the fear and trepidation that so often accompanies the study and performance of Shakespeare. Block by block, the book builds to a fortress of water-tight performance skills, insights and nous. A superb Shakespearian toolkit.'

Emer Casey, Director at Drama For All Stages, Dublin Board Member at Speech and Drama Teachers of Ireland

'*Acting Shakespeare's Language* will be as valuable to university and secondary level Drama teachers and students (from beginner to advanced), as it will be to youth theatres, and to those auditioning for drama school. It creates a sense of the intimate workshop – the advice is precise, direct, friendly and approachable, never patronising or obscure, always concrete. Ideal for lone study, for coaching one to one, or teaching in a class or group.'

Colm Hefferon, Lecturer in Drama Education at Dublin City University

'Too often the discussion about acting Shakespeare is polarised between the iambic fundamentalists on the one hand who emphasise form above everything else, and method actors who say that the only thing that matters is the psychological content. Andy Hinds' brilliant new book shows that good acting in Shakespeare demands both. It's an ideal guide to actors (and directors) approaching the challenge for the first time, but also for the more experienced who want to refresh their skills.'

Stephen Unwin, Founder/Director of English Touring Company, Artistic Director of Rose Theatre, Kingston

CONTENTS

Introduction   xiii

A note on punctuation   xiv

'His and her' etc.   xiv

Chapter One
QUESTIONS, ORDERS AND EXPLANATIONS   1

Objectives   1

Distinguishing 'immediate' and 'overall' objectives   2

Order, explanation or question?   3

Mixing of questions, orders and explanations   6

    Playing explanations, questions and orders 1
    – Romeo and Beatrice   7

'Real' and 'rhetorical' questions   8

    Playing rhetorical questions 1 – Rosalind   9

    Playing rhetorical questions 2 – Paulina   10

    Playing explanations, questions and orders 2
    – Antony and Helena   11

Explanations within orders   13

    Playing explanations within orders
    – Antony and Lady Anne   13

Orders played as explanations   14

Explanations played as orders   15

Explanations within questions   15

    Playing explanations within questions – Edmund   16

KEY POINTS   17

Chapter Two
OPPOSITIONS   18

Oppositions within individual sentences   18

Playing oppositions   19

    'Exaggerate then ease off' exercise – Rosalind et al. 19

Shared oppositions   20

    Playing shared oppositions – Helena and Hermia   20

Speeches built around oppositions   21

    Playing multiple-oppositions within speeches
    – Richard the Third   21

KEY POINTS   23

Chapter Three

IMAGERY AND IMAGISTIC LANGUAGE   **24**

    Play the concrete surface of the image – Romeo   24

    'Addressing a child' exercise – Duchess of Gloucester   25

    Playing imagistic language – Oberon and Hamlet   26

    Playing abstract or 'idea' images – Portia   28

KEY POINTS   29

Chapter Four

ALLITERATION, ASSONANCE AND ONOMATOPOEIA   **30**

Alliteration   30

Assonance   30

    Playing assonance and alliteration – Benedick   31

Onomatopoeia   32

    Playing assonance, alliteration and onomatopoeia
    – Edward the Fourth   32

Assonance and alliteration capturing feeling   34

    Connecting to the feeling in alliteration – Paulina   35

KEY POINTS   36

Chapter Five

'THOU' AND 'YOU'   **37**

General guidelines   37

    Persons of equal station   38

    Lovers   38

    Intimates   38

    Practical or weighty matters   38

    Higher status to lower   39

    Insulting use of 'thou'   39

    Addressing Gods   39

    Plural   39

    Dead or absent characters   40

Shifts between 'you' and 'thou'   40
KEY POINTS   43

Chapter Six
WHAT IS VERSE?   **44**

What is 'verse'   44
Syllables   44
Stressed and unstressed syllables in English words   45
'Feet' in verse   47
'Lines' in verse   48
'Verses' or 'stanzas' within verse   49
Rhyme   50
KEY POINTS   50

Chapter Seven
SHAKESPEARE'S VERSE   **51**

Feet in Shakespeare's verse   51
Verse-lines in Shakespeare   52
Why the iambic pentameter?   53
'Major' sense-units   54
KEY POINTS   56

Chapter Eight
WHY HONOUR THE VERSE?   **57**
KEY POINTS   60

Chapter Nine
ACTING SHAKESPEARE'S VERSE   **61**
Part 1: Playing the Rhythm   **61**

Playing the Rhythm   61
Scanning Shakespeare's lines   62
Introductory scanning practice
– Puck, Lady Macbeth, Richard III   65
Identifying syllables to be 'restored' as strong
– Antonio, Macbeth, Brutus   67
Restoring dropped beats in multi-syllable words
– King and Macbeth   69

Flashing the strong beats   71
Varying degrees of stress   72

Part 2: Irregularities   74
Irregularities in the verse   74
Types of irregularity   74
'Masculine' and 'feminine' endings   79
    Comparing alternative scansions 1 – Helena   81
    Comparing alternative scannings 2 – Hamlet   84

Part 3: Line-Endings and Beginnings   88
End-stopped lines   88
    Playing line-endings and beginnings
    – Romeo and Antipholus   90
Pivotal sense-breaks   92
    Playing pivotal sense-breaks
    – Duchess of Gloucester et al.   93
Multiple mid-line sense-breaks   94
    Swing-boating – Phebe   96
    Playing off-centre sense-breaks – Cassius, Orsino   97
    Pivotal breaks: Interjecting questions – Hamlet   98
Enjambements   99
The caesura   102
Playing the caesura   103
    Playing Caesurae: Interjecting thought bubbles – Macbeth   104
Why enjambements and the caesurae?   105
    Enjambements and caesurae embodying inner conflict
    – Shylock   106
Caesurae and 'self-interruptions'   107
    Self-interruptions – Leontes   107
Other verse forms   110
KEY POINTS   113

Chapter Ten

RHYME   114
Rhyming couplets   114

Rhyme at the ends of speeches, scenes and plays 114

Playing rhyme 115

Playing rhyme 1 – Helena and Hermia 116

Rhyme in dialogue and within speeches 117

Rhymed songs and spells 121

Different rhyming schemes 122

KEY POINTS 123

Chapter Eleven

PRONUNCIATION **124**

Words with apostrophes 124

Pronouncing the 'e' in past tense words
– Richard III et al. 125

Pronouncing words with an apostrophe
– Lady Macbeth et al. 126

Words stressed differently in Shakespeare's day 127

Rhymes that no longer rhyme 129

KEY POINTS 130

Chapter Twelve

**PLAYING SENSE-BREAKS IN PROSE
AND PLAYING PARENTHESES** **131**

Swing-boating; clapping and stamping – Hamlet 131

Experiencing the emptiness – Shylock 133

Playing parentheses, or 'non-essential' sense-units 134

Playing the spine of the sentence – Antony and Calpurnia 135

Playing multiple parentheses – Titania 136

KEY POINTS 139

Chapter Thirteen

ADJECTIVES AND ADVERBS **140**

Adjectives 140

Adverbs 141

Acting adjectives and adverbs 141

Omitting the adjectives etc. – Henry V et al. 142

KEY POINTS 143

Chapter Fourteen

SHORT LINES   **144**

    Shared lines, and free-standing lines   144

        Playing shared lines – Juliet et al.   148

    Short lines and pauses   150

    Pauses other than short-line pauses   151

KEY POINTS   153

Chapter Fifteen

BREATHING THE VERSE   **154**

    Practice with breathing the verse 1 – Antipholus   155

    Practice with breathing the verse 2 – Prince Hal   157

    Breathing irregular lines 1 – Lady Macbeth et al.   160

    Breathing irregular lines 2 – Edmund   162

    Breathing irregular lines 3 – Hamlet   164

KEY POINTS   167

Chapter Sixteen

ACTING SHAKESPEARE'S PROSE   **168**

    Why verse? Why prose?   168

    Shifts between verse and prose   171

    Acting prose   173

        Identifying poetic devices in prose – Hamlet   174

    Structural devices in prose   175

    See-saws   175

    Triads   176

    Headlines   177

    Refrains   178

    Stanzas   179

        Speaking out the structural units – Hamlet   182

        Playing stanzas, headlines, see-saws etc. – Benedick   184

    A note on see-saws   190

    Rhythm in prose   191

KEY POINTS   192

Chapter Seventeen

SOLO SPEECHES   **193**

Prologues   193

Epilogues   195

Soliloquies   195

Key questions to ask when acting a soliloquy   196

Soliloquies which open scenes   198

Trying to get a handle on the situation   201

The balancing of mind and feeling in soliloquies   201

Soliloquy as 'process of enlightenment'   201

Addressees in soliloquies   205

Addressing Solo Speeches to the audience   206

    Addressing the audience – Intimate Mode   206

    Addressing the audience – Formal Mode   209

Non-personal addressees in soliloquies   210

    Addressing non-personal addressees: Objects
    – Antony, Helena and Lear   211

    Non-personal addressees: Absent characters
    – Lady Macbeth   214

    Non-personal addressees: Gods and spirits
    – Edmund and Lady Macbeth   216

Nature of the relationship with addressees   217

    Switching non-personal addresses – Lady Macbeth   218

    Non-personal addresssees: Internal – Claudius   220

    Non-personal addresses: The 'whole self' – Angelo 222

Addressees apart from audience and non-personals   222

    Non-personal Addressees: The universe
    – Malvolio and Angelo   224

    Alternating audience and universe as addressee – Viola   226

The universe feeding back   228

Moments of conception   231

    Receiving from the universe 1 – Angelo   232

Explanations within soliloquies   233

Laying out of already known facts   233

Realising   234

Explaining the realisation   234

Receiving from the universe 2 – Macbeth   234

Receiving from the universe 3 – Malvolio   236

No leaking between steps   238

Flights and landings   239

Standing over the end of soliloquies and speeches   240

Anticipating   241

Steps, flights and landings in Viola's soliloquy   242

Asides   248

Different rules for asides for different occasions   249

Asides in ongoing exchanges   252

KEY POINTS   254

Chapter Eighteen
CONNECTING THE EYES OUTWARDS IN SPEECHES DELIVERED TO AN ONSTAGE CHARACTER OR CHARACTERS

in speeches delivered to an onstage character or characters   **258**

Secondary addressees   258

Connecting the eyes to the universe in regular speeches   258

Connecting the eyes out 1 – Desdemona   259

Connecting the eyes out 2 – Jaques   260

KEY POINTS   263

Last Words   264

Issue productions   264

Index of Exercises   267

Acknowledgements   271

INTRODUCTION

In this book, I wish to pass on to you, in as simple and straightforward a way as I am able, all the ideas, principles and exercises which, over thirty years of teaching and directing, have presented themselves to me as those most effective in helping the actor bring Shakespeare's lines and speeches clearly and dramatically to life. It is written in a way I hope that makes it meaningful and useful, not only to actors and drama students, but also to directors, teachers of drama, and academics.

I thoroughly recommend that as you go through the book, you do each of the short exercises described. Doing the exercises, as opposed to simply reading about them and filing them away for some future use, will provide you with an immediate and *practical* experience of how each principle works in action. By the time you have gone through the book, therefore, you will have not just a list of useful *ideas* about acting Shakespeare, you will already have begun to absorb the various principles and approaches laid out in the book into your system. Without having to think about them any further, you will instinctively begin to employ them, each time you approach the acting of a Shakespeare text. (In the case of some of the exercises you may wish to record yourself on your phone, or another device; or some of them you may want to carry out with a friend or fellow student. But all can be practised on your own, with just as much benefit.)

Also, the book is laid out under very practical and distinct headings, so having finished it, you can come back to it at any time and quickly find the section which will help you with whatever aspect of the text may be giving you difficulty. And for those occasions when you might feel the need for a quick 'refresher', you will find at the end of each chapter, a list of all the key points contained within that chapter. It will also be very simple to remind yourself of the various exercises designed to strengthen your skills in a particular area, as all of those described in the course of the book are listed under various topic headings in a full 'Exercise Index'.

I would like to thank all the students and actors it has been my pleasure to work with over the last few decades. It is through my relationship, and work, with them that I have learnt almost all of what I now am passing onto you.

A note on punctuation

The punctuation in most modern editions of Shakespeare has been created by the respective editors, based on the punctuation in the 1623, and subsequent, editions of the plays. These are known as the 'Folio' editions. The punctuation I use in quotations throughout this book is similarly based on, but is by no means a copy of, the punctuation in the Folio editions. It is a punctuation meant to reveal the meaning of the text as clearly and accessibly as possible to the modern reader/actor/teacher etc.

'His and her' etc.

In the spirit of inclusivity, I have, in instances where it did not prove impossibly unwieldy, employed either the neutral pronoun 'one', 'they', or the phrases 'he or she', 'him or her' etc. In the many cases where it did prove much too unwieldy, I use 'he' to represent any shade of gender.

CHAPTER ONE

QUESTIONS, ORDERS AND EXPLANATIONS

Objectives

It may seem odd to begin a discussion on the acting of Shakespeare's language with a discussion of 'the objective'. The notion of the 'objective', after all, is one with which a lot of teachers, directors, actors and acting students will already be familiar. It is a fundamental tool in acting, directing and actor training generally. There is, however, a very particular reason I wish to do this.

A discussion of objectives will serve as the best means to introduce another, very simple and fundamental observation about language in general. It is the notion I usually introduce to students and actors first when they come to me to learn about acting classic texts. It is an observation which, over the years, I have discovered to be more helpful than any other in bringing clarity and vitality to the acting of Shakespeare's lines and speeches. It is a supremely simple notion that, once stated, is blindingly obvious but which I have not seen discussed in any of the writing on classical acting I have so far come across.

Also, when first faced with acting The Bard, actors can often appear to have forgotten a lot of what they naturally apply to 'ordinary acting'. They feel that there is some whole new set of rules to be followed if only they knew what it was. Even their know-how about the venerable objective can go by the wayside. A discussion on objectives, therefore, will also be of considerable value in its own right.

It is axiomatic that drama is first and foremost about 'action', about characters 'taking action', 'acting'. Those who choose to perform in plays, after all, are known as 'actors'. They are not called 'feelers', or 'emoters', or 'thinkers', or 'intenders'. As so often, the wisdom we seek is in the language we use. And traditionally, of course, the main divisions into which plays are divided are known as 'acts'.

An actor will always want to be in touch with the impulses his character feels inside, which are 'impelling' him to 'do' the actions which he performs. And he or she knows their character never 'gives up', never 'lets up' on their objective. But don't be confused and conclude you must have the wrong objective because you observe the character does not seem to achieve his or her objective, either in an individual scene, or in the drama as a whole; many characters do not. Again, as we have all experienced in real life, even when fully committed to achieving a goal, a person may not accomplish it. Irrespective of whether or not they attain their objective, it is the active and sustained pursuing of the objective that justifies, and makes a character 'live' on stage.

It has always struck me that any guideline for good acting serves as a guideline for a good life. A character never coming off his objective is the equivalent of a person, in real life, honouring and never betraying the promptings of his soul; and allowing himself, purposefully and creatively, to act upon these impulses in the real world.

Distinguishing 'immediate' and 'overall' objectives

One of the issues actors and students regularly ask for help with is clarifying the difference between 'objectives' and 'super-objectives'. The idea that one must never 'come off' one's 'overall,' or 'super-objective' is true, as far as it goes. However, attempting to play one's idea of the 'super-objective' in every scene, and on every line, can create problems.

A character does need to identify what is commonly known as a single 'super-' or, 'overall-objective' which motivates him or her through the 'life-span' of the play. For example, a character's over-all objective could be, 'To gain the crown', 'To win the love of some other character', 'To save one's reputation', 'To avenge oneself on another character' etc. And it is important, in rehearsals, to identify such an 'over-all' objective. The 'over-all' objective provides the actor with an understanding of what they are aiming for, of knowing what they are *doing* within the play as a whole.

Although at any given moment in a play the 'super-objective' is always being pursued, a character will have various *more immediate* objectives throughout the play; more than likely a different one in each scene, a different one in every speech, and a different one on every line. All these objectives are absolutely particular and, at first glance, may appear to have little connection to the super-objective; but they will, and must have a connection. The different objectives played in various scenes, and on individual lines, must each represent a practical means the character is employing, *in that moment,* in pursuit of his or her overall-objective.

As in life, as in drama: to achieve some major goal, there are typically a number of steps to be taken. And the best way to move towards any goal is obviously to commit, moment by moment, and to the fullest of one's ability, to successfully accomplishing each of these individual steps.

Let's say a character's 'overall-' or 'super-objective' within the play is, indeed, 'to gain the crown'. And let's say the character finds himself in a scene where he is with the wife of the king's closest aide. He decides he must convince her that he loves her so that he can ask her, in a later scene, if she will wheedle information from her husband (the king's aide) about the route the king intends to take to the coast the following month…so that he can arrange a murderous ambush. He wants that crown, and therefore all his energy must now go into the pursuit of his *immediate* objective, which is 'to win the lady's trust and affections'. This, his immediate *scene*-objective, is determined and fuelled by his over-all, his super-objective.

And in the very same way, *within* this scene, the would-be assassin may have any number of different speech-by-speech, line-by-line, moment-by-moment objectives. All of these, of course, must still be ways of pursuing both his scene-, and his overall-objective. Since he knows of her devotion to the church, he may choose to convince the lady what a devout Christian he is; and he may elect to do this by narrating a dreamed-up epiphany he had in the Holy Land, when Saint Margaret appeared to him. The overall scene-objective is 'to win her heart'. But within the scene, a more immediate objective becomes to convince her of his Christian piety; and, to this end, the most immediate objective to which he must commit, is to narrate his story about Saint Margaret so passionately and convincingly that the lady believes it, and so will regard him to be a deeply religious man.

In some plays there will be objectives which the character strives to achieve, not through speaking words, but by physical action. Such objectives are normally easy to identify and play. For example. Orlando's immediate objective in the *As You Like It* wrestling-scene will be 'physically to overpower Charles, his opponent'. An immediate objective for Macbeth in his final scene will be to vanquish Macduff in hand-to-hand combat. Another physical objective might be to slip poison in a cup, hide a letter, physically to arouse someone by caressing, or kissing them etc. However, in the vast majority of cases the objective is pursued *at any given moment* by the character speaking words; by saying lines.

This brings me to the fundamental observation about language I mentioned above, as being so helpful in bringing clarity and vitality to the acting of Shakespeare.

Order, explanation or question?

Every human utterance is an explanation, a question, an order.

When delivering lines, then, there are only three types of objective a character can have. These are: 'to explain', 'to ask' or 'to order'.

('Exclamations', such as *'Swounds!'*, *'Alas!'*, *'Pah!'*, or *'God's light!'*, might be thought of constituting a small category of their own. However, as the acting of such short, spontaneous expressions tends to look after itself, I think it more useful to exclude them from this discussion.) Even the most silent physical gestures on stage, such as signalling to another character, or to a ship off-shore, are going to be explanations, questions or orders; or sometimes perhaps the equivalent of an exclamation.

To identify the objective for any line, therefore, you only need ask, 'What am I trying to find out?' (Asking), 'What am I telling someone or something to do?' (Ordering), or 'What am I trying to get someone to understand?' (Explaining). It's always going to be one of these. When acting text, there is nothing else you can be doing. (Apart from uttering an exclamation.) This simplifies things somewhat, does it not?

I have found that to identify, and distinguish what are questions, orders and explanations is a more fruitful way to start working on a Shakespeare line or speech than (as some teachers and directors suggest) to begin by 'scanning' the lines; i.e. by analysing the rhythms. Identifying whether a sentence is an order, explanation or question, and actively and unambiguously playing it as such: this, *more than anything else*, is what I have found gives clarity to an audience. It is what most helps the actor feel a living connection to the line; a connection to what their character is 'doing'; and a connection, therefore, to their character as a whole (a character being the sum total of the acts he or she performs in any play).

In a case where you are having difficulty identifying an *overall*-objective for a scene, you will also discover that it may begin clearly to reveal itself to you, once you identify, and purposefully play, the various *line-by-line* objectives (the individual questions, orders etc.).

You may have noticed that no 'feeling' or 'feelings' have been mentioned in relation to speech- and line-objectives. An objective is *never* 'to express a feeling'. Some actors come to perform classic texts, or to learn about performing them, with their minds full of notions gleaned from various Methods and Schools. Some of these notions are directed towards the accessing of more and more 'truthful' feeling. In principle, this is a good thing. But improperly understood or applied, these notions can lead to 'non-active' acting; to self-indulgent 'emoting'. The results of this are rarely happy; and in the context of acting classic text the results can be particularly unfortunate.

Questions, orders and explanations must be experienced, both by the actor and the audience, as what they are – *purposeful actions*. Feelings, of course, may be said to 'fuel' or drive actions; but they are not such stuff as plays are made on.

The 'raw material' from which music is made is sound; that of dance, movement. 'Human action' is the raw material of drama. We feel that something is 'happening' in a play, and therefore that what we are watching actually *is* a play, only when characters perform actions fuelled by believable motivations, and which have an observable effect on the play's imaginary world. We remain interested only when such actions make us wonder what will happen as a consequence of their being performed.

The sentence, 'I feel sad.' is not to be thought of as an expression, or demonstration, of feeling. It is a purposeful explanation to someone of how one is feeling; an active attempt to get into the head of the listener a precise 'idea' of how one is feeling. An objective is never about the speaker. It is always about what he or she is doing to 'the other'; the person, persons, or thing, which is being asked, ordered or explained to. (I will elaborate on what is meant by addressing 'things' in Shakespeare in due course.)

Obvious examples of utterances in Shakespeare which are *explanations* are:

Jaques: *All the world's a stage...*   *As You Like It 2:7:140*

Portia: *The quality of mercy is not strained...*   *Merchant of Venice 4:1:181*

Puck: *My mistress with a monster is in love...*   *A M. Night's Dream 3:2:6*

Caesar: *Yon Cassius has a lean and hungry look...*   *J. Caesar 1:2:194*

Obvious examples of utterances which are *questions* are:

Calphurnia: *What mean you, Caesar? Think you to walk forth?* *J. Caesar 2:2:8*

Juliet: *... What's in a name? ...*   *Romeo and Juliet 2:2:43*

Desdemona: *... O, good Iago,*
What shall I do to win my lord again?   *Othello 4:2:150*

Shylock: *Hath not a Jew eyes?*   *The Merchant of Venice 3:1:55*

Tamora: *Have I not reason, think you, to look pale?*   *Titus Andronicus 2:3:96*

Obvious examples of utterances which are *orders* are:

Hamlet: *Get thee to a nunnery! Go!*   *Hamlet 3:1:132*

Lady Anne: *Set down, set down your honourable load...*   *Richard III 1:2:1*

Hermione: *Sir, spare your threats...*   *The Winter's Tale 3:2:90*

The drama is carried almost solely on the clarity and precision of these active explanations and questionings and orders. (I use the term 'explanation' rather than 'statement', as I have found that using the words 'explain' and 'explanation' helps students get in touch with the *active* dimension of a line, more readily than if I use the words 'state' or 'statement'.)

Any line or speech, therefore, must be made to work, first and foremost, on this simple, 'grammatical level'. The intention of the actor/character must match, must get behind the grammar. If this grammatical level is clearly achieved by the performer, then so many other aspects of his or her performance tend to look after themselves and fall into place. Surprisingly, this *primary* aspect of utterances is often given least attention.

Mixing of questions, orders and explanations

Questions, orders and explanations are born of very different intentions within us. When spoken, each has a different colour and energy; each creates a different effect in the outside world, both on the character, or characters, being addressed, and on the sensibilities and expectations of the audience.

To take full advantage of this fact, a device Shakespeare frequently uses to vary the colour and energy of his speeches and dialogue is to switch amongst these three types of utterance. An example: Macbeth sees a phantom dagger in the air before him:

Macbeth: (Question: Q.) *Is this a dagger that I see before me,*
The handle toward my hand? **(Order: O.)** *Come, let me clutch thee.*
(Explanation: E.) *I have thee not and yet I see thee still.*
(Question) *Art thou not, fatal vision, sensible*
To feeling as to sight...?   2:1:33

Below is another example of the effective mixing of Q's, O's, and E's. In *As You Like It*, the shepherdess, Phebe, tries to convince Silvius (and herself!) that she is not in love with the boy Ganymede (Rosalind in disguise):

Phebe: (O.) *Think not I love him though I ask for him.*
(E.) *'Tis but a peevish boy:* **(E.)** *yet he talks well*
(Q.) *But what care I for words?*   3:5:109

Following, now, are a group of short and enjoyable exercises designed to strengthen your sensitivity to the distinction between these three different types of utterance; and to provide you with practice in how most effectively to play them. I can promise that doing these exercises (as opposed to simply reading through them) will help you lay a firm, and essential, foundation for acting Shakespearean words.

Playing explanations, questions and orders 1 – Romeo and Beatrice

First of all read these few lines from *Romeo and Juliet*, and be sure you are clear as to their meaning. Then, when I ask you to, act aloud, not only the lines, but also the words 'Question', 'Order' or 'Explanation', right where I have inserted them in the text. Having said, 'Question', play the sentence following as if the character really wants an answer to that question. When you have said 'Explanation' play the line with the focused intention of 'making something clear' to the listener. Having said, 'Order', play the line as if the character genuinely wants that order to be obeyed. Do this at least two or three times:

> **Romeo: Order:** *But soft!** **Question:** *What light through yonder window breaks?* **Explanation:** *It is the east, and Juliet is the sun!*
> **Order:** *Arise, fair sun, and kill the envious moon…*   2:2:2

> *Wait a moment!

When you have done that, act the lines again, this time without speaking the inserted 'Question', 'Order' etc. As you do this, consciously experience how different it feels to explain, to ask, or to order.

> *But soft! What light through yonder window breaks?*
> *It is the east and Juliet is the sun!*
> *Arise, fair sun, and kill the envious moon…*

Now do the same with the lines below from *Much Ado About Nothing*.

Be sure, to begin with, that you know what the lines mean. Then, as you did with Romeo's, act them a few times, speaking aloud the inserted 'Q's' and 'O's' and 'E's'.

Beatrice (alone) has just heard that Benedick is in love with her, and that because she is bound to use it as a means to mock him, it is thought better that she is not told. If you are wondering who Beatrice is talking to in this little speech, you can, for the purposes of this exercise, imagine she is talking directly to the audience:

> **Beatrice: Question:** *What fire is in mine ears?* **Question:** *Can this be true?*
> **Question:** *Stand I condemned for pride and scorn so much?*
> **Order:** *Contempt, farewell; **Order:** and maiden pride, adieu!*
> **Explanation:** *No glory lives behind the back of such.*   3:1:107

Act the lines again, this time without speaking the 'Q's' and 'E's' etc. As you did with Romeo's lines, allow yourself to experience the different taste, quality and weight of each type of utterance:

What fire is in mine ears? Can this be true?
Stand I condemned for pride and scorn so much?
Contempt, farewell; and maiden pride, adieu!
No glory lives behind the back of such...

It may seem unlikely, but a most common mistake when acting Shakespeare is to confuse which type of utterance is which. I often hear questions played as explanations, orders played as explanations etc. In the Beatrice speech above a common tendency is not to distinguish, or play, the different questioning, ordering or explaining intentions in any way at all, but to wash every line over with the same generalised expression of 'excited amazement'. To lose the clarity of what is a question etc., in such a speech, is greatly to reduce its colour, clarity and impact.

'Real' and 'rhetorical' questions

Questions are generally asked in the hope and expectation of receiving an answer; but often questions are asked, not with the desire for a reply, but as a tool of rhetoric; for rhetorical effect. The device works in this way: a question is asked solely in order that a certain idea, or fact, may graphically be caused to percolate in the mind of the person of whom the question is asked.

Take the oft-asked question: 'Is this some sort of a joke?' It is a 'real' question if the speaker is genuinely curious if what is happening has been planned as an amusing entertainment. It is 'rhetorical' when the speaker is pretty sure the situation is *not* a joke. Asking the question puts graphically into the mind of the hearer, the notion that the referred to event, or behaviour, is outlandish; so much so, that it could well be interpreted as being a joke.

Other examples would be: *'Do you think I'm an idiot?'; 'Who do you think you're looking at?'; 'Why do I need to put up with this?'*

In Shakespeare productions, one often hears 'real' questions played either as explanations, or, inactively, as 'expressions of feeling'. But it is rhetorical questions, in particular, which are most often played with a mismatched explanatory energy, or as a means of 'showing feeling'. This is especially unfortunate since, to be most effective, rhetorical questions demand to be asked with not less, but even *more* questioning energy than one might use when asking a real question.

To feel the truth of this point for yourself, see how far you can go playing the 'questioningness' in the examples of modern rhetorical questions cited above. Act each one over a number of times, each time increasing the level of 'interrogativeness', until you cannot play it any harder:

'Do you think I'm an idiot?'; 'Is this some kind of joke?'; 'Who do you think you're looking at?'; 'Why do I need to put up with this?'

You probably found it is almost impossible to exaggerate the questioning intent too much. The more interrogative energy with which one asks a rhetorical question, the more graphically one makes one's point.

Playing rhetorical questions 1 – Rosalind

Here is a sample of two consecutive rhetorical questions from *As You Like It*. Rosalind has just overheard Phebe harshly rebuff the love-smitten Silvius:

> **Rosalind:** *And why, I pray you? Who might be your mother,*
> *That you insult, exult and all at once,*
> *Over the wretched?*   *3:5:34*

The objective of these lines might, at first, be thought of as something such as: 'to insult Phebe', 'to tell Phebe how awful she is' or 'to mock Phebe', or 'to wreak revenge on Phebe for her harsh treatment of Silvius' etc.. You will be getting the point by now, that at the topmost and primary level this is not what these lines are about; they are not accusatory explanations. At the top level Rosalind is *asking* Phebe, 'What extraordinary, blue-blooded lady must *your* mother be, since you believe you can behave in this high-handed way with a good-hearted shepherd offering you love and devotion?'

Deliver Rosalind's lines a few times, and have only in mind, a general, fierce emotional need to lash out and hurt. Get mad, and regard the words as so much 'stuff' you can use to splurge your vengefulness all over this haughty rustic:

> *And why, I pray you? Who might be your mother,*
> *That you insult, exult and all at once,*
> *Over the wretched? ...*

Now, deliver the lines again. This time, 'contain' your desire simply to splurge and lash out. Instead, shape your hot feelings of outrage into a precise, rhetorical instrument, and speak with incisive questioning intention. Exaggerate how much you want to know who Phebe's mother is.

Keep asking, until you sense you have truly got under the 'questioningness' of the lines; till it seems you are truly expecting to be astounded when this shepherdess tells you how extraordinary, and probably royal, her mother is.

Feel how the effect of the rhetoric is realised when you deliver it as a question. Delivered as such, you will sense that your own energy and intention are properly engaged with the line; that they are behind its natural energy and flow.

Playing rhetorical questions 2 – Paulina

Here is a speech from *The Winter's Tale* which opens with a list of rhetorical questions; Paulina enters to tell King Leontes that his barbaric treatment of his queen has resulted in her death. But before she reveals this, she asks what hideous punishment might he contrive for her, as bearer of the worst news he could hear:

> **Paulina:** *What studied torments, tyrant, hast for me?*
> *What wheels? racks? fires? what flaying? boiling*
> *In leads or oils? What old or newer torture*
> *Must I receive, whose every word deserves*
> *To taste of thy most worst?*   3:2:175

How often have I heard these questions played as generalised accusatory statements (explanations); or heard them played as undifferentiated truncheons with which to beat Leontes over the head; as if the content of the lines were something along the lines of, 'You are a horrible, horrible man and tyrant! I hate you, I hate you, I hate you!' or even more simply, 'Blaaaaaaaaaghhh!' When asked what Paulina is doing in these lines, a student will often offer something such as, 'She is expressing her outrage at Leontes'; or, 'She is punishing Leontes...'

But Paulina is not just generally 'expressing outrage'; she is asking which particular type of death and torture Leontes might choose to punish her with, when she has told him the news she is about to give him; news which, surely, will make him want to subject her (the bearer of the news) to the direst torture he has yet devised. As Rosalind did, she needs to *contain* her rage sufficiently so it doesn't get in the way of her ensuring that every detail of every question gets across; questions which are designed, not just generally to beleaguer the king, but to engrave inside his head, a direful anticipation of what this worst-of-all-his-crimes could be. Paulina needs to ask the questions regarding the possible tortures she will receive, as if she really wants specific answers.

The effectiveness of Paulina's rhetorical questions, of course, lies also in the clarity with which she puts them across. If any character's questions, explanations etc. are not delivered sufficiently clearly, he or she may not achieve her objective.

A most productive rule of thumb, therefore, is: 'Always make clarity part of your character's immediate objective'.

When you are sure you know precisely what Paulina's lines mean, act them aloud. Be as angry and outraged as you like; *but*, make your priority, make your objective, 'to get my questions across to Leontes with as much clarity as I can achieve'. That is how you will realise the effectiveness of the questions as rhetorical devices:

> *What studied torments, tyrant, hast for me?*
> *What wheels? racks? fires? what flaying? Boiling*
> *In leads or oils? What old or newer torture*
> *Must I receive, whose every word deserves*
> *To taste of thy most worst?*

Playing explanations, questions and orders 2 – Antony and Helena

Here is a line from *Julius Caesar*; Mark Antony is left alone with Caesar's corpse:

Antony: *Oh, pardon me, thou bleeding piece of earth*
That I am meek and gentle with these butchers.   3:1:254

When asked what the objective of these lines is, an actor will often suggest something such as 'Mark Antony is lamenting to himself the fact that he had to pretend to support the actions of the conspirators who killed Caesar'. These lines do not represent Mark Antony lamenting to himself, or doing anything else to, or for, himself. They constitute an order: an order purposefully directed towards the remains of Caesar. He is ordering the corpse to pardon him.

Of course, Antony is not expecting his order to be instantly obeyed as he would had he uttered a 'real' order to a subordinate. Grammatically speaking, this sentence is indeed an order; but it might be called a 'rhetorical order'. It still must, however, be played with ordering, 'imperative' energy, in order that the device of the 'rhetorical order' can do its work.

Play Antony's lines now. Fully imagine the corpse of your friend Caesar and direct your order to it as if he were alive and could hear and respond to you.

> *Oh, pardon me, thou bleeding piece of earth*
> *That I am meek and gentle with these butchers.*

Sometimes what is an order can be obscured. This is something to look out for.

In *A Midsummer Night's Dream*, Helena believes she has discovered that her best school-friend, Hermia, has ganged up with Lysander and Demetrius to make a fool of her:

Helena: *Lo, she is one of this confederacy!*
Now I perceive, they have conjoin'd all three
To fashion this false sport, in spite of me.   3:2:192

Grammatically, Helena's first line is not an explanation. It would be easy to overlook this and play it with purely explanatory intention. Helena's intention is not to explain that 'This awful Hermia has ganged up with the others against me.' The meaning of '*Lo*' is 'Behold!', and played as such, the first line becomes an order to the audience. The speaker of any order needs to explain specifically what it is he or she wants done, so Helena's line does, of course, contain 'explanatory material'; but, grammatically the line is overall an order and asks to be honoured as such. Expanded the line would say: 'Look, audience, how my friend Hermia is part of this conspiracy against me!'

I want you to act Helena's first line in two different ways now. First of all, play the line a few times, making it unmistakably, and *purely*, an explanation to the audience:

Helena: *Lo, she is one of this confederacy!*

Now play the line again. This time play it actively as an *order* to the audience. Unambiguously tell them what it is you wish them to behold and witness. Do this a few times till you feel you are fully behind the objective of 'I order'.

Do you feel the difference?

Played as the order that it is, the full energy and intention of the line is released. Played merely as an explanation, the invitation to the audience actively to participate in the play's goings-on is lost. Also, we will miss the change in energy from the 'ordering' of this line to the 'explaining' of the two lines which follow it:

Lo, she is one of this confederacy!
Now I perceive, they have conjoin'd all three
To fashion this false sport, in spite of me.

Now act aloud, all three of Helena's lines. Having played the first as an order, play the two following as something you have just realised, and which you want, you *need* to explain to the audience. As you do this, I want you to be sensitive to the shift that occurs inside yourself at the end of the first line, as you change your intention from ordering mode, to the explaining mode. Act all three lines a few times, until you clearly feel this 're-arrangement' occur inside yourself; until you feel you have separated, and 'purified', the lines into an utterance of pure ordering, and one of pure explaining.

Explanations within orders

We saw that there was an explaining component to Helena's first line above, and there will naturally be an element of explanation within *any* order; and this element asks clearly to be played. As I often find that actors/students become confused on this issue, I think it will be useful to look at this explaining aspect of orders in a little more detail.

Playing explanations within orders – Antony and Lady Anne

Antony again:

Oh, pardon me, thou bleeding piece of earth
That I am meek and gentle with these butchers.

In these lines, the first part, *'Oh, pardon me...'* is the core of the order. The next part, *'...you bleeding piece of earth...'* specifies to whom the order is directed. The next part, *'That I am meek and gentle with these butchers...'*, certainly is an explanation; but it is specifying, explaining what it is Antony wants Caesar's corpse to *'pardon'*. The explanation is a necessary part of, is *in support of,* the order. The ordering intention does not die as soon as the most obvious ordering bit is over; it must be carried right through to the end of the explanation.

Below, is an example where, similarly, an explanation forms an important part of what is, overall, an order.

In *Richard III*, Lady Anne addresses the bearers of her father-in-law's (Lancaster's) corpse:

Lady Anne: *Set down! Set down your honourable load...*
... Whilst I awhile obsequiously* lament
The untimely death of virtuous Lancaster.　　　　　　　　　　　　1:2:1

*with appropriate regard for the dead

The grieving Anne orders the pall-bearers to set down the remains of her father-in-law, and, as an essential *part* of the order, she explains *why* she wishes them to do this: she wishes to spend some time grieving over the body. The 'imperative', ordering energy is key and, as in Antony's lines, it must continue and be played *right through* to the end of the explanation which supports it. This may seem obvious when stated in this way, but I can scarcely exaggerate how common it is for actors and students not to do this. Routinely, they will drop the ordering intention and energy when they get to the explaining part, reducing its import to an opportunity for undirected emoting and moaning.

Deliver these lines of Anne now clearly as an order, an order complete with an explanation as to why you want it obeyed. Keep your intention connected to the pall-bearers right through to the end of the explanatory section:

Set down! Set down your honourable load...
... Whilst I awhile obsequiously lament
The untimely death of virtuous Lancaster.

Don't the second two lines become more taut and purposeful when they are uttered in support of, as part of, the order?

Orders played as explanations

Here are two pairs of lines which might not, at first, be understood to be orders with explanatory material.

Phebe again, from *As You Like It.* The smitten shepherdess offers the explanation that Ganymede (Rosalind disguised) is but a peevish boy, and she does so in support of her order that Silvius should not think that she loves him; the whole line-and-a-half is an order:

Phebe: *Think not I love him, though I ask for him:*
'Tis but a peevish boy.   *3:5:109*

Can you see how, if the lines are played right through as an order, that the words, *''Tis but a peevish boy...'* will have much more purpose driving them; they will be presented as evidential support for why Phebe's order might be considered to be justifiable. (I am aware that some editors place a full-stop after *'though I ask for him...'* which would change how one might play the lines; but I choose this common punctuation, as it allows me to employ the lines as a means to illustrate my point.)

From *Julius Caesar:*

Caesar: *Let me have men about me that are fat,*
Sleek-headed men, and such as sleep a-nights.   *1:2:191*

This is another order. Caesar is calling to be surrounded by particular types of men, and, as part of his order, he specifies (explains) which type of men these are to be. Again his order is a rhetorical device; but in order for the device to do the work it is designed to do, it still must be played with ordering energy to its very end. An actor, however, may well play these lines while, inside himself, experiencing them, wrongly, as an explanation; as if they meant: 'I only like men who are fat and sleek-headed to be near me etc.' To play them overall as explanation will muddy the true action in the lines, and therefore, their effectiveness.

Explanations played as orders

Just as an order can be mistaken for, and played as, an explanation, so there are instances where explanations might be mistaken for an order. One has to be vigilant!

Here is a line from *Macbeth*:

Lady Macbeth: *But screw your courage to the sticking place,*
And we'll not fail.   1:7:61

The danger is that such a line is played as a fervid *order* to Macbeth; as if Lady Macbeth's purpose in speaking the words is to make Macbeth *do* something; to order him to bloody well screw his *'courage to the sticking place...'* so the two of them will not fail in their murderous enterprise.

But the pressing objective in these lines is not to make him *do* something; it is to make Macbeth *understand* something; to *explain* to him a crucial truth. The core, or principal part of the sentence, is the explanation, *'we'll not fail...'*. The words, *'But screw your courage to the sticking place...'* exist as an explanation of the circumstance that will ensure the truth of, *'we'll not fail...'*

Unpacked the line might read: 'I am explaining that success will definitely happen, if you but screw your courage etc.' Played while thinking of it as an order means there will be a tension between the line's content and the delivery, with the result of the line being out of focus. When there is alignment between the content and the delivery, when it is played as what it is, an explanation, the line will ring clear and true.

Explanations within questions

Just as there is always an explanatory dimension to orders, so there is often an explanatory element to questions.

From *Romeo and Juliet*:

Juliet: *Shall I speak ill of him that is my husband?*   3:2:97

These words of Juliet do indeed constitute a question, a rhetorical question; but, as do many questions, they have an explanatory element. The asking bit is: *'Shall I speak ill of him...?'* The explanatory part is: *'...that is my husband?'* The explanation part definitely must be played as such. It must in fact be played most strongly as an explanation, *in order* to make absolutely clear the point of Juliet's question.

Playing explanations within questions – Edmund

In *King Lear*, 'illegitimate' Edmund, asks why he should stand plagued by *'custom'* (customary ways), and allow the *'curiosity'* (fastidiousness) of nations to deprive him, simply because he was born out of wedlock – some twelve or fourteen months (*'moonshines'*) before his 'legitimate' brother:

> **Edmund:**   ... *Wherefore should I*
> *Stand in the plague of custom, and permit*
> *The curiosity of nations to deprive me,*
> *For that* I am some twelve or fourteen moonshines*
> *Lag of a brother?*   1:2:2

*because

An actor might be inclined to play these lines with an intention no more particular than to 'express Edmund's general sense of resentment and bitterness'. Or he may play it overall with a distinctly explanatory, rather than interrogative purpose; as if within, he is thinking of the line as meaning, 'I thoroughly resent the fact that I stand in the plague of custom etc.' As an explanation, it can only be a complaint directed at the passive listener.

Edmund's lines, however, offer us a useful example of a question with an explanatory element. Played as a question, the lines involve the listener more actively, challenging them to ponder and seek an answer, a reason, that might fairly justify how the speaker, as illegitimate, is perceived by society. The listener will then be made to realise that any reason they can come up with will probably be found wanting.

The core of the question is: *'Wherefore should I / Stand in the plague of custom, and permit / The curiosity of nations to deprive me...'.* The explanatory bit is, *'For that I am some twelve or fourteen moonshines / Lag of a brother?'* This part provides the listener with information providing the crucial context for Edmund's putting the core question.

Act Edmund's lines a few times now. Keep them alive as a question, right through to their close. Make the explanatory section as clear as you can; spell it out, so the listener has sufficient background fully to appreciate what is being asked:

> ... *Wherefore should I*
> *Stand in the plague of custom, and permit*
> *The curiosity of nations to deprive me,*
> *For that I am some twelve or fourteen moonshines*
> *Lag of a brother?*

QUESTIONS, ORDERS AND EXPLANATIONS – Key points

- An objective is the purpose which fuels, motivates, drives a character's action at any point in the course of a play.
- An 'overall-' or, 'super-objective' is what motivates a character through the entire 'life-span' of a play.
- Throughout the play, a character will have various 'more immediate' scene-, speech-, and sentence-objectives.
- The objective for any sentence is always going to be an explanation, a question, an order.
- An objective is never about expressing or showing feeling.
- Identify each utterance as an explanation, a question etc. Then play each purely as such – right through to the full stop or question mark at the end.
- With all questions: really ask. With rhetorical questions: really ask.
- The explanatory parts of orders and questions need to be spelt out in a way that clarifies, or elaborates on, the 'core' of the question or the order.

CHAPTER TWO

OPPOSITIONS

Great use is made by Shakespeare of 'oppositions'. I use 'oppositions' quite loosely here to refer to words or phrases with opposite, or near-opposite, meanings; or to words or phrases which, in meaning, are not exactly 'the opposite of one another', but which, in the playing, have definitely been set up to be, strongly and deliberately, 'played off' the one against the other.

Oppositions within individual sentences

Here is a line which includes an obvious set of oppositions:

Hamlet: *To be, or not to be, that is the question...*   3:1:56

The oppositions are, of course, *'To be'* and *'not to be'*.

Shakespeare's prose and verse is strewn with such oppositions. Some are obvious and some are less so; but all of them need to be identified and honoured in the playing. There are often two, three or more oppositions in any one line or sentence. In this Lady Macbeth line, there are two oppositions:

Lady Macbeth: *That which hath made them drunk hath made me bold.* 2:2:1

'Them' is opposed to *'me'*, and *'drunk'* is opposed to *'bold'*.

Here is the line with the two oppositions highlighted:

*'That which hath made **them** DRUNK hath made **me** BOLD.'*

There are two oppositions in these lines from *As You Like It*. Rosalind attempts to persuade Silvius how much more worthy he is than Phebe, the object of his abject adoration:

Rosalind: *You are a thousand times a properer man*
Than she a woman.   3:5:51

'You' is opposed to *'she'*; and *'man'* is opposed to *'woman'*.

***You** are a thousand times a properer MAN*
*Than **she** a WOMAN.*

Playing oppositions

When acting oppositions, the first part must be strongly and firmly 'presented', so there is an anticipation from the listener, that something else is coming soon which will meaningfully 'chime against' it. And when the second word is spoken, it, in turn, must receive appropriate 'pointing', so that it seems to bounce off the first word, satisfyingly fulfilling the rhetorical device. When oppositions are given their full rhetorical value in this way, the listener will experience the meaning of the utterance with a greatly increased understanding and enjoyment.

'Exaggerate then ease off' exercise – Rosalind et al.

A very useful method to ensure you are sufficiently honouring oppositions in your playing is first to exaggerate how you present and point them up. You point them up until you feel you are mercilessly pounding them out. Then when you feel you truly can go no further, ease off and act the line again, solely now, with the intention of conveying clearly what you want to get across. You will feel how the experience of the exaggerated version informs the more 'eased-off' version, and will help you to achieve this intention. Playing this 'exaggerate then ease off' game in the sample lines and passages below, will quickly develop your ability to recognise, and properly play, any other of the oppositions in which Shakespeare abounds.

And be prepared: you may find that if you record and listen to what you feel is your most madly exaggerated version, it may need very much less 'easing off' than you imagine. Most are surprised by how far they actually need to go by way of emphasis, fully to release the rhetorical power of oppositions.

(As will be demonstrated, this 'exaggerate then ease off' exercise can be used to help get you in touch with, and enhance your playing of, several other aspects of Shakespeare's language. You already encountered a version of it when you over-emphasised the 'questioningness' of some sentences above.)

Act Rosalind's explanation a number of times, and with each delivery, emphasise the opposition more and more, until you feel it would be impossible to exaggerate them any further.

Rosalind: *You* are a thousand times a properer MAN
*Than **she** a WOMAN…*

Now let go of the over-the-top delivery, allowing the experience of acting them this way, to inform how trenchantly you present your point.

Here are some other samples of 'oppositions'. You will see again that many of the words and phrases are not strictly 'opposites', but demand to be strongly bounced off one another, just as if they were.

Puck from *A Midsummer Night's Dream*, tells Oberon that Titania has fallen in love with Bottom (currently sporting an ass's head). As you read through them, act each one out loud – exaggerating then easing off.

Puck: *My **mistress** with a **monster** is in love...* 3:2:6

In *Julius Caesar*, Calpurnia lists the extraordinary portents making her fear for the safety of her husband:

Calpurnia: *Horses DID NEIGH and **dying men** DID GROAN...* 2:2:23

Romeo imagines the situation if Juliet's eyes were replaced by two of the brightest stars in the firmament:

Romeo: *The **brightness of her cheek** would shame THOSE STARS
As **daylight** doth A LAMP...* 2:2:19

Shared oppositions

The example of oppositions, so far, have all been within lines spoken by one person. But there are very many instances where words or phrases spoken in a line by one character, are opposed by words or phrases in a line spoken by another. In such cases, the oppositions ask to be bounced off each other just as emphatically as they do when they occur within one person's utterance.

Playing shared oppositions – Helena and Hermia

Here is an exchange between Helena and Hermia from *A Midsummer Night's Dream. Within* all of the lines but one, you will find at least one set of oppositions. You will also find that there are instances where opposing words in one line are further opposed by words in the line that follows it. Read the lines and with your pencil, highlight for yourself every opposition that you can identify; both *within* lines, and when shared between two lines:

The two young women are talking of how, no matter what they do to change the situation, Demetrius continues to pursue the love of one, and to reject the love of the other.

Helena: *O, that your frowns would teach my smiles such skill!*

Hermia: *I give him curses, yet he gives me love.*

Helena: *O that my prayers could such affection move!*

Hermia: *The more I hate, the more he follows me.*

Helena: *The more I love, the more he hateth me.* *1:1:194*

Playing shared oppositions should feel like playing an energetic table-tennis game with a well-matched partner. Each opposing word or phrase is a strong ball sent hurtling over the net towards your opponent. Deliver Helena and Hermia's lines out loud (not worrying about knowing any further details about the characters, or the situation they are in). See how forcefully you can play the table-tennis match; then act an 'eased-off' version. You can act both characters, or share the exercise with a partner.

You will by now have begun to feel how satisfying playing such oppositions can be. Playing them engages you with the strength of the characters and their intentions, and engages you powerfully with the person, or persons, you are addressing.

Speeches built around oppositions

As well as in individual lines, and in ongoing exchanges, you will come across entire speeches, or large sections of speeches, which are constructed around opposing words and ideas.

Playing multiple-oppositions within speeches – Richard the Third

In the opening lines of *Richard the Third*, the future king relates, in a lengthy series of oppositions, the stark differences he experiences between the peace that now pertains, and the recently ended hostilities. Here are only the first eight lines of many more containing a veritable glut of oppositions. If you don't have a pencil at hand, this would be a good moment to fetch one. Read these lines over, and without looking ahead, mark with your pencil, A) any oppositions you identify *within* individual lines, and, B) any words or phrases within one line which ask to be played off words or phrases in an adjacent line; you will find examples of both:

> **Richard:** *Now is the winter of our discontent*
> *Made glorious summer by this son of York;*
> *And all the clouds that lour'd upon our house*
> *In the deep bosom of the ocean buried.*
> *Now are our brows bound with victorious wreaths;*
> *Our bruisèd arms hung up for monuments;*
> *Our stern alarums changed to merry meetings,*
> *Our dreadful marches to delightful measures.* *1:1:1*

Perhaps the most obvious is the 'cross-line' opposition occurring in the first two lines:

*Now is the **winter** of our discontent*
*Made glorious **summer** by this son of York.*

Speak these two lines giving emphasis to these oppositions.

Jumping out at one slightly less prominently, but still to be played, are the 'cross-line' oppositions in the third and fourth lines. Keeping things interesting, the *order* of the oppositions in the second line are reversed:

*And all the clouds that (1) **lour'd** (2) UPON OUR HOUSE,*
*(2) IN THE DEEP BOSOM OF THE OCEAN (1) **buried.***

Act these lines till you truly *feel* the 'opposingness' of both these slightly less obvious oppositions; until you feel that you would be making them clear to an audience hearing the lines for the first time.

In the four lines following, there are a number of *internal* oppositions, together with words and phrases in adjacent lines which, although not, in any strict sense, opposites, nonetheless ask strongly to be struck, one off the other.

Here are the four lines marked up (with numbers and different letterings), to indicate, first of all, only the oppositions *within* each line:

Act the passage, chiming loud the opposing words or phrases.

*Now are our (1) **brows bound** with (1) **victorious wreaths**;*
*Our (1) **bruisèd arms** hung up for (1) **monuments**;*
*Our (1) **stern** (2) ALARUMS changed to (1) **merry** (2) MEETINGS,*
*Our (1) **dreadful** (2) MARCHES to (1) **delightful** (2) MEASURES.*

Here are the same four lines marked up, this time, with all the *cross-line* oppositions. Reward yourself by taking a little time, slowly to work through, and fully appreciate, the rich pattern Shakespeare has created in this handful of words:

*Now are our (1) BROWS (2) BOUND WITH (3) **victorious** (4) wreaths;*
*Our (1) BRUISÈD (1A) **arms** (2) HUNG UP FOR (4) monuments;*
*Our (1) STERN (1A) **alarums** (2) CHANGED TO (3) **merry** (4) meetings,*
*Our (1) DREADFUL (1A) **marches** (2) TO (3) **delightful** (4) measures...*

Before reading on, speak the four lines aloud. Relish 'chiming off' each element of the internal and cross-line oppositions.

Boldly playing this cross-bracing of oppositions will not only aid clarity for the audience; it will help both them, and the actor, to get in touch with how keenly Richard suffers as a result of the sudden and violent contrast (the opposition), twixt this time of peace, and the recently concluded strife.

OPPOSITIONS – Key points

— 'Oppositions' refer to words or phrases with opposite, or near-opposite, meanings; or words or phrases which, in the playing, have definitely been set up to be strongly played off, one against the other.

— Strongly and firmly, 'present' the first part of any opposition, so there is an anticipation from the listener that something else is coming which will meaningfully 'chime against' it. The second word in turn must receive appropriate 'pointing' so that it seems to 'bounce off' the first.

— Oppositions can occur within individual lines ('internal' oppositions), and in adjacent lines ('cross-line' oppositions), either when spoken by a single character, or shared by two different characters. Shared oppositions should have the energy of a table-tennis match played by two able opponents.

— 'Exaggerate then ease off' is a useful exercise to ensure you will sufficiently honour oppositions in your playing. Firstly, greatly over-emphasise them; then ease off and act the line more 'naturally', and with the sole intention of clearly getting across your question, or explanation etc.

CHAPTER THREE

IMAGERY AND IMAGISTIC LANGUAGE

I use the term 'image' here, specifically to refer to a' figure-of-speech' whereby one is asked to allow one thing to represent, or stand in, for something else. For example, rather than simply saying, 'He finally understood', one might say 'Finally the penny dropped.' The idea, or the picture and sound, of the penny dropping stands in for the idea of some kind of understanding finally getting through. Instead of saying, 'I've mastered that now', one might say: 'I have that under my belt now.' Having something under one's belt (as one might a hearty lunch) stands in for having thoroughly digested some know-how or skill.

As well as using imagery copiously, Shakespeare also employs what might be called 'imagistic language'; that is, language in which one thing is not being compared to another but which is nonetheless designed poetically to create pictures in the mind of the listener.

Play the concrete surface of the image – Romeo

Just as it is important to play the literal, surface level of questions, explanations etc., it is vital to play the immediate and *concrete surface* of any images or imagistic language. An image will be brought to life and do its work when the top level of its meaning is accurately and objectively explained; when this is done, the audience can receive and 'see' the image, and it can be allowed to do its work.

Romeo sees Juliet appear on her balcony:

Romeo: ... *What light through yonder window breaks?*
It is the East, and Juliet is the sun.   2:2:2

Act Romeo's second line. Explain quite technically to the audience what, as far as you are concerned, Juliet's window represents to you (*'the East'*); and elucidate what Juliet herself represents. No need to play what you reckon to be the general 'love-lorn rapture' that inspires his making the comparison between Juliet and the sun. In hearing him explain, with lucidity and conviction that, 'to him, the window is the East, and Juliet is the sun rising there...', the audience will 'get' how love-lornly enraptured he is. There is no suggestion that the delivery of his line should not be highly-coloured by the intensity of Romeo's rapture. What is proposed is that making clear and getting across the 'top' meaning of the image must take priority. When playing any image, the clarity of the words must not be obscured, or overwhelmed by a demonstration of whatever powerful feeling the character may be experiencing. If you have the facility, record yourself and have a listen. Did you 'get' it?

'Addressing a child' exercise – Duchess of Gloucester

I'd like you now to try an exercise (one I regularly use), which can help one understand just how much 'clear explaining' is required when acting Shakespeare. It is particularly helpful for clarifying the delivery of his imagistic language, but you can use it to help clarify any aspect of his language. I call it 'Addressing a child'.

In *Richard the Second*, the Duchess of Gloucester wishes to convey to John of Gaunt just how precious is each of King Edward's sons:

Duchess: ... *Edward's seven sons, whereof thyself art one,*
Were as seven vials of his sacred blood,
Or seven fair branches springing from one root...   *1:2:11*

The duchess is using imagery here to help make Gaunt see her point, so as to 'frame' his view of the value of Edward's offspring. She works to do this, by explaining to him that Edward's seven sons compare to seven vials of Edward's sacred blood; then doubles up on her 'comparing imagery' by explaining that Edward also compares to the root of a tree, and that his seven sons compare to seven branches *'springing'* from that same tree.

The job here is not to overwhelm any resistance in Gaunt, purely with the force and vehemence of your delivery (at the expense of the *content* of what you are saying). The job is for the actor to invest all her powers of clear explaining to make these comparisons as lucid as possible, so that when she has succeeded, Gaunt will be more receptive to the argument she goes on to make. In a case such as this, it is almost impossible to go too far in terms of clearly 'spelling-out' the images.

Speak these lines aloud a few times (recording yourself, if you can); and as you do, I want you to imagine that the person you are addressing is very young, say four or five, and is perhaps not even the brightest tot you've had to parley with. As well as this, imagine that you only have this one go at etching each detail of your comparisons in this infant's mind – otherwise, some fearful disaster will befall the two of you. I'll allow you to specify your own special catastrophe. Go far beyond what you think would be natural, as you exaggerate your s-l-o-w and careful attempt to spell your meanings out:

Edward's seven sons, whereof thyself art one,
Were as seven vials of his sacred blood,
Or seven fair branches springing from one root...

If you have been able to record, listen to your slow, 'to a child' delivery, as if it were your first time hearing the lines. You may find it doesn't sound as 'overdone' as you might have anticipated. How much of this 'exaggerated' way of acting the lines might you, in fact, usefully retain?

Now, act the lines again more 'normally'. The exercise will have improved your feeling of being connected to what you are attempting to explain, and will have enhanced the clarity of its delivery. If you *can* record and listen back to these, or any other lines you apply the exercise to, and there are still points where you reckon your listener might 'need more help', keep delivering them till you feel every point is so clearly presented that the most empty-headed person, even hearing it for the first time, will fully 'get it'. As with oppositions, I have often heard a student who is doing this exercise say that he feels ridiculous acting the lines in such a grotesquely over-explanatory way; only to hear everyone else in the class call out, 'No! We still aren't quite getting it. Help us even more!'

Playing imagistic language – Oberon and Hamlet

Here are a few well-loved, 'poetic' lines from *A Midsummer Night's Dream* where I might use the same exercise:

Oberon: *I know a bank where the wild thyme blows,*
Where oxlips and the nodding violet grows,
Quite over-canopied with luscious woodbine,
With sweet musk-roses and with eglantine:
There sleeps Titania sometime of the night,
Lull'd in these flowers with dances and delight...   2:1:249

Oberon's references to the various scented flowers in this speech are not, strictly speaking, 'images'; not in the sense of one thing standing in for another; Oberon uses the words 'oxlips' and 'woodbine' to refer to the flowers themselves. But I chose the speech, as it contains language intended to create pictures in the mind of the listener.

Performing such a speech, the temptation can be to make one's tone and delivery 'all flowery', so as to 'match' the perceived 'floweriness' of the language.

I have often said to an Oberon that there is no need to infuse the delivery of the words with a tone reflecting 'the truly, madly, deeply felt appreciation of how beautiful that bower and these flowers are'. One needs to regard the imagistic language as a 'practical tool' used to get specific and concrete details into the heads of the hearer. Oberon needs to get technical and horticultural. He must explain, with the precision of an expert, the exact combination of flora which characterise this particular bower; and do it in such a way that the specifics of every flower are transmitted into the minds of Puck and the audience; so that they will 'see' that bank; so that it will be instantly identifiable by Puck when he comes across it. If you go 'poetic on it', you are telling the audience that the tone of general 'poeticness' you are smearing over the words, is what they should attend to; and that, really, the words could probably just as easily be a whole lot of other words, for all the difference it would make; how that bank looks and smells will not be graphically and fully transmitted into their minds.

Here is another passage where the 'talking to a child' exercise might also be used with profit:

Hamlet: *How weary, stale, flat and unprofitable*
Seem to me all the uses of this world!
Fie on't! ah fie! 'Tis an unweeded garden,
That grows to seed; things rank and gross in nature
Possess it merely.   *1:2:133*

These lines include two short outbursts in which the young prince exclaims his angry loathing for the world (*'Fie on't! ah fie!'*). The danger here is that the actor will also want to use what follows as a means to exclaim said feeling. He may feel his job is to churn up within himself a deep feeling of disgust, and then to bloat the delivery of the words with as much of this disgust as he can dredge up. My advice to anyone attempting to pursue such a goal is: desist. The prince needs rather to harness his disgusted anger, and use it to fuel a precise explanatory intent; an intent to make concrete in the listener's imagination, the picture of a shamefully neglected garden. As did Oberon, the young prince needs to get technical and horticultural: this garden is *'unweeded'*; it has *'gone to seed'* etc.

It is by having a clear image of this garden put into their heads, that the listeners will have a clear idea of the disgust that Hamlet feels; a much more powerful idea than if he had said, simply and unmetaphorically, 'I'm sick of this world'; or if he tried to lather his lines with nauseation. And the idea put into the listener's head will not merely be an intellectual, *abstract* understanding of how the prince feels; it will be a colourful, *visual* and *felt* understanding.

Playing abstract or 'idea' images – Portia

The images examined so far have been quite 'visual'; the task to transmit 'pictures' into the listener's head. In these lines from *The Merchant of Venice*, the images Portia wishes to convey are of a different type; they are not pictures, but 'ideas'. The images are more 'cerebral' – drawn from the dry world of accounting.

Shortly after Bassanio has chosen the casket giving him the right to her hand in marriage, Portia speaks the lines below. Take a look at this rather lovely speech, and get to know what Portia is saying. She is telling Bassanio how, for his sake, she wishes she were so much better than she is. She tells him that she wishes – not for herself, but for him – that she were many times more rich, many times more fair; that in order to stand high in his estimation (*'account'*) she would wish her virtues and properties to be *beyond 'account'* (beyond calculation and keeping score of). But the truth is, she says, that when 'all of her' is totted up, it does total *something*; and stated in *'gross'*, what it all adds up to, at the very most, *'Is an unlesson'd girl, unschool'd, unpractis'd…'*:

Portia: *…for you*
I would be trebled twenty times myself;
A thousand times more fair, ten thousand times more rich;
That only to stand high in your account*,
I might in virtue, beauties, livings**, friends,
Exceed account; but the full sum of me
Is sum of something, which, to term in gross***,
Is an unlesson'd girl, unschool'd, unpractised… 3:2:152

* estimation   ** means of support   *** whole amount

The comparisons Portia makes here can indeed be classed as 'imagistic'; and it will come as no surprise when I suggest that the cold, technical specifics of these 'accounting' images must be transferred vividly into the minds of the listener.

How clearly Portia gets across to Bassanio, the technical, *surface* meaning of this sequence of 'accounting' images, is exactly how successfully she will convey to him how highly she estimates him, and how unworthy of him she feels.

One needn't think, 'Oh, she is full of love for Bassanio and wants to 'express her love to him', so the emphasis must be on 'showing' this feeling to him. Again, the images must be thought of as practical tools; not as sounds to be used to create a general soundscape of love and romance. (This passage is a definite candidate for 'Talking to a child'.) Better to think,

'How, in terms of sums and accounting, can I spell out to him that, when all of me is tallied in an account book, I wonder if I add up to enough to deserve high standing in his estimation'. This of course can be done in many different ways; and, again, I'm not, of course suggesting that the love she has for Bassanio will not inform her voice and demeanour; or that, in the way she speaks the lines, she might not let Bassanio, and the audience, know that she is slightly bemused herself that she is employing such mathematical language to describe something so heartfelt. But, whatever else might inform the way these lines are acted, the priority, again, must always be to make sure Bassanio clearly grasps the accounting images; thereby allowing the 'image tools' to do the work they have the power to do.

Act Portia's lines aloud, focussing on elucidating the maths of how she feels standing before the man she wants to choose the right casket.

Portia: *...for you*
I would be trebled twenty times myself;
A thousand times more fair, ten thousand times more rich;
That only to stand high in your account,
I might in virtue, beauties, livings, friends,
Exceed account; but the full sum of me
Is sum of something, which, to term in gross,
Is an unlesson'd girl, unschool'd, unpractised...

IMAGERY – Key points

— Play the concrete surface of the image, not the feeling or idea you believe is underlying, or inspiring, the image. The character may be in a state of high feeling as he or she speaks any lines containing images; but to show this feeling is never your objective or priority.

— The feeling may, and naturally will, inform your delivery but not to the extent of diminishing the lucidity of how you explain your images – be they visual, or 'idea' images.

— 'Addressing a child' exercise: thoroughly **exaggerate** your sl-o-w attempt to convey the images to a child; if you fail, some terrible consequence will ensue. Then deliver the lines 'normally'.

CHAPTER FOUR

ALLITERATION, ASSONANCE AND ONOMATOPOEIA

Alliteration

Alliteration is the device of deliberately grouping together words containing the same consonants.

The content of the saying, *'Practice makes perfect'*, is packaged in a way, both to present its meaning snappily to the listener, and to render it simpler to remember. The same applies to the saying, *'A stitch in time saves nine'*. Part of the packaging is the strong rhythm; but what also works to imprint the content of such sayings on our brains is the alliteration which they contain.

In the first saying, we have the two key words both beginning with 'p': *'**P**ractice makes **p**erfect'*. But we also have the hard 'kt' sound occurring in both key words, together with the similar sounding 'k' sound occurring in the middle word: *'Pra**ct**i**c**e ma**k**es perfe**ct**'*. We also have two hard 's' sounds ending the first and third words: *'Practi**c**e makes perfe**c**t'*. A lot of alliteration in a three-word sentence. The economy of words, the snappy rhythm, and the alliteration, all combine to create this 'once heard, hard to forget' axiom.

Assonance

Assonance is the device of deliberately grouping together words containing the same vowel sounds.

'A stitch in time saves nine.' In these five words we have two examples of assonance; or depending how one pronounces the opening *'A'*, we have three examples. There are the short, 'i' sounds: *'A st**i**tch **i**n time saves nine'*: then the more obvious longer vowel sound, 'ai': *'A stitch in t**i**me saves n**i**ne'*: and, if you pronounce the first *'A'* as 'ay' (as in 'hay'), then you have a further assonance: *'**A** stitch in time saves nine.'* As well as the assonance, I'm sure you can sense the alliteration created by the three 's' sounds, and the three 'n' sounds (as well as the 'near-alliterative' 'm' of *'time'*. *'A stitch in time saves nine.'* A whole lot of assonance and alliteration. And, I think, it is true that it would be quite hard to say either of these two sayings in such a way that their rhythm, conciseness and alliteration would not be able do their work.

Take this line from one of Brutus' speeches in *Julius Caesar*:

'It is the bright day that brings forth the adder…'   2:1:14

It is not quite so condensed as the two common sayings above, but it certainly is a line that is easy to listen to, and whose content is relatively easy to remember. In it there are the two strongly placed 'br's': *'It is the **bright** day that **brings** forth the adder…'*; and less obvious, but still actively doing some work, are the two 'd' sounds: *'It is the bright **d**ay that brings forth the a**dd**er…'*.

You can hear how less readily ingested, and remembered, the line would be if Shakespeare had written, instead, for instance:

'It is the bright morn that leads forth the adder…'.

You may be wondering is there any point worrying about assonance and alliteration when acting, as it is true that just by speaking the lines, you won't be able to avoid playing any they may contain. There is indeed some point to this question since, before you come to act the words, Shakespeare has arranged them, and the sounds from which they are made, in such a way as to create his alliterative and his assonantal effects. However, it does do to develop an eye, and an ear, for these devices, as a *conscious* use of them can greatly enhance a line's clarity and impact.

Playing assonance and alliteration – Benedick

In the line below, the alliteration is less marked; but becoming aware of it, and consciously using it, will help bring out the balance of the line, and transmit its meaning more emphatically. It is Benedick again from *Much Ado About Nothing*, wondering if he could ever end up having the same love-infected vision as Claudio:

Benedick: *May I be so converted and see with these eyes?*   2:3:19

Altogether, there are four 's' sounds in the line, but the two *key* 's' sounds are the 's' of '*so*' and the 's' of '*see*'. By saying the line, you will feel how the 's' of '*so*' in the first part of the question, strikes off the 's' of '*see*' in the second half. Aware of the weight-balancing job the '*so*' and the '*see*' are doing, you can slightly 'present' them, *use* them to help achieve that sense of really 'nailing' the line. Act the line now with this in mind:

*May I be **s**o converted and **s**ee with these eyes?*

Notice also, how the length of the assonant 'ee' sounds, in the two strongly stressed words, '*see*' and '*these*', gives the listener time to take in, and be with, the horror that Benedick feels about young Claudio's disgustingly distorted vision. These two long 'ee' sounds are there to be fully played, fully experienced, perhaps even slightly elongated. This will increase the force of the phrase of which they are part, so that, *'see with these eyes'* means something more akin to, *'actually manage to see with such God-accursed eyes'*.

Try that now, allowing yourself fully to experience the long 'ee's:

May I be so converted and see with these eyes?

There is the further assonance of the 'aye' sound in *'I'*, and the 'aye' sound in the word *'eye'*. Can you sense how each of these matching long vowels acts as a book-end at either end of the line; they provide it with a containing frame.

Act the line again with this framing dynamic particularly in mind:

May I be so converted and see with these eyes?

There is, of course, the sheer physical satisfaction to be had from consciously pointing up and relishing any assonance or alliteration in the lines you act; but, I needn't, I'm sure, say that any 'playing up' mustn't be so strongly played as to draw attention to itself as more important than the meaning. The devices need only be relished to the extent that they help you feel more viscerally in touch with the words' meanings, and with the feelings that lie behind them; to the extent that helps lucidly to convey these meanings and feelings to the audience.

Onomatopoeia

Onomatopoeia (pronounced *on-oh-mat-o-pay-a*) is the device of deliberately choosing, and sometimes grouping together, words that sound like the thing the word refers to, or which in some other, often mysterious, way are suggestive of this. Words that are obviously onomatopoeic are 'hiss', 'sizzle', 'chop', 'big and bouncy', 'neigh', 'plump', 'wild and windy weather', 'glut' and 'gutted'. Often onomatopoeic sounds will be combined with alliteration and/or assonance.

Playing assonance, alliteration and onomatopoeia – Edward the Fourth
Here are a few of Edward the Fourth's lines from *Richard the Third*. Edward rhetorically asks which one of his lords had tried to dissuade him from condemning his own brother to death, by reminding him how nobly and unselfishly the same brother had always behaved towards him:

> **King Edward IV:** ... *Who told me when we both lay in the field*
> *Frozen almost to death, how he did lap me*
> *Even in his garments and did give himself,*
> *All thin and naked, to the numb cold-night?*   2:1:111

The words *'field'* and *'Frozen'*, both sharing an initial 'f', are placed side by side in two strongly stressed positions, the end of one line and the beginning of the one that follows:

> *Who told me when we both lay in the field*
> *Frozen almost to death, how he did lap me...*

Act these two lines now: you will feel that this device helps greatly to implant the sense of what is being described in a listener's mind. And, perhaps you can sense too, that apart from being alliterative, the actual *sound* of the 'f's' is onomatopoeic. They somehow connect to the sense in us of chill and cold, both for the actor and the listener. In English, 'f' is used in a number of cold-associated words: 'freeze', 'founder', 'frost', 'frigid'.

In the third line we have another good example of alliteration being used to re-enforce the key balancing words on either side of a line.

Play these words now, strongly presenting the two 'g's', and you will experience how doing this provides a solid and balancing anchor for both sides of the line:

> *Even in his **g**arments   and did **g**ive himself...*

To me, Edward's fourth line offers a moving instance of the evocative power of alliteration and onomatopoeia working together:

> *All thin and naked, to the numb-cold night.*

Again, apart from the obvious alliteration, there is, to me, considerable onomatopoeic power in the combination of the five soft 'n' sounds. They evoke the tender, child-like vulnerability of exposed human flesh:

> *All thin and naked, to the numb-cold night?*

And stabbing into these soft 'n' sounds, the two hard, alliterative 'k' sounds are similarly onomatopoeic:

> *All thin and naked, to the numb cold-night?*

They evoke, on the one hand, the bones of a skeleton sticking through the thin covering of freezing, suffering flesh; and, on the other, evoke the ice-cold air which pierces it.

To get the most out of such a line, or lines, so replete with alliteration and onomatopoeia, it can be very useful to slow your delivery right down, and apply the 'exaggerate then ease-off' routine. Try it now with Edward's line below. Slow your delivery down, enabling you consciously to 'over-relish' any assonance, alliteration or onomatopoeia. Wring all the juice from them you can; till you really *feel* the sounds fully active in your mouth:

All thin and naked, to the numb-cold night...

When you have done this – yes – ease off and deliver the line again, focussing, this time, only on making yourself clear to your lords. The experience of the first, 'over-relished' delivery will serve you in ensuring the listener really 'gets' just how exposed your beloved brother was prepared to make himself so that you might be warmed.

And now have a go at acting all four of Edward's lines; allow your lips, tongue and teeth to relish the physical sensation of connecting to the alliteration and the onomatopoeia. Have as your primary focus, however, that of making your rhetorical question as clear and meaningful to the listener:

... Who told me when we both lay in the field
Frozen almost to death, how he did lap me
Even in his garments and did give himself
All thin and naked, to the numb cold-night?

Assonance and alliteration capturing feeling

We have seen how assonance and alliteration contributes to making a line more catchy and memorable; and that particular sounds, and sound combinations can, of themselves, also help to evoke the things being spoken of. The way a writer arranges sounds can also actively embody particular *feelings;* and can embody and reflect *character.* And again, often the words and sounds arranged to this end, will involve alliteration and/or assonance.

Have you ever been in full passionate or angry flow, and stopped suddenly frustrated because the 'right' words for what you want to say aren't quite breaking into your consciousness; then suddenly have a phrase break through and, as you utter it, feel with great relief and satisfaction, 'Yes! That says it! That satisfies me!' Any satisfying words, or phrases, that have come to you are likely to contain some alliteration, or assonance; and apart from these making what you want to say easier to grasp, and easier to remember, the chiming sounds may also help you feel you are giving satisfying expression to the very particular *feeling,* and *intensity* of feeling, that is giving rise to the utterances. At some level, every character is *choosing* their words, and as each human, and precisely how they feel, is unique, then no two characters will choose precisely the same words to express what they are feeling. A character other than you would have found, and been satisfied with, not *your* words or phrases, but quite different ones. And in the universe of Shakespeare, characters tend to enjoy the gift of fluent access to the words which best give expression to what they are feeling, and to what they want to get across. They readily call up all the words, phrases and sentences that make them feel, 'Yes, that's it! That satisfies!' And as well as coming from the top, literal meaning of the words they use, the satisfaction they experience will be due also to how the words have been ordered to create certain groupings, and patterns, of particular consonants and vowels. So it is indeed good, therefore, to ask if any assonance, alliteration or onomatopoeia in your lines is doing any more than simply making what you say pithy and memorable (though this, in itself, is a good thing). Is their use also indicative of a particular colour, or intensity, of feeling on the part of the character speaking the lines? Often they will be; and playing them with a sensuous, muscular *relish*, will help put you in contact with the unique quality and strength of those feelings; it will put you in touch with why he or she *needs*, and at some level is *choosing*, this particular combination of assonantal, onomatopoeic or alliterative sounds. It can help connect you, in a felt way therefore, with who the character *is*.

Connecting to the feeling in alliteration – Paulina

Here is the opening line from Paulina's speech in *The Winter's Tale* in which she wishes to make Leontes know and feel the extremity of his guilt for having caused the death of his innocent queen:

> **Paulina:** *What studied torments, tyrant, hast for me?* 3:2:175

Act this line. You can't say it to too quickly, can you? It is too densely clotted with its four 't's', the two 'st's and the related 'ts'.

> *What STudied tormenTS tyrant, haST for me?*

It is as if Paulina cannot pack enough 't's' or 'st's' into the line satisfactorily to embody the titanic outrage, and need to hurt which very nearly overwhelm her. At this moment, Paulina's spirit needs, and chooses, these percussive, stabbing words; and having chosen them, she will wring all the satisfaction out of them that her speaking apparatus will allow.

ALLITERATION, ASSONANCE AND ONOMATOPOEIA – Key points

- Alliteration is the device of deliberately grouping together words containing the same consonants.
- Assonance is the device of deliberately grouping together words containing the same vowels sounds.
- Onomatopoeia occurs when words, or groups of words, sound like, or are somehow suggestive of, what the word refers to. Very often onomatopoeic sounds will be combined with alliteration and/or assonance, as in, 'wild and windy weather'.
- Any of these devices, on their own, or in different combinations, can render any utterance more pithy and memorable. But their presence can be indicative also of the underlying feelings (and intensity of feelings) giving rise to your character needing, and at some level choosing, this particular combinations of assonantal, onomatopoeic, or alliterative sounds. Playing these with muscular relish will help put you in touch with these feelings.

CHAPTER FIVE

'THOU' AND 'YOU'

You may have noticed when reading Shakespeare's plays that characters address each other in one of two ways: they use 'thou', 'thee' and 'thy'; or they use 'you' and 'your'. I'm sometimes asked if these forms of address are interchangeable: does Shakespeare choose one rather than the other, merely on the basis of which sounds better in any particular context? This is a fair question as, in many instances, Shakespeare's characters can switch several times between one form and another within one short scene; or even within one speech.

In Early English, (circa 450-1066) the distinction between 'you' and 'thou' was simple and clear: 'thou', 'thee' and 'thy' were singular; 'you' and 'ye' were plural. After the Normans invaded England in 1066, when French became the language of government, and of more 'refined' literary expression, English absorbed more and more French words; and it probably then also assimilated the French distinction between 'tu' and 'vous'.

'Thou', became the equivalent to the French, 'tu'; and 'you' the equivalent to the French 'vous'.

'You' was more formal.

'Thou' was the form generally used between intimates and lovers.

But by the 1400s, long before the period when Shakespeare wrote his plays (c.1591-1613), the distinction between the use of 'you' or 'thou' had already begun to break down. The choice of one over the other was becoming more random. And by 1700, the use of 'thou' had all but disappeared from the spoken language. On most occasions, however, it is clear that Shakespeare is using the distinction between 'you' and 'thou' with deliberate dramatic intent. There are some occasions where it will always remain conjectural if the choice of one or other has been made for reasons of musicality, or is, indeed, simply random.

General Guidelines

Here are the general guidelines as to what the use of either 'thou' or 'you' may signify in Shakespeare:

Persons of equal station

– 'You' is used amongst persons of equal station. From *Julius Caesar*:

Cassius: *I know that virtue to be in **you**, Brutus,*
*As well as I do know **your** outward favour.*   1:2:90

Amongst his fellow tradesmen in *A Midsummer Night's Dream*, Quince distributes the roles for the play to be performed before the court:

Quince: *No, no, **you** must play Pyramus; and, Flute, **you** Thisbe.*   1:2:51

Lovers

– 'Thou' is the form used by lovers; Romeo and Juliet use it almost exclusively:

*O Romeo, Romeo, wherefore art **thou** Romeo?*   2:2:33

Intimates

– 'Thou' is the form chosen also by those who share a non-sexual, but affectionate bond. In *As You Like It*, the inseparable cousins, Rosalind and Celia, often (though by no means exclusively) use, 'thou':

Celia: *O, my poor Rosalind, whither wilt **thou** go?*
*Wilt **thou** change fathers? I will give **thee** mine.*   1:3:86

Practical or weighty matters

– 'You' can also be the form used between intimates, when the subject matter is weighty, and/or where there is some practical business to be sorted out.

In *Much Ado About Nothing*, Beatrice has asked Benedick to '*Kill Claudio*' for shaming his intended bride, Hero. Having, just before, declared his love for Beatrice, and begun to address her as 'thou', Benedick immediately reverts to 'you', as more appropriate to the planning of such a portentous matter:

Benedick: *Think **you** in your soul the Count Claudio hath wrong'd Hero?*

Beatrice: *Yea, as sure as I have a thought, or a soul.*

Benedick: *Enough, I am engaged; I will challenge him. I will kiss **your** hand, and so I leave **you**.*   4:1

Higher status to lower

– 'Thou' is also the form often used when someone addresses a person of lower status than his or herself. It might be used by a king to a subject, a father speaking to his child, a lord to a servant etc. And regularly the lower status character will address the upper status person with, 'you'.

From *Henry VI Part 2*:

Sir Humphrey: *Villain, **thy** father was a plasterer;*
*And **thou**, **thyself**, a shearman, art **thou** not?*   4:2:128

A messenger delivers the news to Lady Macbeth that King Duncan is on his way: she uses 'thou' and 'thy'; he addresses her as 'you':

Messenger: *The king comes here tonight.*

Lady Macbeth: ***Thou**'rt mad to say it.*
*Is not **thy** master with him? who, were't so,*
Would have inform'd for preparation.

Messenger: *So please **you**, it is true…*   1:5:31

Insulting use of 'thou'

If a character wants to insult or condescend to a peer then he might use 'thou'. In *Twelfth Night*, Toby advises Sir Andrew that he can raise the heckles of Cesario (Viola disguised as a boy) by addressing him as 'thou' (of course, the insulting irony of Toby's addressing Sir Andrew himself as 'thou' is lost on the weak-brained knight):

Sir Toby: *If thou '**thouest**' him thrice, it shall not be amiss.*   3:2:42

Addressing Gods

– 'Thou', is the form usually employed when addressing God or Gods. Edmund in *King Lear*:

Edmund: ***Thou**, Nature, art my Goddess; to **thy** law*
My services are bound.   1:2:1

Plural

– 'You', (or sometimes 'ye') is the form used also when more than one person is addressed, of whatever status. At the banquet, Macbeth addresses his lords collectively as 'you', and also when speaking to the two murderers. And, of course, Mark Antony uses 'you' in his oration to the assembled Roman people:

Antony: *Friends, Romans, countrymen, lend me your ears...*   3:2:74

Dead or absent characters

– Characters who would normally use 'you' when addressing a particular character, will often use 'thou' and 'thee' if addressing the same character when he or she is dead, or absent. Lady Macbeth talks to her absent husband:

Lady Macbeth: *... Hie thee hither,*
That I may pour my spirits in thine ear...   1:5:25

Banquo addresses the absent Macbeth in his soliloquy:

Banquo: *Thou hast it now, King, Cawdor, Glamis,*
As the Weird Women promis'd...   3:1:1

Later, Macbeth addresses Banquo's ghost:

Macbeth: *Thy bones are marrowless, thy blood is cold:*
Thou hast no speculation in those eyes.   3:4:93

Shifts between 'you' and 'thou'

In the first scene of *As You Like It*, Orlando, and his brother Oliver, begin by addressing each other stiffly as 'you':

Oliver: *Know you where you are, sir?*

Orlando: *O, sir, very well: here in your orchard.*

Oliver: *Know you before whom, sir?*   1:1:40

Shortly after these strained exchanges, the rankling animosity between the brothers suddenly breaks out in physical assault; and at precisely that point, Oliver switches to addressing Orlando with the insulting 'thou':

Orlando: *Come, come, elder brother, you are too young in this.*

Oliver: *Wilt thou lay hands on me villain?*   1:1:53

This exchange offers another example of how, within the same conversation, a shift from one form of address to the other may signify a shift in the feeling or temper of the relationship between the characters. The shift may be from warmth to distance, from formality to closeness, from love to suspicion, or from an intimacy to a more objective discussion of some practical business at hand (as in the Benedick and Beatrice exchange quoted above). Noting these shifts, therefore, can provide information for directors and performers, about changing dynamics within a character or scene.

One conversation between Rosalind and Celia in *As You Like It* provides a further example of how such a shift represents a change in the tone of a relationship; the shift, this time, is from 'you' to 'thou'. Affectionately addressing Rosalind with 'thou' and 'thee' Celia works hard to brighten the spirits of her currently disconsolate cousin. Not feeling playful, or closely connected to anyone, at the moment, Rosalind addresses Celia using 'you':

Celia: *I pray **thee**, Rosalind, sweet my coz, by merry.*

Rosalind: *Dear Celia, I show more mirth than I am mistress of, and would **you** yet I were merrier? Unless **you** could teach me to forget a banished father, **you** must not learn me how to remember any extraordinary pleasure.*

Celia: *Herein I see **thou** lovest me not with the full weight that I love **thee**.*

1:2:1

Later in their conversation, when Celia manages to restore a flow of relaxed and playful intimacy between her and her cousin, Rosalind suddenly again addresses Celia with 'thou':

Rosalind: *Nay, now **thou** goest from Fortune's office to Nature's.* *1:2:39*

An exchange often used to exemplify the significance of switches between the different forms, is an earlier section of the Benedick and Beatrice scene just cited. These two duelling wits have always addressed one another using 'you':

Beatrice: *I wonder that **you** will still be talking, Signor Benedick: nobody marks **you**.* *1:1:112*

(The one time she does use 'thee' addressing Benedick, he is absent. *3:1:111*)

But in the scene where, at last, he finally declares his love to Beatrice, Benedick switches several times between addressing her with 'you' and 'thou'; and one (mostly) can discern a logic in these switches. For his initial, relatively dispassionate observations about his love, he uses 'you'; but when he presses his love more personally and directly, hoping for more intimate contact, he changes to 'thou'. Insecure, Beatrice keeps her cards self-protectively to her chest, and persists in her use of 'you':

Benedick: *I do love nothing in the world so well as **you**: is not that strange?*

Beatrice: *As strange as the thing I know not. It were as possible for me to say I loved nothing so well as **you**...*

Benedick: *By my sword, Beatrice, **thou** lovest me.* (An attempt at the intimacy he hopes for.)

Beatrice: *Do not swear, and eat it.*

Benedick: *I will swear by it that **you** love me; and I will make him eat it that says I love not **you**.* (His offer rejected, he has reverted to the previous less personal form.)

Beatrice: *Will **you** not eat your word?*

Benedick: *With no sauce that can be devised to it. I protest I love **thee**.* (Another attempt to establish intimacy.)   *4:1:269*

Going by the 'you/thou' logic in Benedick's lines, one might understandably expect Beatrice to switch to 'thou' when she, too, finally opens her heart, and declares her love for Benedick; but she continues in her use of 'you':

Beatrice: *I love you with so much of my heart that none is left to protest.*
                                                                  4:1:286

In such an instance, one must speculate as to what individual psychology, if any, induces Beatrice to choose 'you' at such a moment.

To conclude: any alternating uses of 'thou' and 'you' which you encounter are probably telling you that some change in the tenor of the conversation is occurring. You do need, therefore, to question each shift in the light of the general guidelines outlined above, and to draw your own conclusions as to what dramatically (if definitely, indeed, anything) it may signify. And be prepared for the reality that, reaching a conclusion may not always be as straightforward as one might wish; and that, in some cases, any two commentators are likely to arrive at different conclusions.

'THOU' AND 'THEE' – Key points

- 'You' is more formal: the form generally used between those of equal social standing; and the form used by someone of lower social status addressing a person of higher standing.

- 'Thou' is the form generally used between intimates and lovers; or by a high-ranking person addressing someone of lower station.

- 'You' can also be the form used between intimates, when the subject matter has little personal content; when, for example, some business or serious issue is to be dealt with.

- 'You' (or sometimes 'ye') is the form used when more than one person is addressed, of whatever status.

- 'Thou', is the form usually employed when addressing dead or absent persons, or Gods.

- A shift from one form of address to the other will often (but perhaps not always) signify a shift in the feeling, or temper, of the relationship between characters.

CHAPTER SIX

WHAT IS VERSE?

A fear beginners usually have when approaching the acting of Shakespeare is a fear of not knowing 'how to act the verse'. And some students, when they first come to me, are not entirely certain as to what precisely is the difference between 'verse' and the other thing called 'prose'. I will assume, therefore, that the reader knows little, or nothing about verse in general, nor any more about Shakespearean verse in particular.

What is 'verse'

'Verse' is a term used to refer to a type of language which is different to 'prose'. The form of language we use in everyday exchanges is prose; the type of language you hear in a news broadcast is prose. Verse is more regularly structured than prose, primarily, but by no means exclusively, in terms of the artfully controlled regularity of its rhythm. In prose, the rhythms are random.

Looking through any Shakespeare play-text, you will notice that, in some sections, each line on the page has a capital letter, and that the lines do not run fully over to the right-hand margin. And, in other sections, you will notice that the text is laid out as it would be in a novel, the print extending from margin to the margin. The sections where the lines run across to the right hand margin are in 'prose'; sections where each line begin with a capital letter are the sections in 'verse'. Most Shakespeare plays comprise a mixture of both prose and verse, albeit in widely differing proportions.

Syllables

If we break any word up into the various meaningful 'sound-parts' that make it up, then we are isolating the 'syllables' that make up the word. The word 'audience', for example, is made up of three sound-parts, three syllables: 'Au', 'di' and 'ence'. 'Dramatic' has three syllables: 'Dram', 'at' and 'ic'. 'Shopping' is made up of two syllables: 'shop' and 'ping'. 'Actor' is made up of two syllables: 'act' and 'or'. 'Algebra' has three: 'Al', 'ge' and 'bra'. 'Mathematics' has four: 'Math', 'e', 'mat' and 'ics'.

Stressed and unstressed syllables in English words

The syllables that make up any word in English can be either 'stressed' or 'unstressed'. Say the word 'Richard' aloud as you would naturally say it. The quality, the feel of the 'Rich' part is different from the 'ard' part. There is a feeling of 'leaning on', a sense of a forward and outwardly directed pressure on, this syllable. And there is a sort of 'letting go,' or feeling of 'releasing back into oneself', on the 'ard'. A 'leaned-on' syllable such as 'Rich' is variously referred to as 'carrying a stress'; as 'having a strong stress'; as 'stressed'; as 'being a strong beat'; or simply as 'strong'. A syllable such as 'ard' is referred to as 'not carrying a stress'; as being 'unstressed'; as 'having a weak stress'; as 'being a weak beat'; or simply as 'weak'. The word 'Richard' therefore, is made up of one strong, or stressed, syllable, and one weak, or unstressed, syllable: '**Rich**-ard'. (For clarity, I will, throughout, present stressed syllables in bold.)

The word 'Shakespeare' has the same stressed-unstressed arrangement as 'Richard': '**Shake**-speare'. So has 'Ireland'–'**Ire**-land'; or 'wicked'–'**wick**-ed'; or 'husband'– '**hus**-band'.

You can hear, I'm sure, that the three-syllable word 'dramatic' comprises one strong stress – the second one: 'dram-**at**-ic'.

'Algebra' has two strong stresses; one on the first syllable ('al') and one on the last syllable 'bra': '**al**-ge-**bra**'.

'Mathematics' has four syllables, with two strong beats; one on the first syllable, 'math'; and one on the third syllable, 'mat': '**math**-e-**mat**-ics'.

Of course, there are a lot of words of merely one syllable (box, nice, tyre, eat, bad, short, heart), and when one pronounces such words on their own, they have the feel of a stressed syllable. For example, if a non-English speaker points at a box and asks, 'What's the word for one of those?', the way in which you speak the word 'box', in reply, would have the feel of a stressed syllable. But when used as part of a sentence comprising a number of different words, a one-syllable word can find itself either stressed or unstressed, depending on the circumstances in which it occurs in that sentence. There will be examples to illustrate this observation as the discussion continues.

Because English words are made up of such stressed and unstressed syllables, it becomes possible, when writing sentences, to choose certain words over others, and to arrange them in a particular order, such that the strong and weak syllables fall in a set pattern; in a regular rhythm. Nursery rhymes provide clear and simple examples of words arranged so that the stressed and unstressed syllables of the words of which they consist form an easily discernible rhythm.

It is for that reason, when first introducing students and actors to Shakespeare's verse, that I begin by examining a few of the best known of these rhymes. The easiest way to develop a vocabulary for discussing Shakespeare's verse, is firstly to examine verse which is simpler, and which most English speakers remember from when they were at school.

Here is the first verse of 'Mary Had a Little Lamb':

Mary had a little lamb,
Its fleece was white as snow,
And everywhere that Mary went,
The lamb was sure to go.

The first line of this rhyme has four stressed syllables and three unstressed:

Ma-*ry* **had** *a* **lit**-*tle* **lamb**...

The second has three stressed and three unstressed:

Its **fleece** *was* **white** *as* **snow**...

Read this other example of a nursery rhyme aloud:

Simple Simon met a pieman
Going to the fair;
Said Simple Simon to the pieman,
'Let me taste your ware.'

The first line has four stressed syllables and four unstressed: four strong beats and four weak beats.

Sim-*ple* **Si**-*mon* **met** *a* **pie**-*man*...

The second line has three stressed and two unstressed:

Go-*ing* **to** *the* **fair**...

The third line has five unstressed and four stressed:

Said **Sim**-*ple* **Sim**-*on* **to** *the* **pie**-*man*...

The fourth has three strong beats and two weak beats:

'Let *me* **taste** *your* **ware.'**

Notice that if one were saying the second and third lines of this little verse, as part of an everyday conversation, one might *not* put a strong stress on the word '*to*': one may say them stressed in this way:

Go-*ing to the* **fair**; *said* **Sim**-*ple* **Sim**-*on to the* **pie**-*man*...

In order to maintain the regular rhythm of any verse, one sometimes needs to give a strong stress to a syllable, or short word, that in an ordinary situation, one might speak as *un*stressed. I have underlined them:

> **Go**-*ing* **to** *the* **fair;**
> *Said* **Sim**-*ple* **Sim**-*on* **to** *the* **pie**-*man*

'Feet' in verse

In the little poems above, what creates the 'rhythm' is that there is a particular grouping of stressed and unstressed syllables which is regularly repeated. Here is the third line of the 'Mary' poem:

> *And* **eve**-*ry*-**where** *that* **Ma**-*ry* **went**...

In this line, the syllable-grouping which is constantly repeated is that of a single *unstressed* syllable, followed by a single *stressed* syllable. The 'unit' which, when repeated, provides the line's readily heard rhythm is: 'dee dum'...

...and there are four of these units in this line:

> *[And* **eve**-*]* *[ry-***where***]* *[that* **Ma**-*]* *[ry* **went***]*

[Dee dum] [dee dum] [dee dum] [dee dum]

And three in the following line:

> *[The* **lamb***]* *[was* **sure***]* *[to* **go***]*

[Dee dum] [dee dum] [dee dum]

In discussions of verse, any such 'rhythm-unit' is referred to as a 'foot'. I always think of 'feet' as regular steps within the verse; like regular steps within a dance.

This 'dee dum' is a foot commonly chosen by writers of verse in English, and it is referred to as an 'iamb' (short for *iambus*, from the Latin). The stress is on the first syllable, the 'i' (pronounced as in 'I, Claudius'); the 'b' of 'amb' is sounded: '**i**-amb'.

There are a number of other common types of feet, of course. Read aloud the two opening lines of 'Lochinvar', by Sir Walter Scott:

> *Oh, young Lochinvar is come out of the West*
> *Through all the wide Border his steed was the best.*

You can hear the rhythm here is: Dee dum dee dee dum dee dee dum dee dee dum etc. The basic 'rhythm-unit', the 'foot' the poet elects to use in this poem has three syllables, not two. Each foot is made up of two unstressed syllables, followed by one stressed: 'dee dee dum'. Scott chose this type of foot, no doubt, to capture the sense of the thrusting young hero galloping through the landscape on his way to claim his love:

*[Oh, **young**] [Loch-in-**var**]   [is come **out**]   [of the **West**]*

[Dee dum]   [dee dee dum]   [dee dee dum] [dee dee dum]

*[Through **all**] [the wide **Bor**-] [der his **steed**] [was the **best**.]*

[Dee   dum] [dee dee dum]   [dee dee dum] [dee dee dum]

I know when you look at the scansion above, instead of there being a full foot, a full 'dee dee dum', at the beginning of each line, there appears instead to be a 'dee dum', an iamb. But, I think, if you listen carefully to the way you instinctively speak the lines, you will realise you are marking in a silent 'dee' at the start of the second line, before the sounded 'dee dum'; before you say, *'Through all'*. Although not sounded, for the chosen rhythm of the lines to be maintained, this 'virtual' beat (as such silent beats are sometimes called) asks to be marked. Also, at the beginning of the first line, one can regard a silent 'dee' as being, as it were, implied. Here is the verse then, scanned with the virtual beats represented:

*[Oh, **young**] [Loch-in-**var**]   [is come **out**]   [of the **West**]*
(dee)   [Dee dum]   [dee dee dum]   [dee dee dum] [dee dee dum]

*[Through **all**]   [the wide **Bor**-] [der his **steed**] [was the **best**.]*
(dee)   [Dee dum]   [dee dee dum]   [dee dee dum] [dee dee dum]

(Another commentator may regard each of these two lines as simply consisting of one iamb, one 'dee dum', followed by three 'dee dee dums'. But I shan't ask you to take sides in such a momentous controversy; sufficient to say, the basic foot from which the 'Lochinvar' lines are constructed is 'dee dee dum'. This type of foot is known as an 'anapaest' and I mention it here only as a representative of the other possible types of feet that versifiers use, apart from the 'dee dum', the iamb.)

'Lines' in verse

In the case of all the snatches of verse so far presented, you can see that each new line finishes well before reaching the right-hand margin of the page. The poems are arranged in 'lines' of a fixed and regular length; and to re-enforce this (as the traditional convention dictates) each new line is introduced with a capital letter. (Of course, in more modern verse, the convention of having a capital letter at the beginning of each line is commonly disregarded.)

But even without seeing it written down, or in print, when the poem is spoken, you can *hear*, not just its regular rhythms, but you can hear where each line ends, and the next one begins. You readily pick up that the poem proceeds in lines of pre-determined lengths; that is, of a *pre-determined number of syllables*. Combined with the regular arrangement of the syllables, this grouping of the words into lines of a regulated length provides further conscious *form* to the poem: it breaks the language up into regular and predictable chunks, allowing the content of the verse to be even more digestible and memorable.

Consider the difference if the 'Simple Simon' and 'Mary' poems were written without a regular rhythm, and without set line-lengths: in 'normal', or more 'naturalistic' language; in prose:

> *Simple Simon met a pieman on his way to the fair and asked him if he could taste some of his ware.*

> *Mary had a little lamb which had snow-white fleece, and no matter where Mary went the lamb would always go as well.*

Neither sounds as energetic, pithy or purposeful, does it? Not so much fun to speak, or listen to.

And imagine if you recited one of these rhymes, fully in its proper verse form, to a focus-group of toddlers, but spoke it 'flatly', without placing an emphasis, or leaning, at least a little, on the strong stresses. The infants will be disappointed. They will sense that the recitation is missing a vital and pleasure-giving element that could, and ought to, be there.

'Verses' or 'stanzas' within verse

As well as being divided up into 'rhythm-units' or 'feet', and into individual 'lines' consisting of regular numbers of these feet, one other common (though not essential) characteristic of 'verse' is that, fixed numbers of lines can be grouped together into 'verses' or 'stanzas', as in:

> *Mary had a little lamb,*
> *Whose fleece was white as snow.*
> *And everywhere that Mary went,*
> *The lamb was sure to go.*

> *It followed her to school one day*
> *Which was against the rule.*
> *It made the children laugh and play,*
> *To see a lamb at school.*

> *And so the teacher turned it out,*
> *But still it lingered near etc.*

With the exception of a few instances that may be argued for, it is only in songs, or in the odd spell, that Shakespeare arranges his poetry into verses or stanzas.

Rhyme

Another verse-device which has probably come into your mind in the course of the discussion, is that of choosing words, so that the ends of verse-lines rhyme. Here are our little poems with the rhymes marked in bold:

Mary had a little lamb,
*Its fleece was white as **snow**,*
And everywhere that Mary went,
*The lamb was sure to **go**.*

Simple Simon met a pieman
*Going to the **fair**;*
Said Simple Simon to the pieman,
*Let me taste your **ware**.*

You may already have noticed that in the 'Simon' poem, rhyming is happening not only at the end of the lines, but also occurs *within* the first, and second, lines:

*Simple **Simon** met a **pieman**,*
Going to the fair;
*Said Simple **Simon** to the **pieman**,*
Let me taste your ware.

This is known as 'internal' rhyme, and represents the last of the devices deployed in the making of verse that I wish to introduce. There are, of course, a number of other devices that verse avails of, but most of these are also used in prose; for example, oppositions, assonance, alliteration and onomatopoeia.

WHAT IS VERSE? – Key points

- The elements which, more than any other, define traditional verse are rhythm, line-lengths, rhyme, and stanzas. There are other devices used in verse, but these are also to be found in prose.

- Rhythm is created by the repetition of 'rhythm-units' made up of different combinations of stressed and unstressed syllables, such as, 'dee dum' (an 'iamb'). The iamb is a rhythm-unit very common in English verse.

- A 'rhythm-unit' is referred to as a 'foot'.

- Lines consist of a fixed number of 'feet'.

- The use of the above devices renders the content of any verse more easily memorised by the speaker; and more memorable, and more readily digestible, for the listener.

CHAPTER SEVEN

SHAKESPEARE'S VERSE

Feet in Shakespeare's verse

The rhythm-unit used by Shakespeare (mostly) when creating his verse is the same as the rhythm-unit used in the 'Mary' poem, the iamb:

[And eve-] [ry-where] [that Ma-] [ry went]

[dee dum] [dee dum] [dee dum] [dee dum]

[The lamb] [was sure] [to go.]

[dee dum] [dee dum] [dee dum]

I want you to act the lines below aloud, and ask you to approach them exactly as you would the lines of a nursery rhyme: that is, making very clear to the listener that they are lines of verse which have a strong regular rhythm.

In *Antony and Cleopatra*, Enobarbus describes the first time Antony saw the Egyptian queen:

Enorbarbus:
The barge she sat in, like a burnished throne...   2:2:191

Antony addresses the corpse of his friend, Julius Caesar:

Antony: *Oh, pardon me thou bleeding piece of earth*   3:1:254

Earlier in *Julius Caesar*, Cassius relates to Brutus how the near-deified Julius got very humanly ill:

Cassius: *He had a fever when he was in Spain...*   1:2:119

Oberon in *A Midsummer Night's Dream*, describes how he intends to use the love-inducing juice from a magic flower he has asked Puck to fetch:

Oberon: *I'll watch Titania when she is asleep,*
And drop the liquor of it in her eyes...   2:1:177

You will have found that all of these lines are indeed made up of the same rhythm-units of one stressed and one unstressed syllable; the same 'dee dum's' as in: *'Its fleece was white as snow'*; the same iambs. As one does with the 'Simon' poem, in order to maintain the rhythm of any verse, one sometimes has to award a strong stress to a syllable, or short word, that in normal conversation you would speak with a weak stress. Since I asked you to approach these lines as lines of rhythmic verse, I imagine you instinctively found yourself doing this. You probably put a strong stress, for example, on the words 'when' and 'was' in Cassius' lines, words which you might give very little, or no, stress to in regular conversation. I have underlined them:

He **had** a **fev**-er **when** he **was** in **Spain**...

Here is one way a person may say this line as part of everyday speech:

He **had** a **fev**-er when he was in **Spain**...

Or in Oberon's lines, you may well have given a strong stress to the small words 'when', 'is', 'of' and 'in' (underlined):

I'll **watch** Ti-**tan**-ia **when** she **is** a-**sleep**,
And **drop** the **liqu**-or **of** it **in** her **eyes**...

Here are all four lines with their iambic rhythm clearly marked. Act them aloud again, pointing up the rhythm:

Oh, **par**-don **me** thou **bleed**-ing **piece** of **earth**...

He **had** a **fev**-er **when** he **was** in **Spain**,

The **barge** she **sat** in, **like** a **burn**-ished **throne**

I'll **watch** Tit-**an**-ia **when** she **is** a-**sleep**...
And **drop** the **liqu**-or **of** it **in** her **eyes**...

Verse-lines in Shakespeare

We have already learnt that in verse, a rhythm-unit is referred to as a 'foot'; so the 'Mary' line, '*Its* **fleece** *was* **white** *as* **snow**' would be said to comprise three 'feet'. The line length that Shakespeare uses is one containing *five* feet, and a line with five feet is referred to as a 'pentameter'.

The word pentameter comes from classical Greek: the '*pent*' part of the word indicates '*five*', as it does in *pent*agon (a five-sided shape), or in *Pent*ateuch (the first five books of the bible). The '*metre*' part of 'pentameter' (again from the Greek) indicates 'measure' or 'unit of measurement'; so 'pentameter' means 'comprising five units of measurement'. In the case of verse, the unit of measurement is the 'foot'. One of the 'Mary' lines consisting of four feet would be referred to as a 'tetrameter' (Greek, '*tetra*': four): '*And* **eve**-ry-**where** *that* **Ma**-ry **went**...'. A line with three is referred to as a 'trimeter': '*The* **lamb** *was* **sure** *to* **go**...'. As each unit of measurement (each foot) in most

Shakespeare lines is an iamb, his verse-lines are referred to as being 'iambic'; they are 'iambic pentameters'.

Here are some of the verse-lines from above, laid out with their iambic pentameter structure made 'visible':

Antony: *[Oh, par-] [don me] [thou bleed] [-ing piece] [of earth]...*
    [dee dum] [dee dum] [dee dum]   [dee dum] [dee dum]
     iamb   iamb   iamb   iamb   iamb
      1   2   3   4   5

Cassius: *[He had] [a fev-] [er when] [he was] [in Spain]...*
    [dee dum] [dee dum] [dee dum] [dee dum] [dee dum]
     iamb   iamb   iamb   iamb   iamb
      1   2   3   4   5

Oberon: *[I'll watch] [Tit-a-] [nia when] [she is] [a-sleep],*
    [dee dum] [dee dum] [dee dum] [dee dum] [dee dum]
     iamb   iamb   iamb   iamb   iamb
      1   2   3   4   5

Most of Shakespeare's verse is 'unrhymed', and unrhymed verse, particularly when it is composed of iambic pentameters, is referred to as 'blank verse'. The first use of blank iambic pentameters in English literature is in a translation of book two and four of Virgil's Aeneid by Henry Howard, Earl of Surrey. It was first published in 1547, some years, as it happens, after his execution for treason; but scholars believe it was composed around 1540. And the first known use of unrhymed iambic pentameters in an English *drama* is in the play *Gorboduc* by Thomas Norton and Thomas Sackville (1561). So thirty years later when Shakespeare began his writing career, blank verse was still a relatively recent arrival.

The vast majority of Shakespearean verse-lines are indeed iambic pentameters, but there are instances of verse-lines consisting of other lengths and other types of feet. Not exclusively, but by and large, these different feet and line-lengths are reserved for songs and spells (as with stanzas); for speeches spoken by faery characters; and for the comic verse in the play-within-a-play in *A Midsummer Night's Dream*.

Why the iambic pentameter?

It has often been proposed that the iambic pentameter is best suited to drama because, with its ten syllables, it corresponds to the number of syllables any English speaker, on average, tends to speak on one breath.

I recently put this piece of received wisdom to the test, and listened carefully to a large number of news reports, political debates, celebrity and political interviews, conversations on daytime television, conversations and arguments between people on the bus etc. What I observed was that, more often than not, the average number of syllables spoken on one breath was significantly greater than ten. What was also evident was that, generally speaking, the number of syllables used in one breath increased with A) the education and social status of the speaker, B) the formality of the situation, C) the weight or urgency of the topic, and D) the degree of emotion driving the talk.

Shakespeare plays, even from the first lines of their opening scenes, usually involve heightened emotion, formality of situation, persons of high rank and education, and situations of great personal, or political, moment. I wonder, therefore, has the line length less to do with the duration of *breath* English-speakers use in speech, and more to do with the length of the major *sense-units* that, on average, English-speakers need, and use when constructing sentences with which to communicate with one another.

'Major' sense-units

The length of an iambic pentameter snugly accommodates such major sense-units: units around the size of the '*main* chunks of sense', or 'sense-units' from which an English-speaker, *on a loose average*, will build his or her utterances.

I'm using 'sense-unit' here to mean, not necessarily a complete sentence, although it could be a complete sentence. '*Mary had a little lamb*', for example, is a complete unit of sense; and it could also stand on its own as a complete sentence. The line, '*And everywhere that Mary went*', can be considered a complete sense-unit, but is not a complete sentence: it is a unit of sense that is part of, that goes into making up, a complete sentence.

An English-speaker will always, of course, use many sense-units which are shorter, and ones that are longer, than those containable within a line of blank verse; but I am talking now about the rough average. Below are some examples of lines where a major sense-unit can be seen neatly to be contained within a single pentameter line:

Hamlet: *To be, or not to be, that is the question...*   *3:1:56*

Macbeth: *Is this a dagger which I see before me...?*   *2:1:33*

Desdemona: *What shall I do to win my lord again?*   *4:2:150*

The above are sense-units which fit into the iambic pentameter, and which could also stand as complete sentences.

The following two lines from *Richard the Third* and *Hamlet* represent complete sense-units accommodated by an iambic pentameter, but which are *not*, in themselves, complete sentences:

Cassius: *For once, upon a raw and gusty day...*   *J. Caesar 1:2:100*

Hamlet: *Be thou a spirit of health, or goblin damn'd...*   *1:4:40*

In my view then, a ten-syllable pentameter is more a 'neatened-up version', a distilled and regularised version of one of these English major sense-units. It is a form that provides a near 'fits-all' template easily accommodating these average-length major units-of-sense.

When English sense-units are made to fit into verse-lines which have *fewer* than ten syllables, rather than sounding elegantly distilled, they will tend to sound artificially contracted. One will be more aware of them being 'made to fit' into the line. And with this, when lines consist of fewer than ten syllables, each new line will more quickly follow another. This, inevitably, will, begin to draw attention to the lines, 'as lines', drawing attention to the 'artifice' of the verse. The combined effect of these factors is that the verse will sound more 'constructed'; more artificial, and less like humans talking. Shorter lines are fine and fun for songs, poems, proverbs, spells and ditties etc.; but they are not the most suitable for drama. Can you imagine sitting through a play composed of lines of only four, or three, stressed syllables per line? Two hours of the equivalent of *'Mary had a Little lamb'* or *'Ding dong bell / Pussy's in the well'*? What a difference a 'dee dum' or two makes.

Verse in drama asks for a form which, although artificially concentrated, and controlled, will not draw *too much* attention to itself; will not *sound* too artificial; will not sound too different from how people talk. The pentameter's accommodating, pre-fab structure invites a writer to distill their characters' explanations, questions etc. into units more regularised than in everyday speech; but not so regularised as not to give a convincing, *artistic representation* of how humans in the real world construct their spoken exchanges.

Such condensing, and regularisation, can add a definite musicality to any utterance. This, in itself, can be immensely pleasurable to listen to. But, such distillation can also invigorate a character's speech with an added forward impetus; inject it with an increased pointedness and purpose. Artfully created, and intelligently performed, this distilled and regularised version of human discourse can more securely penetrate the awareness of an audience. It can more readily hold their attention than 'normal speech'; and it can do this while still offering an acceptably convincing artistic impression of normal speech.

SHAKESPEARE'S VERSE – Key points

- Most Shakespearean verse-lines are iambic pentameters, i.e. each line consists of five feet; each foot is an iamb, a 'dee dum'.
- Other line lengths, and types of foot, mostly are reserved for songs, spells, speeches spoken by faery characters, and for the comic verse in the play within a play in A Midsummer Night's Dream.
- The ten-syllable pentameter is a distilled and regularised version of one of the major sense-units that, on average, English-speakers use when constructing sentences. Its prefab structure invites a writer to distill his or her characters' explanations, questions etc. into units more regularised than in everyday speech; but not so regularised as not to give a convincing, artistic representation of how humans talk.

CHAPTER EIGHT

WHY HONOUR THE VERSE?

B efore beginning a detailed discussion on how to act Shakespeare's verse in a way that 'honours' it, I think it worthwhile to devote a little space to defending the idea of *why* one should bother honouring it, in the first place.

I remember one young talented actor telling me in class that I was stifling his individuality and creativity, by suggesting to him that a particular Shakespeare line he was delivering asked to be stressed with a particular rhythm. As others sometimes do, this student wondered if it would be more spontaneous and fresh, not to worry about the lines as being verse, and pretty ancient verse at that. Wouldn't it be more exciting and *truthful*, he suggested, to deliver the lines within the natural idiom and rhythm of his own modern way of speaking? My simplest, and shortest, answer to that is: No.

Following such logic a performer might as well say, 'Why do I even have to say the actual words the author has written. Why, as a unique and creative individual, can I not just say what occurs to me on the night; in the moment?' This would be an interesting proposition if plays were about the actors who perform them.

Some directors and actors, however, do try as hard as possible to disguise the fact that what is being spoken is verse. They attempt to force the text into sounding 'like what people talk like today' – so as not, they say, to alienate the audience. It is as if the more colloquial it sounds, the more accessible, and 'truthful', it somehow is going to be. But Shakespeare didn't compose his poetry as a vehicle for his players to sound like 'man or woman in the street in the twenty-first century'. And what do you do when acting in a Shakespeare play, and your character's lines rhyme? Or even rhyme in such a way that your own, and another character's, lines form a highly-wrought sonnet? How do you make that sound 'naturalistic'? Though some will try. And, in any case, no-one speaks in everyday life the way characters do in *any* play, ancient or contemporary. To be in any way effective, even the most 'naturalistic' dramatic writing is actually highly artificial: written and re-written, crafted and distilled, to create an artful 'indication', or illusion, of contemporary speech.

To decide that an audience will be alienated if you don't strive to sound 'contemporary' by ignoring the verse is, to me, akin to believing you will alienate a young listener if you honour the verse of 'Simple Simon', by reciting it with the strong regular rhythm in which it is composed.

By way of expanding on this point, I would like you speak the first 'Simon' line below, *not* honouring the rhythm as one normally would, but instead, strongly emphasising the beats which are marked in bold:

Sim-**ple** Si-**mon** met a pie-**man,** going **to the** fair.

Here is a less exaggerated misrepresentation of the intended stresses:

Sim-ple **Sim**-on met a **pie**-man, going to the **fair.**

Delivered in either of these ways, there is an obvious war going on between the way the line has been created (or has evolved) to be said, and the way it actually is being said. It is, of course, highly unlikely that anyone would propose reciting this rhyme as in the first version above. I exaggerated to make a point. But the second version represents how the words might indeed be delivered as part of a 'naturalistic', 'modern' conversation. It is not, however, how 'Simple Simon' asks to be said.

And it is not just that the clarity of the line's meaning is reduced by delivering it in this 'naturalistic' fashion. Nor is it out of some cold academic rigour, or snobbery, that one believes the rhythms, as writ, need to be observed. The issue is: when the rhythms in 'Simon' are not observed, what is lost is an experience of the particular 'voice' with which the content of the poem is expressed. Listening to the poem's strict, highly artificial rhythms, we hear the voice of a sunny and unconflicted individual; of someone dwelling in a world where strife and adult troubles, rarely, if ever, occur. By honouring the constraints of the rhythm, and the rhyme, a speaker can get in touch with the particular quality of this voice, and sense the soul of which the voice is an expression. And he or she can reveal this to the listener.

Having written a number of plays myself, I know that in those moments when I am putting words in the mouth of a character which is already well-developed in my imagination, I will hear his or her very specific and unique voice. That voice rises up as embodying the unique soul, feelings, motivations and conflicts which animate the character, and which impel him to do what he does in the course of the story of the play. And it is not just the literal content of what he says, or even any idiosyncratic vocabulary he might use, that reveal a character's unique inner-life: it is also very much the *particularity of the rhythms* that he uses when he is talking.

And each individual does not have only one characteristic rhythm. As well as speaking with an individual rhythm in relaxed, everyday situations, we all use different rhythm patterns when in various social or professional situations, and in different emotional, or psychological states. We use differing rhythms depending on whether we are feeling excited or depressed, confident or insecure, lying or telling the truth, at war or at peace within ourselves etc. Shakespeare had a particularly good ear for hearing, and accurately transcribing, the uniqueness of his characters' voices; so if, as well as accurately communicating the content of the lines, you also observe the particular rhythms he has given each of them, you will begin to sense the ways in which the character is different from you. You will sense that Shakespeare's characters express themselves not in *your* personal and contemporary rhythms, but in their own; that each is a different soul from you. Attempting to use your own contemporary speech patterns when speaking Shakespeare's verse means, therefore, that you will hinder your ability to feel your character's feelings and intentions with any accuracy, or with the appropriate degree of intensity. You will be less able to sense who he or she *is*.

Sometimes I hear an audience member remark that the actors in a Shakespeare production did not, *thankfully*, act the text 'as if it were verse'; that they delivered the lines just as if they were speaking 'normally', in a real human situation. Usually when I hear this, it has not at all been the case that the actors have imposed a contemporary naturalistic way of speaking on the lines; it is precisely the opposite.

What has happened is that the cast, first of all, have taken the trouble to work out precisely what their lines mean, and so actually understand themselves what it is they are wishing to convey by acting them. Secondly, they have, in fact, very much been honouring the verse. They have not, indeed, been 'pumping the verse out' in a way that brings attention to itself *as verse*, and which tends to override the meaning and intention of what they are saying, and which unfortunately can, indeed, make it sound so much like, you know, *Shakespearean*. What they have been doing is honouring the verse, but in a way that allows it to marry with, and to serve, the feeling and the active intention in their lines. Acted in this way, the lines have come across as not simply clear, but as clearly *appropriate* to purpose; appropriate to the various characters' situations, and to the various qualities and intensities of feelings which drive them. It's by virtue of the fact that not just Shakespeare's words, but his rhythms, so appropriately embody his characters' feelings and intentions, that the lines they speak come across so lucidly and 'natural sounding'. It is not because the actors have imposed a 'contemporary-like' delivery on the verse.

In *All's Well That Ends Well*, young Bertram refers to *'love's own sweet constraint'* (4:2:16). And sweet is how one should come to regard the constraints of the iambic pentameter.

> **WHY HONOUR THE VERSE?** – Key points
>
> – Observing Shakespeare's rhythms and line lengths allows the rhythms to work **you**. It allows you to begin feeling more like someone else; to begin feeling, with the appropriate degree of intensity, your character's feelings and intentions.
>
> – It allows such feelings and intentions to be much more clearly and effectively communicated to the audience.

CHAPTER NINE

ACTING SHAKESPEARE'S VERSE

Part 1

PLAYING THE RHYTHM

I have identified rhythm, fixed-length lines, stanzas, and rhyme as the key components of verse. And asked to identify the single most profitable of these components to honour when it comes to acting Shakespeare's verse, I would plump unhesitatingly for rhythm.

Playing the rhythm

If then asked, 'What is the single most important thing to accomplish when it comes to honouring the rhythm?', I would say, 'The primary requirement of honouring the rhythm of verse-lines is simply to identify which are the strong, and which the weak, beats in any line; and to make this clear when it comes to acting those lines.

I want you to say the first verse of the 'Mary' poem aloud; but not in the normal way. I want you to say it whilst omitting many of the beats meant to be spoken as strong. Put a strong stress only on the syllables I have indicated in bold:

*Ma-ry had a lit-tle **lamb**,*
*Its **fleece** was white as **snow**,*
*And **eve**-ry-where that Ma-ry **went**,*
*The **lamb** was sure to **go**.*

Spoken in this way, you will hear that there are a number of instances of three-, four-, or five-in-a-row *weak* stresses. In the context of this little poem, these runs of weak syllables do seem rushed and gabbled, do they not? This could be how a person may say the lines, in idle everyday conversation; in an instance where it wasn't of too much importance whether the listener was taking in all of what was being said. But recited with all these consecutive weak beats, the poem will disappoint, and have but a very slippery hold on our group of under-fives.

Acting Shakespeare's verse-lines without honouring all of the strong and weak beats is the equivalent of reciting 'Mary Had a Little Lamb' in something like the way exampled above; and it is equally likely to lessen the line's grip on any audience.

Scanning Shakespeare's lines

As was briefly referred to earlier, the task of identifying which beats are strong and which are weak, is known as 'scanning' the line; or as 'scansion'.

On the face of it, one may imagine scanning to be a pretty straightforward activity; and in many cases it is. Hasn't Shakespeare done that work for us by carefully arranging the words in a particular order – so that the stresses within the words form a regularly repeating, and audibly discernible, pattern? But with at least as many lines as not, identifying the strong and weak beats will require the application of a certain amount of know-how.

And even with all the know-how that is available to help us scan, it is surprisingly true, that if you ask a number of different people what should be the 'correct' scansion of even the most straightforward Shakespeare verse-line, you are likely to receive a variety of different answers. In fact, I am constantly astonished by how others scan lines, and, no doubt, many others would similarly be dumbfounded by the scansions I propose. Ultimately, therefore, you will need to learn how to make your own decisions. The best I can do, therefore, is to provide you with appropriate, and sufficient, equipment to do this.

I will first look at a pair of lines which present less challenge as to how to reach a scanning decision. Then I will go on to examine other less straightforward lines, where reaching a confident decision about scansion will require some extra thought. With these more challenging lines, I will propose various ways I believe they may be scanned, and explain why. Exposure to what possibilities there can be in a number of different cases, will quickly help you to develop your own 'ear' for which scanning, to you, seems most effective for a particular line.

So, what then is the best way to go about deciding which syllable is strong and which is weak? As a very general principle, I suggest that the actor or student does not, to begin with, sit down with a pen or pencil and mark the weaks and strongs on the page. Being asked to begin by scanning the lines can lead to the misapprehension that the actor's first responsibility is, in some slavish, abstract way, to serve 'THE VERSE'. This is not the case: the verse is there to serve the actor, and the character he or she is playing. The verse provides the actor with the means to get the character's intention across with as much clarity, appropriate energy, colour and intensity as possible.

Rather than by scanning lines, then, I usually recommend approaching the verse by first establishing what one's lines *mean* overall; and being certain of the precise meaning of each individual word. When this is clear, next to establish is: What is the *active intention* in each sentence; what is the objective? And as discussed earlier, this will reveal itself to be a specific order, question, or explanation that your character wants to get across to his or her addressee. When you are confident about your objective for each sentence, act the lines aloud. Act them in the way that feels most natural to you; in the way that feels most *effective* as regards getting your question, order or explanation across as clearly as possible.

Having done the preparation, you will, to a certain extent, tend to say the lines with the arrangement of weak and strong stresses Shakespeare intended. However, I do stress 'to a certain extent'. Doing this will bring you perhaps sixty-five, or seventy percent of the way; but not all of the way. Unfortunately, the thirty, or thirty-five percent you may miss can radically reduce the power the verse holds. This is where you must call on your 'verse know-how'; so you can assess if the way you are stressing the lines is indeed the optimum way. Precisely what this 'know-how' is, forms the content of the remainder of this chapter.

I will continue to indicate a strong stress by having it printed in bold, and mark a weak stress by allowing it to remain in regular type; but when reading about the scansion of verse in other contexts, you will find different methods used to mark the syllables. One very common method, is to place / above the stressed syllables and – over the unstressed, as in:

/ –   / –   / –   /
Ma-ry had a lit-tle lamb

Another system you may come across is one which places x above the stressed beats and – above the weak, as in:

x   –   x   – x   –   x
Ma-ry had a lit-tle lamb

I would like to offer you an illustration of how the principles I have just outlined, may be put in to practice.

Here are the opening two lines from Richard the Second's *'hollow crown'* speech.

Richard: *No matter where. Of comfort no man speak.*
Let's talk of graves, of worms, of epitaphs...   *3:2:144*

First establish the objective for each sentence (is it a question, order or explanation?):

–   *'No matter where' is an explanation meaning, 'It does not matter where.'*

- *'Of comfort, no man speak' is an order meaning 'Don't any man speak of comfort.'*
- *'Let's talk of graves, of worms, of epitaphs…' is an order.*

Now, without analysing the rhythm in advance, or trying to 'get it right', act the lines aloud a couple of times; in the way that *naturally occurs to you*.

Having done that, and without looking ahead, I want you to identify which syllables you are stressing as strong, and which as weak.

To help you more clearly sense this, repeat the lines out loud a few more times, exaggerating the rhythm. Really let the listener know which are the strong beats. Acting the lines in this over-emphasised way will allow you to sense more easily which syllable you tend to play as strong and which as weak. In this instance, or in any of the scansion exercises which follow, don't worry about sounding too nursery-rhymey or mechanical. I am not for a moment suggesting that this is how, in the end, you should be acting the lines. This is an exercise.

When you are clear on the 'strongs' and 'weaks' you are playing, mark them with your pencil. I am asking you to 'scan' the lines *as you are naturally tending to say them.* (You can use one of the systems of symbols described above, or simply invent your own way of marking them.) Marking the beats in this visual way will help you to 'see' how you are stressing the lines.

Now count these strong stresses. In all, how many strongs have you given the lines? And how many weaks?

I would scan the lines with five strong, and five weak, as in:

*No **mat**-ter **where**. Of **com**-fort **no** man **speak**.*
*Let's **talk** of **graves**, of **worms**, of **ep**-i-**taphs**…*

This gives each line five consecutive iambs.

*[No **mat**-] [ter **where**.] [Of **com**-] [fort **no**] [man **speak**.]*
*[Let's **talk**] [of **graves**,] [of **worms**,] [of **ep**-] [i-**taphs**…]*

Perfect iambic pentameters.

Just speaking these lines of Richard's with the appropriate ordering or explaining intention will have resulted in the majority of you scanning the lines as I, and most, would scan them. It brought us one-hundred-percent to the rhythm in which Shakespeare heard his characters say them. But, as I suggested earlier, in many other cases it will not be quite as straightforward.

Sometimes when you act a particular line in the way your instinct first suggests, you may find you are giving the line more, or fewer, than the five strong beats that constitute the standard iambic pentameter. You may find you are giving it only four or three. Or maybe only two. Or six or seven. It is, however, much more usual, for one to stress *fewer* than the five strong beats standard for the pentameter, than to stress more.

If you are putting a strong stress on fewer than five beats, then you will be speaking three or more syllables in an row as weak, as 'off-beats': just as you were doing when I asked you to recite the 'dysfunctional' version of the 'Mary' poem above, as in:

> **Ma**-*ry had a lit-tle* **lamb**
> *Its* **fleece** *was white as* **snow**

I would like now to look closely at this critical notion of playing too few strong stresses and too many weak in a verse-line.

Introductory scanning practice – Puck, Lady Macbeth, Richard III

For the purpose of demonstration, I want you now to act out loud Puck's line below. Again, I want you to over-emphasise any strong beats I ask you to play, and to 'throw away' the unstressed beats, i.e. give them very little emphasis.

Firstly, act the line putting a strong stress *only* on the syllables I have indicated in bold:

> **Puck:** *My* **mis**-*tress with a* **mon**-*ster is in* **love**...   3:2:6

This is conceivably how, on first instinct, a student or actor might say it. Scanned in this way the line has only *three* strong stresses. You can also see that it now has two sets of three *consecutive* weak beats. To present this visually, here is the line again, with the two sets of consecutive weak syllables underlined:

> **Puck:** *My* **mis**-<u>*tress with a*</u> **mon**-<u>*ster is in*</u> **love**...

And here are the two sets in isolation:

> -*tress with a*
> -*ster is in*

Deliver the line again this way, three or four times. Get a feel of how it is to act it with just the three strong stresses in this way.

Can you get a sense that in the three-in-a-row weak-beat sections, the delivery seems suddenly to 'skitter' along, slightly free-wheeling and out of control? I call this 'skidding'. It is as if the authority presiding over the line has temporarily loosened its grip.

And now act the line again, this time, as scanned below: with a strong stress now added to the word '*with*'. This will mean that there are four strong beats, and only one set of three-in-a-row weak beats.

*My **mis**-tress **with** a **mon**-<u>ster is in</u> **love**...*

Act it a few times in this way.

To me, it still feels as if the line is not quite being allowed to achieve its full potential; as if an essential building block is missing; or that, for a while, the line has slipped its reins or harness. Speaking the line in this way, the actor will come across as less engaged with what he wants to explain, and so as less authoritative.

Now act the line in a third way. Add another strong beat on the word *'is'*, so creating five alternating weak and strong beats; I want you really to *emphasise* those five, strongly stressed syllables.

*My **mis**-tress **with** a **mon**-ster **is** in **love**...*

And here is the line presented with the five feet artificially separated:

*[My **mis**-] [tress **with**] [a **mon**-] [ster **is**] [in **love**.]*

In the three-strong-beat-only version of Puck's line, we were 'dropping' two syllables which should be played as strong. In the final version these two syllables have been 're-instated', or 'restored', as strong. With the dropped strong beats restored, can you sense, as you act it, that the line now feels 'replete'; 'filled in'; 'plumped out'. Act it again:

*My **mis**-tress **with** a **mon**-ster **is** in **love**...*

Here is Lady Macbeth attempting to bolster Macbeth's resolve:

Lady Macbeth: *But screw your courage to the sticking place...*　　　　　1:7:61

It would not be uncommon to hear this line spoken with only four beats, and with three consecutive unstressed syllables, as in:

*But **screw** your **cour**-<u>age to the</u> **stick**-ing **place***

Here the three (skidded) short syllables are *'age to the'*.

Act the line in this way, over-stressing the four strong beats, and running together the syllables *'-age to the...'*:

*But **screw** your **cour**-<u>age-to-the</u> **stick**-ing **place***

Which is the syllable in this line that needs to be restored as a strong beat?

The candidate I think that calls out for restoration is the word *'to'*.

Act the line aloud again, this time also putting an emphatically strong stress on the word *'to'*:

*But **screw** your **cour**-age **to** the **stick**-ing **place***

Again, do you sense the line seeming more filled out; sounding more like a verse-line; more akin to the child-pleasing delivery of 'Mary had a Little Lamb'? Again, don't fret for now about it sounding nursery-rhymey.

One more example from *Richard the Third*:

Richard: *A horse! A horse! My kingdom for a horse!*   5:4:7

As it 'naturally first comes to one', some might speak this line with four strong beats, and a run of three unstressed:

*A **horse**! A **horse**! My **king**-<u>dom for a</u> **horse**!*

But I prefer it acted with five; with a strong on '*for*':

*A **horse**! A **horse**! My **king**-dom **for** a **horse**!*

As we proceed with this examination of the verse, you will quickly become used to hearing when you speak too many consecutive syllables as unstressed.

Identifying syllables to be 'restored' as strong – Antonio, Macbeth, Brutus
With the lines that follow, first be sure you are clear exactly as to what each of them means, establishing if they constitute a question, order or explanation.

Then identify, and mark, which set, or sets, of three consecutive syllables you think might be in danger of being skidded over. My own suggestions will follow eventually…don't look ahead! When you have decided which three consecutive syllables are in danger of being skidded, identify which of the three is the one that has been 'dropped' and asks to be restored as a strong beat.

The first line I want you to do this with is Antonio's line from *The Merchant of Venice*:

Antonio: *In sooth*, I know not why I am so sad.*   1:1:1

*truth

And now do the same with the following two lines from *Macbeth*. Identify the possible three-in-row weaks, then identify the syllable that should be restored as strong.

Macbeth ruminates on Banquo's great prudence:

Macbeth: *He hath a wisdom that doth guide his valour…*   3:1:52

And finally, mark the likely run of three weaks and so on in this oft-quoted Brutus line from *Julius Caesar*:

Brutus: *There is a tide in the affairs of men…*   4:3:216

Here are the lines marked, first of all, with my suggestions as to which are the three-in-a-row syllables some might play as weak; and secondly, marked as I think it would be better played – with the dropped strong syllable restored.

In order really to feel the difference between the two versions, act all three of the lines again now, with all of the different scansions.

Three-weak-syllable version of Antonio's line:

*In **sooth** I **know** not **why** I-am-so **sad**.*

With the lost strong beat (*'am'*) restored:

*In **sooth** I **know** not **why** I **am** so **sad**.*

There are two different ways I think one might hear the Macbeth line delivered with too few strong syllables. First act it as stressed thus:

*He **hath** a **wis**-dom-that-doth **guide** his **val**-our…*

Then stressed in this way:

*He **hath** a **wis**-dom-that-doth-guide-his **val**-our…*

In this version there are *five* in-a-row weak syllables. It is not so uncommon to hear lines delivered in such a skiddy way. Not a good thing.

And finally, act it with the lost strong beats (*'that'* and *'guide'*) restored:

*He **hath** a **wis**-dom **that** doth **guide** his **val**-our.*

To me, the versions of the lines with five strong syllables, as opposed to four or three, all sound more filled out and authoritative.

As regards the Brutus line, I have heard it argued that the line should be scanned not as a regular pentameter but as one that Shakespeare deliberately wrote, and wanted to be spoken, as an 'irregular'; as having only four strong beats, as in:

*There **is** a **tide** in the af-**fairs** of **men**…*

To my ear, delivering the line with only four strong stresses sounds 'gabbley' in the middle; is equivalent to not having a strong stress on the word *'had'* in the first line of our 'Mary' poem, as in:

*Ma-ry had a **lit**-tle **lamb**…*

I would restore a strong stress to the small word, *'the'*, so filling out the line. (In the circumstance of this line, *'the'* will be pronounced more as 'thee', as it normally will be when occurring before any word which begins with a vowel):

*There **is** a **tide** in **the** af-**fairs** of **men***

Restoring dropped beats in multi-syllable words – King and Macbeth
Not always, but often, it is small, one-syllable words that are acted as weak, and which require a strong stress – those small connecting words that in everyday conversational prose one may well skid over, to no ill effect; words such as: 'to', 'it', 'is', 'and', 'in', 'not', 'if', 'that', 'on', 'then', 'no', 'so' etc. In Puck's line the two syllables in danger of being dropped, and which, therefore, might need restoring, were the words *'with'* and *'is'*. In Lady Macbeth's line the word was *'to'*. In Richard's it was *'for'*.

On other occasions, the syllable in danger of being dropped will often be one occurring *as part* of a word made up from a *number* of syllables.

In the line below, the ailing King in *All's Well That Ends Well* talks to Helena who has come to him, offering to heal the illness which all doctors in the realm have failed to cure:

King: (… We thank you, maiden,)
But may not be so credulous of cure.   2:1:114

I can imagine this line being delivered with only three strong beats and two sets of three-in-a-row weak beats, as in:

*But **may** not-be-so **cred**-ul-ous-of **cure**.*

Say the line aloud a few times with only these three stresses. Acted this way it does sound very skiddy, does it not? There is a small, single word in this line which requires elevating; but also a syllable which is part of a multi-syllable word. The small word *'be'* needs to be restored; and also, the third syllable of the word *'credulous'*. This word needs to be acted with two strong beats, as in: **cred**-*ul*-**ous**.

Act the line now giving the two 'lost' strong beats the same emphasis as the other strong beats:

*But **may** not **be** so **cred**-ul-**ous** of **cure**…*

So, as well as one-syllable words sometimes needing to be re-assigned as a strong beat, often it is a syllable or syllables which form part of a three-, four-, or more syllable word.

Act out loud this line spoken by Macbeth when he sees the phantom dagger:

Macbeth: *I see thee yet in form as palpable*
As this which now I draw…   2:1:40

Depending on the circumstances, the final syllable of the word *'palpable'* may or may not, in everyday speech, receive a strong stress. But in order to fill out Macbeth's verse-line, the third syllable of *'palpable'*, I would say, definitely asks to be honoured as a strong beat. Say the lines again as scanned below, with two strong stresses on 'palpable':

> I *see thee yet in form as palp-a-ble*
> As *this which now I draw...*

And, now, act them again, this time omitting the strong stress on the 'ble' of 'palpable':

> I *see thee yet in form as palp-a-ble*
> As *this which now I draw...*

I miss the final strong beat. Without it, the end of the first line sounds sludgey, undefined.

Summing up: If when you act a line as you are naturally first inclined, you find that you are only giving a strong stress to two, three or four syllables (and therefore have a run, or runs, of consecutive weakly stressed syllables), then you can be sure that, *in the majority of cases*, you are 'dropping' a syllable or syllables which needs be 'restored' as strong. I do say, in the great majority of cases.

When I come to examining Shakespeare's 'irregular' verse-lines in the next chapter, it will be seen that, in some instances, a run of three weak syllables is probably what Shakespeare heard. But, these will usually occur in a line which is irregular, in having more than ten syllables – perhaps eleven, twelve, or more. Even when they contain a run of three consecutive weak syllables, therefore, these longer lines can still have (at the least) the five strong stresses of the pentameter. Of course, different ears and different sensibilities will prefer different things, and you will find commentators who would regard the 'fewer than five' strong beats in some, or all, of the lines examined above, as quite acceptable; and who would suggest retaining them and leaving the lines with four only stresses. I seem to be a little bit more enamoured of the iamb and, much more frequently than not, feel that an occurrence of three side-by-side weaks will act as a 'puncture' in a line; will reduce the buoyancy or tautness supporting the focused intention that drives it.

And let me quickly stress again here that 'filling in', honouring all of what should be strong beats, is not done for its own sake; because one wants to 'speak the verse beautifully'. As was proposed in the chapter on 'Why honour the verse?', by acting the lines with the properly filled-out stress patterns, you will find that the lines begin to have a felt effect on you. You will begin physically to feel the emotional impulses (and the particular strength of the impulses), which *give rise* to the character's need to get across their specific questions, orders and explanations.

Flashing the strong beats

An exercise I often use to help a performer connect more fully to the rhythm of any line, or run of lines, is to hold their hands up in the air in front of their chest as they are about to speak the lines. Then, on each *weak* beat, they gather energy up, or draw it in, by making a fist; and on the strong beats, they *very energetically* release the gathered up energy by opening the fist and widely spreading their fingers. This I call 'flashing the strong beats'. It is an exercise you can use with any line, or lines, (even prose-lines), and which has got to be done with great energy; there is no value in being limp or self-conscious about it. This rhythmic gripping and releasing *makes visual* the strong pulsing of the verse-line. It also gives you a strong *physical* sense of this pulse.

Try the exercise with these few lines below now. Really *flash!* those strong beats. Most benefit will be gained by slowing the delivery right down to begin with – three or four times slower than normal. Grant each strong beat its own separate pool of time and space; take time fully to experience the weight and, as I sometimes call it, the 'plumpness' of each one of them. When you have flashed the lines slowly a few times in this way, gradually speed up the delivery until you are speaking them at a more natural pace – but while *still* continuing to flash, *right* in the heart of each strong beat. When you can comfortably say the line, or lines, at this more natural pace, while still remaining accurate with your flashes, let go of the exercise, and act the lines minus any flashing. You will feel a distinct difference between the pre- and the post-pulsing. You will feel much more bodily connected to, and involved in, the rhythm:

Lady Macbeth:
But **screw** *your* **cour-** *age* **to** *the* **stick-** *ing* **place**
FLASH   FLASH   FLASH   FLASH   FLASH

Richard the Second:
A **horse!** *A* **horse!** *My* **king-** *dom* **for** *a* **horse!**
FLASH   FLASH   FLASH   FLASH   FLASH

Enorbarbus: *Antony and Cleopatra 2:2:191*
The **barge** *she* **sat** *in,* **like** *a* **burn-** *ished* **throne**...
FLASH   FLASH   FLASH   FLASH   FLASH

Viola: *Twelfth Night 3:1:159*
By **in-** *no-***cence** *I* **swear** *and* **by** *my* **youth**...
FLASH   FLASH   FLASH   FLASH   FLASH

When acting the sample lines above, as I urged, with strong and equal emphasis on each strong beat, you will, no doubt, have felt and sounded less like a person talking to someone, and more like a young child pounding out a recitation with the rest of the class. You may have felt as if the 'jingliness' of the 'dee dum, dee dum' rhythm was taking over from the importance of the line's content. Sometimes, one does attend performances where the actors feel they really have to 'play the verse', and pump out that iambic for all it's worth, each strong beat awarded its fair share of emphasis. Far from enhancing our engagement with, and understanding of, the text, this steady thrashing out of the 'dee dums' quickly becomes tedious to the ear, and can actually incline us to 'zone out' from the performers, and from the meaning of their lines. So what is one supposed to do?

It has only been for the sake of clarifying some basic principles that I have, so far, been pressing you, strongly and equally, to emphasise every strong beat and not to worry about sounding jingly. Now it is time to worry about precisely that.

Varying degrees of stress

With the exercises above under your belt, you will be ready to take on board the next important principle. The principle is that, although all the strong beats must indeed be identified, and played as such, each one does not need to be hammered on with precisely the *same* emphasis. And indeed, most of the different systems that have been devised for scanning verse, not only offer symbols for marking stressed and unstressed syllables, but provide also, signs for representing two, or sometimes three different *degrees* of stress on strong beats. (For those who might be interested, information on these systems can easily be accessed on the web; simply search 'scansion', or 'scanning verse'.)

You will remember that when discussing the idea of restoring missing strong beats we restored the word *'to'* as a strong beat in this Lady Macbeth line; as in:

> But **screw** your **cour**-age **to** the **stick**-ing **place**...

Say the line aloud again, and as you have done before, focus on really 'pumping' the five strong beats. Give each of them the same amount of space and heavy emphasis; even the *'to'*.

> But **screw** your **cour**-age **to** the **stick**-ing **place**...

You might sound a bit like a robot, delivering the line in this way.

Now act the line aloud again. This time, I want you to keep in the back of your mind that you are still going to honour all the strong beats as identified, including the *'to'*, but... *but,* at the same time, your *main* focus will be 'what it is I want to explain to Macbeth'. What you want to explain to him is that if he but keeps his nerve, and his resolve, the two of them will not fail in their plot to murder Duncan. Focus on making your explanation to him clear:

> But **screw** your **cour**-age **to** the **stick**-ing **place**
> (And we'll not fail…)

Playing the line with an awareness of the beats, but with the primary focus on what you want to convey, you will probably have awarded to the word, 'to', a lighter stress than you did to the other four stressed beats. In support of best getting the meaning of the lines across, you are honouring the strong beats, but you are also, instinctively, awarding each one of them its appropriate *degree* of stress.

The line now begins to sound more 'natural' when performed in this way; more as if a real human being is talking. But because the 'to' syllable *has* been honoured, albeit more lightly, the line still maintains its integrity, fullness and poise, as verse.

So you need not fret. I am not suggesting you need to sit down and work out in advance the exact degree of stress you are going to allot to every individual syllable in your lines. That way madness lies. Once you are clear which syllables you will act as strong, focus on the clarity of what you want to get across and the appropriate degrees of emphasis will tend to look after themselves.

Key points for 'Acting Shakespeare's Verse parts 1, 2 and 3 will be listed at the end of Part 3: page 113.

Part 2

IRREGULARITIES

Irregularities in the verse

You may have observed already that some of the lines I have, so far, used for demonstration purposes did not conform strictly to the iambic pentameter rule of ten syllables arranged as five consecutive 'dee dums'; a few, for example, had an irregular eleven, or more, syllables. You will find that a substantial proportion of Shakespeare's verse-lines do not fully conform to this, or other 'rules' of the iambic pentameter.

I have written versions of Greek tragedies in iambs and, as would be the case with any writer, I know on any occasion I departed from the strict 'dee dum, dee dum' of the iambic, it was done primarily on instinct: it was done because it *felt right*. It is not the case that a writer decides, 'Oh, I must make sure to put an extra syllable or two in this line to indicate a particular feeling underlying the line'; or, 'Perhaps I will put three weakly stressed syllables in a row in that line to point up a particular meaning.' As he writes, a writer becomes aware, not only of what it is one of his characters wishes to say; he is also aware of the *nature* of his characters; of their underlying motives, and of the emotional state they are in at any point in the play; or he is in the process of discovering it. So, given that the writer has a reasonable 'ear', the form of the lines he instinctively starts to hear, and finally provides for any character, is going to reflect all of these things. The relative regularity or irregularity of any verse-lines, for example, will occur as a reflection of, as an embodiment of, the speaker's character, motives, state of mind etc. It is prudent, therefore, for actors and directors to presume, before they presume anything else, that there is a good reason for any irregularities in a character's lines. Often a full understanding of why a line is irregular in a particular way will instinctively be felt, simply by honouring the irregularities in how you act the line. The irregularities will 'work on you' and give you the information. But it is good to have a conscious knowledge of the different types of irregularity; and to have the know-how to work backwards from any irregularities, in order to deduce possible understandings of what it is in the character, and their emotional circumstances etc., that has given rise to them.

Types of irregularity

There are not so many different ways in which a line of verse can be irregular. The principal irregularities are:

- variations in the number of syllables in a line (more or less than ten)
- variations in the ordering of the strong and weak syllables (weak, or strong, syllables occurring side-by-side, instead of strictly alternating, one after the other).
- variations in the number of strong stresses in a line (usually more, occasionally fewer, than the regular five).

When it comes to acting lines with an irregular *rhythm*, you will simply need to honour the irregular arrangement of the strong and weak beats, as closely as you honour the arrangement in lines which are perfectly regular. And as regards honouring the different lines of irregular *length* that you will encounter, well, you don't really have a choice, as that is how they are composed. But *why* and to what effect Shakespeare varies the line lengths, and what information the various line-lengths might be offering the actors; these are topics I will be examining in due course.

Act aloud the Lenox line, from *Macbeth*, below. You will see that, even though in the second line there are a full five strong beats, two consecutive weak beats remain: '*ing*' and '*with*'. I have underlined them:

Lennox describes the unnatural sounds that have been heard in the air the night of Duncan's murder:

Lenox: (...strange screams of death,)
And **proph***-e-sy-*ing with* ac-cents* **ter-rib-le**...   *2:3:55*

(A choice might be to make this line regular by eliding the '*y*' syllable in '*prophesying*', so giving the word only three syllables, as in '**proph**-*e-sying*'. Such a delivery will not cause outrage in the stalls; but, to my ear, the contraction sounds odd and a tad forced; and for the reason also of maintaining clarity for the ear of a contemporary audience, my vote goes to the full, four-syllable option.)

In Lenox's line, the occurrence of two consecutive weak beats is to be explained in terms of Shakespeare 'sneaking in' an *extra* weak syllable amongst its five regular iambs. Here is the line scanned with the extra weak beat enclosed in round brackets:

[And **proph**-*]* *[e- **sy**-]* *(ing)* *[with* **ac**-*]* *[cents* **ter**-*]* *[rib-**le**]*
[dee dum] [dee dum] (dee) [dee dum] [dee dum] [dee dum]
iamb   iamb   (dee)   iamb   iamb   iamb

It is as if the '*ing*' of '*prophesying*' is a little pebble strewn in the way of the smooth and regular pulse of the iambs. It momentarily disrupts the rhythm but does not destroy it: the drive of the iambic pulse is strong enough to power on regardless, taking the little hiccup in its stride. An audience will still sense the essential beat of the iamb in the line; and the player will still feel that he is explaining, ordering or explaining within an iambic rhythm. However, the disruption to the regularity of the verse rescues it from becoming too predictable and monotonous; it injects a degree of the relative randomness characteristic of everyday speech.

Here are a half- and full line from *Twelfth Night*. Orsino explains to Viola how much he has opened himself to her:

Orsino: *… I have un-clasp'd*
To thee the book even of my sec-ret soul.   *1:4:13*

Listen carefully to yourself as you act what Orsino says, a few times; then, with your pencil, mark which syllables you are inclined to play strong and which weak. Don't read on until you have done this.

Below is how most, I reckon, will tend to act it:

*… I **have** un-**clasp'd***
*To **thee** the **book** ev-en of my sec-ret **soul**.*

You will see that the second line here is irregular in a few different ways. First of all, if you count the syllables, you will find it has eleven syllables instead of ten. Secondly it contains two consecutive strong syllables. And thirdly there are three consecutive weak syllables. The three consecutive *weak* beats are: *'-en of my'* ; the two side-by-side *strong* syllables are: *'book'*, and the *'ev'* of *'even'*.

The rhythmic irregularities are the result of two things. The first is that Shakespeare has arranged the words so that the 'dee' and the 'dum' in the line's third foot are reversed: rather than a regular iamb, he has, irregularly, made the third foot a 'dum dee', and not a 'dee dum'.

    *[the **book**]*   *[**ev**-en]*
    [dee dum]   [dum dee]
    iamb   trochee

A 'dum dee' foot is referred to as a 'trochee' (pronounced *tro-* as in 'trophy', and *-chee* as in 'key': 'tro-chee'). In case you are wondering (or worrying): in order fully to honour the verse in your acting, it is not necessary to remember the technical term for this, or any other type of foot. You need only become aware of which syllables are best played weak, and which strong, and to play them as such.

The second factor creating the rhythmic irregularities in Orsino's line is that Shakespeare (as he did in the Lenox quote above) has included an extra syllable.

I will look firstly at the two consecutive strong beats (*'the **book** ev-en'*).

Often when Shakespeare replaces an iamb with a trochee as he does here (meaning there will be two strong beats side by side), it is because he wishes to point up some meaning in the line by bringing added attention to a particular word or phrase. I'm sure you can sense this in Orsino's line. The strong syllable, *'ev'* pushes back against the strong syllable *'book',* bringing the word *'even'* into high relief. It emphasises the word, in such a way, that it strongly conveys just how out-of-the-ordinary is the degree to which Orsino has revealed himself to Viola. Act the line again with this in mind. You will get it:

> *... I have un-clasp'd*
> *To thee the **book** ev-en of my sec-ret soul.*

And now to look at those three consecutive weak beats. Earlier, I mentioned that when it seems that three consecutive weak beats are indeed what Shakespeare intended, these will normally be encountered in lines made up of an irregular eleven syllables or more. Orsino's eleven-syllable line offers a perfect instance where three-in-a-row weaks are most likely what Shakespeare heard as he was writing. I can imagine someone arguing that because Orsino wants to spell out what he wants to convey to Viola, in slow, simple words, it would be preferable to keep a *strong* stress on the *'of',* in the Duke's second line, as in: *'ev-en **of** my **sec-ret soul**...'*. Although this would give the line an irregular six strong syllables, the line would remain *more* regular, in the respect that it would not have the run of three-in-a-row weak beats, and so retain more of an iambic pulse. Act Orsino's words again with six strong stresses in the second line:

> *... I **have** un-**clasp'd***
> *To **thee** the **book** ev-en **of** my **sec-ret soul**.*

To my ear, adding this sixth stress seems to burst the bounds of the iambic pentameter, and renders speaking the line, a little like hard work.

The extra syllable that Shakespeare has slipped into Orsino's second line is the *'of'*. This is again a little pebble thrown into the unregarding flow of the pentameter. All this going on in one line might be confusing and difficult to grasp when expressed in words; so here are the lines laid out in such a way as, visually, to make their construction clear. Again I have placed the extra syllable between round brackets. Take a little time to examine and absorb the details of this way of understanding, and scanning, the lines:

> *... [I **have**] [un-**clasp'd**]*
> [dee dum] [dee dum]
> iamb   iamb

*[To **thee**] [the **book**]   [ev-en]   (of)   [my **sec-**]   [ret **soul.**]*
[dee dum] [dee dum]   [dum dee] (dee) [dee dum] [dee dum]
  iamb   iamb   trochee (extra) iamb   iamb

It is interesting to note that, in order to speak any two strong beats one after the other, we have to play a little *silent,* or virtual, weak beat between them. We put in a tiny moment of silence; and within this moment, it is as if we gather up the strength to pronounce the second strong syllable. By doing this, we create a tiny moment of anticipation. This moment of anticipation then assists in highlighting any syllable that follows it. Act Orsino's line again, carefully listening to yourself, and you will notice the silent weak beat you put in between the '***book***' and the '***ev-***'. You needn't worry too much about this when you come to acting two (or occasionally more) strong beats together: it happens automatically. It would sound weirdly rushed and strange to speak the two strong beats one after the other as quickly as you would a weak and strong. Try it yourself and see:

*... I **have** un-**clasp'd***
*To **thee** the **book** ev-en **of** my sec-ret **soul**.*

Below is the Brutus line cited earlier in a different context. Act the line; then again, without reading on, mark where you hear yourself acting two strong beats side by side:

It is the bright day that brings forth the adder...

Did you note, that apart from having eleven syllables, there are *two* occasions in this line where a pair of strong beats occur together?

*It   **is**   the **bright day** that   **brings forth**   the **ad - der**...*
[dee dum] [dee dum] [dum dee] [dum dum] [dee dum] (dee)

Can you see how the occurrence of the pair of two side-by-side strongs solidly helps to highlight the key words, and therefore the meaning of this proverbial line? Also, the two silent beats occurring between both of the strong/strongs significantly slows the line down at the important points, so we have extra time to take in the line's two key phrases: '*bright day*' and '*brings forth*'. When it comes to performance, therefore, the actor can consciously use these two irregularities to help his character lay out the line's content with maximum clarity. He will want to relish the alliteration, and create a certain space for the two double strongs; present them with a weight sufficient to point up the argument in the line.

A scansion of Brutus' line reveals an irregularity not yet mentioned: it contains another type of foot irregular to the iambic pentameter: the 'spondee'.

*[It **is**]*	*[the **bright**]*	*[**day** that]*	*[**brings forth**]*	*[the **ad-**]*	*(der...)*
[dee dum]	[dee dum]	[dum dee]	[dum dum]	[dee dum]	(dee)
iamb	iamb	trochee	spondee	iamb	(extra)

You can see that a spondee is a foot consisting of two strong beats.

You will also notice that, in this instance, the line's 'extra' beat, is a weak syllable tacked on at the very end.

In the remainder of this section, several other examples of lines closing irregularly with an unstressed syllable will be encountered; so before going on, I would like to give a little attention to this phenomenon. It is an irregularity of length, creating (necessarily) an irregularity of rhythm.

'Masculine' and 'feminine' endings

A line ending with a strongly stressed syllable, as does a regular iambic pentameter, is referred to as having a 'masculine' ending. A line which ends with an unstressed syllable, as does Brutus' line, is known as having a 'feminine' ending.

Scan this question of Macbeth:

Macbeth: *Is this a dagger which I see before me...?*   2:1:33

You will have noted the unstressed beat at the line's end: *'be-**fore** me...?'*
Feminine endings are very common in Shakespeare.

This line where Varro reassures Brutus, in *Julius Caesar*, has a feminine ending:

*So please you, we will stand and watch your **pleas**-ure.*   4:3:247

The first four lines of Hamlet's most well-known soliloquy all have eleven syllables, and feminine endings:

*To be or not to be, that is the **quest**-ion:*
*Whether 'tis nobler in the mind to **suf**-fer*
*The slings and arrows of outrageous **for**-tune*
*Or to take arms against a sea of **troub**-les*
*And by opposing, **end** them.*   3:1:56

As a phenomenon on their own, there is nothing you need particularly to do about feminine endings except to speak them. The effect of their occurrence is to lend a looser, slightly less formal edge to the lines of which they are part.

And now to return to the discussion on consecutive strong beats.

The witches have foretold that after Macbeth has gone, Banquo will be father to a line of kings. Macbeth rages at the fact that he may have shattered his own peace of mind by killing Duncan, only to benefit another's heirs; he rages that he has:

Macbeth: *Put ran-cours in the ves-sel of my peace,*
On-ly for them… (Banquo's sons)   3:1:66

These lines offer another example where Shakespeare introduces an irregularity to a line in a way which helps to support its meaning. You will have spotted that the second line begins with an irregular trochee, a 'dum dee'. This creates a further instance of two consecutive strong syllables; but two which straddle the end of one line, and the beginning of another. Acting the lines you will feel how the *'On-'* of *'On-ly'* assertively pushes back against the word *'peace'*, at the end of the previous line. This puts a strong spotlight on the *'On-ly'*, helping to capture Macbeth's fury that the great sacrifices his crimes have entailed really may have been for the benefit of another man's sons.

Two consecutive strong syllables are regularly to be found straddling lines within one character's speech in this way. They are often also found straddling the end of one character's lines, and the beginning of a line spoken by another.

You will note that the Macbeth line below opens with a trochee (dum dee), and therefore with a strong beat:

Macbeth: *Who can be wise, amaz'd, temperate and furious,*
(Loyal and neutral, in a moment? No man.)   2:3:106

[***Who*** *can*]   [*be* ***wise****,*]   [*a-****maz'd****,*] etc…
  trochee   iamb   iamb

By examining the context in which the line is delivered, one can see why Shakespeare chose to do this. In the course of the uproar following Duncan's murder, Macbeth says he regrets the rage leading to his killing the grooms. Without giving Macbeth a second to think, Macduff asks him why he has done such a thing, and it is in answer to this bald question that Macbeth speaks the lines we are examining:

Macbeth: *O, yet I do repent me of my fury*
That I did kill them.

Macduff: *Wherefore did you so?*

Macbeth: *Who can be wise, amaz'd, temp'rate and furious,*
Loyal and neutral, in a moment? No man.   2:3:104

Hearing Macbeth immediately push his strong, *'Who'*, against Macduff's strong final *'so?'*, one senses his unnatural haste, his over-eagerness to cover up his real motives for killing the grooms – so that they cannot now be subject to an interrogation which might result in their being cleared, possibly diverting suspicion to himself:

> *Where-fore did you so? / **Who** can be wise...?*

In the case of most of the examples above, the scansions put forward are ones that, I believe, are likely to be agreed by a lot of the actors and directors approaching them. But, there are many cases where two or three different scanning choices might be argued for, and with equally convincing reasons put forward to justify them.

Comparing alternative scansions 1 – Helena

I wish, now, to give you the opportunity to decide on a scanning scheme of your own for some short verse passages; then to take you through some of the alternative ways in which I consider the passages might be scanned. The experience of 'comparing and contrasting' the virtues or drawbacks of the various versions will further develop your 'iambic pentameter ear'; equip you to begin approaching any future scanning decisions with confidence.

In these next few lines from *All's Well That Ends Well*, lowly Helena finally admits that she is hopelessly, and inappropriately, in love with the Countess' son, Bertram. First read Helena's explanation for meaning. Then listen to yourself speaking her lines aloud, a few times – until you know where you want to place the weak/strong stresses. When you are clear about that, mark them with your pencil:

> **Helena:** *Then I confess, before high heaven and you,*
> *That before you, and next unto high heaven*
> *I love your son.*
> *My friends* were poor but honest: so's my love.*   1:3:186

* relatives, family

In an attempt to keep the lines as regular as possible, one might decide to act them stressed as presented below. Following this scheme, act the lines and endeavour to make them 'work' for yourself:

> *... Then **I** con-**fess**,*
> *Here **on** my **knee**, be-**fore** high **heav**-en and **you**,*
> *That be-**fore** you, and **next** unto **high heav**-en*
> *I **love** your **son**.*

This serves as one attempt to marry the 'meaning content' to the requirement of the iambic pentameter. It is hardly, is it, the most harmonious of matches? In the second line, I think, you'll agree that to say *'Here **on** my **knee**...'* sounds like a case of the rhythm being made more important than the sense. Here, the sense asks to go against the regular iambic rhythm; it asks for *'**Here** on my **knee**...'* More like a real person talking, isn't it?

It would probably not be how I would choose to act it, but in the second line, I can imagine someone arguing for a strong stress on the *'high'* before, *'heaven'*, as in:

> *... Then **I** con-**fess**,*
> ***Here** on my **knee**, be-**fore high heav**-en and **you**...*

The result is a rather uncommon occurrence of *three* strongs in a row (*'-**fore high heav-** '*); but as Helena wishes to emphasise just how great is the authority before which she avows her love (*'high heaven'*), I think an actor might wish to speak the line in this way. This, of course, makes the line even more irregular: it already has eleven syllables; now it has three consecutive strong beats, as well as an irregular six strong beats overall. This, however, still does not destroy the sense of an underlying iambic pentameter. Act the line this way and see how it feels to you:

> *... Then **I** con-**fess**,*
> ***Here** on my **knee**, be-**fore high heav**-en and **you**...*

In the third line it would be hard *not* to keep a strong stress on the word *'high'* before *'heaven'*, as in: *'...and **next** unto **high heav**-en'.*

(A quick note here about the word *'heaven'.* Some would suggest giving Helena's second line a regular ten syllables by eliding the second *'e'* in *'heaven'*, making it *'heav'n'*, and this is certainly a choice. While in other circumstances it might be the better option, in this instance the two syllable version works for me. Such elision is also sometimes called for with other words, for example with the name Juliet. To suit his rhythms, Shakespeare usually (not always) hears this name spoken as two syllables; as in *'**Jul**-yet'*. The pronunciation of words with 'elidible' syllables is to be determined on the basis of the rhythmic context in which each occurs.

I'd like to offer you a few more options on these lines of Helena. Here is the option, suggested above, for her first words:

> *... Then **I** con-**fess**...*

But here is another option:

> *... **Then** I con-**fess**,*

This version gives the word, '*Then*' greater weight, lends it the force of, 'Well, in *that* case then!'

In the third line, instead of '*That be-fore you…*', another option would be:

*That be-fore you, and **next** unto **high heav-en**…*

Act the line in this way. Playing this arrangement of stresses, do you feel how the two pairs of strongs (*'fore you*' and '*high heaven*') bring into robust relief, the key elements of the point that Helena is endeavouring to make, i.e. that the Countess stands only below Bertram in her love, and that Bertram stands only below her love for God and Heaven?

And to offer one final option for these lines; in the third, I have added a strong on the first word, '*I*', so making the opening foot of the line a spondee, a 'dum dum':

*I **love** your **son***

So here are the lines laid out in one version which does help Helena make her explanation clearer to the Countess than the one I first presented:

> *__Then__ I con-**fess**,*
> *__Here__ on my **knee**, be-**fore high heav**-en and **you**,*
> *That be-**fore you**, and **next** unto **high heav**-en*
> *I **love** your **son***

How does this compare to how you scanned it?

Were I acting the lines, however, I would probably lose the strong stress on the '*high*' of the first '*high heaven*'. The occurrence of two '*high heav-en's*' in two consecutive lines, seems too ponderous to me:

> *__Here__ on my **knee**, be-**fore** high **heav**-en and **you**,*

What do you think?

And perhaps I would also lose the strong on the '*I*' in the last line. Perhaps it would be better left as it first was: '*I **love** your **son**…*' Act all the lines again with these amendments.

> *__Then__ I con-**fess**,*
> *__Here__ on my **knee**, be-**fore** high **heav**-en and **you**,*
> *That be-**fore you**, and **next** unto **high heav**-en*
> *I **love** your **son***

What do you think?

Before moving on to the next, and last, scanning exercise, I feel inclined to repeat here that asking you to review different scanning options for any passage is done, not with any intent to confuse, but by way of fulfilling my intent to develop your iambic pentameter 'ear'. Having absorbed some know-how, and with some practice under your belt, you will, on approaching any fresh text, find yourself instinctively rummaging within the lines as you work, and successfully unearthing what is the optimum scansion for your character, for the audience, and for the verse.

Comparing alternative scansions 2 – Hamlet

When you understand the meaning of these Hamlet lines below, take your pencil, and listening to yourself act them (and without reading on), mark your strong and weak stresses:

> **Hamlet:** *To be or not to be, that is the quest-ion*
> *Wheth-er 'tis nob-ler in the mind to suf-fer*
> *The slings and ar-rows of out-rage-ous for-tune*
> *Or to take arms a-gainst a sea of troub-les*
> *And by op-pos-ing, end them...*   3:1:56

Here is one way I have heard the first line performed:

> *To **be** or **not** to **be**, that **is** the **ques**-tion...*

No matter how lightly one might play the strong stress on the *'is'* in this version, it will always come across as if with deliberate emphasis. This makes Hamlet sound as if he is in the middle of an ongoing conversation with someone; one where the subject of whether 'to be or not' has already been on the table. It is as if he were saying, 'Yes, you are quite right. That indeed *is* the question.'

Below, however, is how one mostly hears the line delivered:

> *To **be** or **not** to **be**, **that** is the **ques**- tion...*

The line has eleven syllables and has a feminine ending but, scanned this way, it is irregular also in that the iamb (dee dum) in the fourth foot has been replaced with a trochee (dum dee), resulting in two consecutive strong syllables, followed by two consecutive weaks;

> *[To **be**] [or **not**] [to **be**,] [**that** is] [the **ques**-] [tion...]*
> iamb   iamb   iamb   trochee   iamb   extra syllable

This provides another good example of how, when the iambic beat is disrupted with two consecutive strong syllables, attention will be drawn to the second of those syllables. In this instance, the strongly stressed *'that'* pushing off from the strongly-stressed, *'be'*, gives it the significance of 'yes, *that*, more than any other, is (the question)...'.

> *To be or not to **be**, **that** is the ques-tion...*

The second line, too, has eleven syllables and another feminine ending. How did you scan it? This is what I hear:

> *Wheth-er 'tis nob-ler in the mind to suf-fer...*

Starting the line irregularly with a trochee, and therefore a strong beat, grabs our attention, so we will be attentive as Hamlet elaborates on his headline question (*'To be or not to be'*). I have seen it proposed that this line should be scanned with four only strong stresses and a run of three weak stresses, as in:

> *Wheth-er 'tis nob-<u>ler in the</u> mind to suf-fer*

I prefer it filled out with five strong beats (lighter stress on *'in'*):

> *Wheth-er 'tis nob-ler in the mind to suf-fer*

Some propose that the Prince's next line is, again, one to be played with only four strong stresses, so creating another run of three-in-a-row weaks. Act it this way:

> *The slings and ar-<u>rows of out</u>-rage-ous for-tune*

Performed this way, the three consecutive weaks come across to me as a patch of gabbled skiddiness in the line; a patch in which the character loses a slight control over his utterance. I prefer to hear the *'of'* acted with a strong stress (lightly touched). Act it with this scansion and feel the difference: the line will feel more filled out as a line of verse; the character will sound more needfully engaged with the meaning of what he is putting out:

> *The slings and ar-rows of out-rage-ous for-tune*

The next line also has eleven syllables...

> *Or to take arms against a sea of troub-les...*

...and, I think, might possibly also take a strong beat on its first syllable (*'Or'*). Playing it strong will, on its own, grant this small word an emphasis. But what will bring it into even higher relief is the fact that, when you act it with a strong stress, there will, unavoidably, be a sense of a comma coming after the word. Listen as you do this and you will feel it:

> *Or to take arms a-gainst a sea of troub-les...*

This scansion, of course, gives the line six strong stresses. An alternative (one I have often heard played) is to act the first two syllables as weak. (For anyone interested, a foot containing two weak beats is referred to as a 'pyrrhic'.)

> *[Or to] take arms a-gainst a sea of troub-les...*

Something to bear in mind when considering the merits of this version is that the line which precedes it ends also with a weak syllable:

*The slings and ar-rows of out-rage-ous **for**-tune...*

This results in three weak syllables in a row, albeit straddled over the end of one line and the beginning of the next. What do you think?

*The slings and ar-rows of out-rage-ous **for**-<u>tune</u>*
*<u>Or to</u> **take arms** a-**gainst** a **sea** of **troub**-les...*

Personally, I don't like the rushed splodginess this injects between the lines.

Another option, and one which neither overly enthuses me, is to give the line five strong stresses by retaining the *'Or'* as strong, but creating a run of three weaks on *'a sea of'*.

Have a go at acting it this way (the run of weaks is underlined):

***Or**, to **take arms** <u>a-gainst a</u> **sea** of **troub**-les...*

Not the most elegant option; a skiddy gabble in the middle.

And finally, the half-line which ends our passage. Was this how you scanned it?

*And **by** op-**pos**-ing, **end** them...*

The only other real possibility is to make the opening foot a trochee (dum dee) instead of an iamb (dee dum). Doing this lends a strong emphasis to the first, *'And'*, which again invites the player to act the sense of there being a comma after the word. Act the line this way:

***And** by op-**pos**-ing, **end** them...*

Which do you prefer? As will often be the case, it is not advisable to make a final decision on the scansion of any individual line until it is considered, and acted, in the context of the other lines around it.

Here, now, are three different versions of the full Hamlet passage below. Do any of them correspond with your own original scansion? Act each of the three versions over until you get a sense of which, for you, achieves the optimum balance between 'clarity of what you want to get across', and honouring the lines as verse. I am not proposing that any of these options is the one I would consider optimum for acting the passage; but trying them will help you further to develop your 'ear':

The first version has the greatest number of strong stresses:

*To **be** or **not** to **be**, **that** is the **ques**-tion*

> *Wheth-er 'tis nob-ler in the mind to suf-fer*
> *The slings and ar-rows of out-rage-ous for-tune*
> *Or to take arms a-gainst a sea of troub-les*
> *And, by op-pos-ing, end them...*

This second version has the fewest strongs:

> *To be or not to be, that is the ques-tion*
> *Wheth-er 'tis nob-ler in the mind to suf-fer*
> *The slings and ar-rows of out-rage-ous for-tune*
> *Or to take arms a-gainst a sea of troub-les*
> *And, by op-pos-ing, end them...*

This third is a mixture of the previous two:

> *To be or not to be, that is the ques-tion*
> *Wheth-er 'tis nob-ler in the mind to suf-fer*
> *The slings and ar-rows of out-rage-ous for-tune*
> *Or to take arms a-gainst a sea of troub-les*
> *And, by op-pos-ing, end them...*

If you absolutely had to choose one to act, which would it be?

Now, having had your attention drawn to these various options, take your pencil and, without consulting the scanning versions above, and putting your original scansion out of your mind, scan the lines the way *you* think they best should be performed:

> *To be or not to be, that is the ques-tion*
> *Wheth-er 'tis nob-ler in the mind to suf-fer*
> *The slings and ar-rows of out-rage-ous for-tune*
> *Or to take arms a-gainst a sea of troub-les*
> *And by op-pos-ing, end them...*

Is this how you scanned it first (page 84)? Or is it different?

Having examined what is involved in honouring the rhythm (regular or irregular) of Shakespeare's verse, I will look at what is involved when we endeavour to honour the other main element that makes Shakespeare's verse, verse: the fact that it is written in 'lines' of a fixed length: the ten syllables, the five iambic feet of a strict pentameter.

Key points for 'Acting Shakespeare's Verse' Parts 1, 2 and 3 will be listed at the conclusion of Part 3 (page 113).

Part 3

LINE-ENDINGS AND BEGINNINGS

Read aloud these lines from the *Mary* rhyme again:

Mary had a little lamb,
Its fleece was white as snow,
And everywhere that Mary went
The lamb was sure to go.

In the case of this, and most nursery rhymes, each verse-line contains a major sense-unit. To remind you, I am using 'sense-unit' to mean a discrete and substantial 'block of meaning', one which may represent a complete sentence, but which may represent a major unit-of-sense that is *part of*, that goes into making up, a complete sentence.

'*Simple Simon met a pieman*' is a major sense-unit, and one that could stand on its own as a complete, though simple, sentence. '*Going to the fair*', is a major sense-unit, but not a complete sentence; it is a major unit-of-sense that goes into making up a complete sentence.

To drive home the notion of the ends of lines coinciding with the ends of complete sense-units, here are the words of the 'Mary' poem, organised into lines whose endings do *not* coincide with the end of a sense-unit:

Mary had a little
Lamb its fleece
Was white as
Snow, and everywhere
That Mary
Went, the lamb etc.

When the end of a verse-line coincides with the end of major sense-unit, it is described as being 'end-stopped'.

End-stopped lines

Notice how, when you recite the 'Mary' rhyme, by means of a slightly increased emphasis, you tend to let the listener know that that last word in any line, indeed, *is*, the last word. By doing this you are helping to reveal the form of the poem to the listener; to 'exhibit' its line-structure. And it is easy to spot that the words are arranged so that those which are key to what is being said are often placed at the ends of lines:

Mary had a little lamb,
Its fleece was white as snow.
And everywhere that Mary went
The lamb was sure to go.

You may also sense that each line feels as if it is driving towards the destination of this last key word (or 'words' as it sometimes is). Notice this as you speak the first lines of the Simon rhyme:

Simple Simon met a pieman,
Going to the fair
Said Simple Simon to the pieman,
'Let me taste your ware.'

Since the end of each line in these nursery rhymes coincides with the end of a major sense-unit, it is obvious that the start of each line is going to coincide with the *beginning* of a new sense-unit. So when you deliver such a poem, you will instinctively have the sense of a fresh 'launching off' at the opening of each line; the sense of a gathering up of a fresh energy that impels you into this new line.

You can find a solid sense of this if you imagine that the little poem is not a monologue, but is actually a dialogue between the speaker and another person; and that this other person says something at the end of each line which freshly gives rise to the next one. For example, after delivering 'Mary Had a Little Lamb', you might imagine the listener saying, *'So?'*, and, in response to this you deliver the second line: *Its fleece was white as snow*; and so on. Act the 'Mary' rhyme aloud as laid out below, complete with the inputs from the listener I have supplied. You can act both speaker and listener, or you and a partner can share the parts:

Mary had a little lamb,	So?
Its fleece was white as snow.	Well?
And everywhere that Mary went	What?
The lamb was sure to go.	I see.

Acted this way, you can begin to feel the separateness of each major sense-unit, and to sense the gathering up of new energy that launches each one off towards its intended destination; towards the final word.

Try the same trick with Simple Simon:

Simple Simon met a pieman	Where?
Going to the fair;	So?
Said Simple Simon to the pieman,	What?
Let me taste your ware.	And the pieman said? Etc.

Deliver it again now, without the inserted questions, but still retaining the awareness of 'gathering up' an energy at the start of lines, which drives each one to its landing place:

Simple Simon met a pieman
Going to the fair;
Said Simple Simon to the pieman
Let me taste your ware

The few notions thrown up in this brief examination of lines in nursery rhymes, will provide the basis for a discussion on 'playing the line' in Shakespeare's verse.

Playing line-endings and beginnings – Romeo and Antipholus

Below are examples of lines, or short segments of longer speeches, from some of Shakespeare's earlier plays. When you are certain as to their meaning, notice how, just as with the nursery rhymes, A) the end of each line coincides with the end of a major sense-unit; and therefore the beginning of each new line coincides with the *beginning* of a new sense-unit, B) the words *key* to what the character wishes to convey fall at the ends of the lines, and, C) the thrust of each line drives towards this final word or words.

I want you to act these passages aloud a few times, each time bearing a different thing in mind.

Firstly, I want you to focus on the notion that the drive in each verse-line tends towards the final word or words. To assist you in developing an awareness of this, I'm asking you really to over-emphasise these significant last words (highlighted in bold).

Two lines, already encountered, from *Romeo and Juliet* (1594-95):

Romeo: *But soft, what light through yonder **window breaks**?*
*It is the East, and Juliet is the **sun**!*   2:2:2

In *The Comedy of Errors* (1592-3), Antipholus of Syracuse, just arrived in Ephesus, instructs his manservant, Dromio:

Antipholus: *Go bear it to the Centaur*, where we **host****,*
*And stay there, Dromio, till I **come to thee**.*
*Within this hour it will be **dinner-time**:*
*Till that, I'll view the **manners of the town**,*
*Peruse the traders, gaze upon the **buildings**,*
*And then return and sleep within mine **inn**,*
*For with long travel I am stiff and **weary**.*   1:2:9

* an inn   ** lodge

Now, I want you to focus on the fact that the opening of each line coincides with the beginning of a major sense-unit. Play the game we played with the 'Mary' and the 'Simon' poems: saying lines as if in response to questions. Again, you can have a partner ask the questions, or you can simply ask and respond to them yourself. Do give yourself a moment to take each question in, and to feel the impulse to respond. This will encourage in you the sense of taking a firm hold of the intention which launches you into each new line. As I have urged with other exercises, don't be concerned for now about the lines sounding nursery-rhymey or over-worked:

Romeo: *But soft, what light through yonder window breaks?*
Dunno. Tell me.   *It is the East, and Juliet is the sun!*

Antipholus: *Go bear it to the Centaur, where we host,*
And do what?   *And stay there, Dromio, till I come to thee.*
What will you be doing?   *Within this hour it will be dinner-time:*
Indeed. So?   *Till that, I'll view the manners of the town,*
Is that all?   *Peruse the traders, gaze upon the buildings,*
And then what?   *And then return and sleep within mine inn,*
Sleep?!   *For with long travel I am stiff and weary.*

Now I want you to act these lines aloud again, this time *without* the added questions; without seeing the end-words printed in bold. Consciously bear in mind that you are 'speaking verse', in exactly the way you would if you were delivering 'Mary Had a Little Lamb'. Exaggerate this as much as you wish for now. Still sense the drive in each line to the final word or words; deliberately lean on these final words; and, at the beginning of each line, have a sense of taking hold of the intention which launches you into it:

Romeo: *But soft, what light through yonder window breaks?*
It is the East, and Juliet is the sun!

Keep gathering up at the starts, and driving to, and leaning on, the final last key word or words:

Antipholus: *Go bear it to the Centaur, where we host,*
And stay there, Dromio, till I come to thee.
Within this hour it will be dinner-time:
Till that, I'll view the manners of the town,
Peruse the traders, gaze upon the buildings,
And then return and sleep within mine inn,
For with long travel I am stiff and weary.

Of course, when performing, one mustn't be too obvious about this gathering up, and driving towards the end word or words. I deliberately asked you to over-emphasise these aspects of your delivery for the sake of getting the hang of the principle. But in the same way that there is always the danger of over-emphasising, and drawing undue attention to the *'dee **dum**, dee **dum**'* of the verse, so also there is a danger in over-marking the end and beginning of lines. The idea is not to be a slave to this aspect of the verse – the pointing can be ever so subtle, almost subliminal. But *use* it. Use it in a way that *assists* you in clearly getting across your questions, orders and explanations. As with scanning the lines, with a little practice, you will find yourself marking line-endings and beginnings instinctively, and with the pointedness appropriate to conveying your meanings.

I want you to go back and speak the lines aloud just one more time now. This time, still point up the ends and beginnings etc., but only to the extent that helps you to make clear what you want to get across.

Apart from marking line-endings and line-beginnings, there is another important aspect of 'playing the line' I now wish to draw your attention to.

Pivotal sense-breaks

Looking at the major sense-units contained within the lines above, you will find each is made up of two smaller, or 'minor' sense-units, each of which pivots satisfyingly around a 'sense-break'. I have marked this sense-break in some random lines from the passages just examined:

It is the East, || and Juliet is the sun!

Within this hour || it will be dinner-time:

And then return || and sleep within mine inn...

It has been argued that the existence and consistency of such breaks in Shakespeare lines is, at least to some extent, a hangover from Old English (circa 450-1066) and Middle English (1066-1450) verse. In these periods, such a sense-break was a strict, built-in requirement of the verse-line, probably developing as a means of allowing the poems to be more easily memorised for live recitation. This break was referred to as the 'caesura' (from the Latin word 'to cut'). When referring to Shakespearean and later verse, the term caesura is now more usually employed to refer to a sense-break in the line that is 'complete'; a sense-break likely to be indicated by means of a colon or semi-colon; or a break in the line where one sentence ends and another begins, and which, therefore, will be marked by a full stop. (The caesura, in this sense of the word, will be discussed a little later in this chapter.) But even without considering the legacy of Old and Middle English verse, it is the case that in English, or any language, there is anyway going to be a sense-break in most utterances consisting of more than four or five words; and as Shakespeare's verse-lines comprise an average of around six or seven words, there is going to be a sense-break of some sort in each of them.

'Marking' these sense-breaks in your acting will bring the structure of any line into bold relief, greatly enhancing its clarity and muscularity.

Playing pivotal sense-breaks – Duchess of Gloucester et al.

To help you develop a feel for the 'bi-partite' structure of such major sense-units, I'd like you to act the lines below aloud; and as you do, leave a little pause where the sense-break occurs:

The Duchess of Gloucester, from *Richard the Second*, berating John of Gaunt:

Duchess: *Finds brotherhood in thee* || *no sharper spur?*
Hath love in thy old blood || *no living fire?*　　　　　　　*1:2:9*

And a line from later in the same play:

John of Gaunt: *This precious stone,* || *set in the silver sea.*　　*2:1:46*

Hamlet: *To be, or not to be,* || *that is the question...*　　*3:1:56*

Macbeth: *Is this a dagger* || *which I see before me...?*　　*2:1:33*

Desdemona: *What shall I do* || *to win my lord again?*　　*Othello 4:2:151*

Paulina: *What studied torments, tyrant,* || *hast for me?*
　　　　　　　　　　　　　　　　　　　The Winter's Tale 3:2:175

I always feel these sense-breaks provide a line with a pivot comparable to that of a see-saw, or old-fashioned weighing scales. It is as if the weight of the two smaller sense-units hanging off either side of the pivot provides the line with a point of tension, a point around which to balance.

You will experience this balancing function palpably in the opening of Richard the Third's speech. Act these lines aloud, and as you do I want you to make a short pause where the internal sense-break is marked, and also at the end of each line. Acting the passage in this way will give you a strong sense that each line contains one self-contained major sense-unit, and that each of these can be broken down into two smaller, or *minor* sense-units:

Richard: *Now is the winter || of our discontent ||*
Made glorious summer || by this sun of York, ||
And all the clouds || that loured upon our house, ||
In the deep bosom || of the ocean buried. ||
Now are our brows || bound with victorious wreaths ||
Our bruised arms || hung up for monuments...   1:1:1

Even out of context, one recognises that the following groupings of words from Richard's speech constitute small blocks of coherent meaning: *'Now is the winter'*, *'bound with victorious wreaths'* and *'Our bruised arms'*. These are minor sense-units, any of which could form part of a major sense-unit or complete sentence. The following groupings of words are *not* sense-units of any stripe: 'bag over is', 'frequently who pullover', 'mansion again perspire'.

Here is Katherine, from *The Taming of the Shrew*, exhorting wives to respond more compliantly to their lords, and explaining why they ought to. Act Katherine's lines, leaving again a short pause, both where the pivotal sense-breaks are marked, and at each line's end:

Katherine: *Fie, fie! || unknit that threat'ning unkind brow, ||*
And dart not scornful glances || from those eyes, ||
To wound thy lord, thy king, || thy governor: ||
It blots thy beauty || as frosts do bite the meads, ||*
Confounds thy fame || as whirlwinds shake fair buds, ||
And in no sense || is meet or amiable. ||
*A woman moved** || is like a fountain troubled, ||*
Muddy, ill-seeming, thick, || bereft of beauty...   5:2:137

* meadows   ** in a bad temper

Multiple mid-line sense-breaks

Usually there is only one clear sense-break in any one line; but there can be more than one.

Here are two other examples of verse-lines with multiple sense-breaks; I have marked these.

From Richard the Third:

Richard: *A horse! || A horse! || My kingdom for a horse!*   5:4:7

And a line from *The Winter's Tale*. King Leontes (depending how one interprets this line) is either describing the horrible depths of his own status as a 'horned' cuckold, or he is offering a view of his wife, Hermione, as a treacherous adulteress:

Leontes: *Inch-thick! || Knee-deep! || O'er head and ears a fork'd one.*   1:2:186

But while every sense-break to some extent asks to be acknowledged in the playing, I do tend to encourage the actor to feel if there is a 'primary' sense-break: a break that seems to be the 'main' one; the one on either side of which the two halves of the line hang in some sort of balance; and to give this sense-break priority in the playing. Look back at the two examples given above and decide which break you would choose as the *pivotal* one.

In these lines, the pivotal break, I think, suggests itself quite readily. As you have probably done, I would place the sense-breaks as follows:

Richard: *A horse! A horse!* || *My kingdom for a horse!*

Leontes: *Inch-thick! Knee-deep!* || *O'er head and ears a fork'd one.*

Sometimes, however, which break is best to play as pivotal may not be so immediately obvious. You may have noticed that in the Katherine passage just quoted, there are lines which also divide themselves into three or four units; for example:

To wound thy lord, || *thy king,* || *thy governor...*

Muddy, || *ill-seeming,* || *thick,* || *bereft of beauty...*

And you may have wondered, too, if the point I marked as the principal pivot point in these lines would be better placed elsewhere. For example, in the line below, I placed the pivot after the word, *'king'*:

To wound thy lord, thy king, || *thy governor...*

Might the pivot be more meaningfully placed after *'lord'*, as in:

To wound thy lord, || *thy king, thy governor...*

Or in this line, might the pivot be better located after, *'ill-seeming'*, as in:

Muddy, ill-seeming, || *thick, bereft of beauty...*

...instead of after *'thick'*, where I placed it:

Muddy, ill-seeming, thick, || *bereft of beauty...*

Test these possibilities for yourself. Play the lines aloud both ways; act them until you feel one suggesting itself to you as the way that better supports what Katherine wishes to get through to her listeners:

To wound thy lord, || *thy king, thy governor...*

To wound thy lord, thy king, || *thy governor...*

Muddy, ill-seeming, || *thick, bereft of beauty...*

Muddy, ill-seeming, thick, || *bereft of beauty*

Swing-boating – Phebe

Swing-boating is an exercise I often use, and one which rarely fails to help an actor, or student, sense and reveal the pivotal sense-breaks. You can use it with any piece of iambic pentameter verse you may be working on.

This is how it goes: as you deliver the first part of each line, swing from the waist letting the arms fly out as if you were slinging the content of the half-line out through the length of your arms and releasing it through the tips of your fingers. See the words sail out and splat forcefully against the wall of the room. Or even see them flying straight through the wall and out into the open air beyond. Be sure to release and send out the very *last word* of the line – there can be a tendency to allow the end of each half-line to 'drop', to have less energy. 'See' it; 'watch' that last word sail out with as definite an energy as the rest of the line, and strike that wall. Then swing round and fling the second half-line out towards the opposite wall. And again, be sure to fling out the last word with as much force as the others. Your body, as the line, will be pivoting around the mid-line sense-break. The swinging will put you in vividly felt contact with the break and, hence, with what I refer to as the 'meaning architecture' of the line. (This 'full-blast version' of the exercise can be done with text you have already learnt, but for lines or speeches where you are not 'off-book' and need to hold the text in one hand, simply scale it down slightly. You may need to swing less vigorously, allowing only one of your arms to swing out.)

Having established what they mean, have a go at swing-boating the Phebe lines below, from *As You Like It*. (Unless you happen to know the piece by heart you will only be swinging one arm.) I have marked in the 'lefts' and 'rights'.

Shepherdess, Phebe, tries to convince Silvius (as well as herself) that she has not been smitten by the arrogant youth, Ganymede (Rosalind in disguise):

Phebe:
(Swinging right) Think not I love him, || *(Swinging left) though I ask for him:*
(Right) 'Tis but a peevish boy; || *(Left) yet he talks well;*
(Right) But what care I for words? || *(Left) Yet words do well,*
(Right) When he that speaks them (Left) || *pleases those that hear.*
(Right) It is a pretty youth: || *(Left) not very pretty:*
(Right) But, sure, he's proud; || *(Left) and yet his pride becomes him:*
(Right) He'll make a proper man...   *3:5:109*

A more discreet version of this exercise which you may prefer to use, particularly if you don't have a lot of room, is smartly to clap your hands together, and/or stamp your foot to mark each break. Your claps or stamps must not be 'on', must not coincide with, a word in each half-line. Each must be sounded smack-dab in the middle of the break, like a quick extra beat *inserted between* the end of one half, and the start of the next. As with the 'Flashing the strong beats' exercise, your claps, or stamps should not be self-conscious, or half-hearted. Clap! Stamp! (If you are in a situation where you are at risk of disturbing others, you will be able, I'm sure, to think of even more discreet adaptations of the exercise. You could, for example, lightly tap your pencil on your desk or table, or instead of stamping your foot at each break, you could simply press it firmly into the floor instead.)

When you have completed the exercise (swinging, clapping, and/or stamping) perform the lines again, but 'normally' now, no longer aiming to mark the breaks in an exaggerated way. Invest your focus only on the questions, explanations and orders that Phebe wishes to get across to Silvius. You, and any one listening, will hear a distinct improvement both in clarity, and in your engagement with the text and its meanings:

> *Think not I love him, though I ask for him:*
> *'Tis but a peevish boy; yet he talks well;*
> *But what care I for words? Yet words do well,*
> *When he that speaks them pleases those that hear.*
> *It is a pretty youth: not very pretty:*
> *But, sure, he's proud; and yet his pride becomes him:*
> *He'll make a proper man…*

Playing off-centre sense-breaks – Cassius, Orsino

Most mid-line sense-breaks occur somewhere around the line's centre, after the second or third foot. But breaks are sometimes placed *off-centre*. Not only are such off-centre breaks a means to add variety to the shape of verse-lines; they are a means Shakespeare uses to focus the intended *meaning* of a line more sharply.

In the fourth line of the passage below from *Julius Caesar*, the sense-break happens near the beginning, right after the first foot; this is referred to as an 'initial' sense-break.

Speak the lines aloud and you will experience how the short introductory, '*For once…* ', helps Cassius to grab the attention of Brutus (and the audience); it invests the listener's interest in what is to follow.

Cassius is endeavouring to impress upon Brutus just how very 'human' is this Caesar whom the Roman people are close to deifying:

Cassius: *I was born free as Caesar;* || *so were you:*
We both have fed as well || *and we can both*
Endure the winter's cold || *as well as he:*
For once, || *upon a raw and gusty day,*
The troubled Tiber || *chafing with her shores...*

Interestingly, when it comes to acting off-centre sense-breaks, in order for the line to retain its balance, you will find that the short part of the line asks to be played with a little more 'weight', to be given a little more 'space', so that the longer part does not seem to 'outweigh' it. The image of a see-saw plank is particularly apt here. When the plank is pivoted on its support off-centre, to remain balanced, the weight placed on the short side must be heavier than any weight placed on the long side. Note also that when acting such lines, the break itself naturally asks to be marked in a noticeably more pronounced way.

In order to gain a felt understanding of these points, speak aloud the Orsino and Cassius lines below, going as far you can, A) as regards clearly marking the sense-break, and B) as regards, giving each short side of the line, sufficient weight and space to act as balance to the weight and length of the longer side.

In Orsino's line, it is the second part of the line which is short. (A pivotal break placed towards the end of the line is referred to as a 'terminal' sense-break.)

Orsino: *If music be the food of love* || **play on...**

Richard explains to the audience how the fearful activities of war have given way to the trivial and amorous pursuits of peace. (Note how the initial sense-break here fulfils much the same 'attention-grabbing' function as it did in the Cassius passage.) Weigh the short side of the line, and give the sense-break full value:

Richard: *Grim-visaged war* || *hath smooth'd his wrinkled front*;*
And now, || *instead of mounting barded steeds*
To fright the souls || *of fearful adversaries...*

*brow

Pivotal breaks: Interjecting questions – Hamlet

Apart from swing-boating, and clapping and stamping, another means of getting feelingly in touch with the sense-breaks in any lines, and hence in touch with their 'meaning architecture', is to use the 'Inserting a question' exercise *(described above: page 89 and 91).* Instead of asking questions at the beginning of complete lines, you interject an appropriate question before the new *half*-line so that the half-line comes out as if in an active, energetic response to the question asked. For example:

Hamlet:
To be, or not to be: || (What about 'to be or not to be?') *that is the question...*
Whether 'tis nobler in the mind || (Whether **what** is nobler in the mind?)
to suffer
The slings and arrows || (What slings and arrows?) *of outrageous fortune*

The questions should be posed forcefully by a partner, or by yourself, and your response back should be just as forceful. Consciously make each half-line you speak something you very much, and very clearly, want to get across in response to each question. The speech then becomes an intense series of exchanges. I often use this exercise, improvising a question I feel might give rise to each half-line, the student making his or her delivery of the half-line a full-hearted response. If I don't feel that the student's half-line comes across as a sufficiently energetic and active response to my question, I keep repeating the question until it does.

Use 'Inserting questions' with any speech, or indeed single verse-line, that you have to deliver; you will get used to dreaming up questions to ask before each sense-unit – as you can see from my examples, they do not have to be literature! Having applied the exercise to any piece of text, you will find when you deliver it without the questions, that without having to think about it, you will be making good use of the pivotal breaks (again, no matter how subtly). You will be connecting to the satisfying balance in each line; and realising it for the audience.

Enjambements

I have suggested above that the length of the major sense-units in English roughly coincides with the length of Shakespeare's pentameter, and how comfortably, therefore, they can fit within it. And in the earlier plays such as *The Taming of the Shrew* and *Richard the Third* this, indeed, is mostly what we find. Increasingly, however, from the middle to the later plays, we discover that each major sense-unit is not always slotted neatly into one line. Often now the unit 'straddles' lines, i.e. the first half of a major unit begins in the *middle* of one line and finishes at some point in the next. There are three such instances in this short Macbeth passage, where he talks of the threat Banquo represents to him:

Macbeth: ... *There is none but he*
Whose being I do fear: and under him
My genius* is rebuked; as it is said,
Mark Antony's was by Caesar...   *3:1:53*

* guardian spirit

You can see that the second halves of the first three lines are minor sense-units which do not *complete* a major sense-unit (as in an end-stopped line):

There is none but he...

and under him...

as it is said...

Instead, these half-lines represent the first half of a major sense-unit which is completed in the *following* line.

Here are the three 'line-straddling' sense-units complete:

... There is none but he / Whose being I do fear:

... and under him / My genius is rebuked;

... as it is said, / Mark Antony's was by Caesar...

The occurrence of a major sense-unit running through the end of one verse-line and into another is referred to as an 'enjambement' (a French word meaning 'straddling' from the French word 'jambe' for 'leg' – and pronounced the French way). Running major sense-units through lines in this manner does 'cut across' the neat 'containedness' of the regular, end-stopped verse form, and this can produce an enlivening tension between the verse and the 'matter' for which it is the container. The increasing use of enjambements represents one of the ways in which Shakespeare progressively is inclined to 'loosen the grip' of this strictly regular end-stopped form. Regular, end-stopped lines may have been perfect for the simpler, boldly-outlined, and un-self-questioning characters of the early plays. The greater fluidity introduced to the verse by enjambements indicates that what the characters in later plays want to convey, cannot quite be packaged within the confines of such a tidy consistently repeated form. The characters need some greater degree of flexibility, and freedom, as regards how they put out what they want to get across. With enjambements the verse is moved a little further towards the greater structural variousness of everyday speech.

Of course in later plays there are still many neatly end-stopped lines:

Portia: *The quality of mercy* ‖ *is not strained...* ‖   *M. of Venice 4:1:179*

Macbeth: *We have scorch'd the snake,* || *not kill'd it…* || *3:2:13*

But to illustrate how numerous enjambements are in middle and later works, I have, in another *Macbeth* passage below, numbered the points where one major sense-unit begins mid-line, then straddles the beginning of the line which follows. To achieve a strong awareness of these major mid-line sense-breaks, act Macbeth's lines aloud, taking a short pause at each numbered point. Unusually, I am not asking you to pin down the precise meaning of each line in this particular passage! Scholars still surmise, and argue, about some aspects of its meaning. Essentially, Macbeth is observing that if the planned assassination of Duncan could (by virtue of being performed) eliminate any negative consequences, then it would be better to get it over with as quickly as possible. But things, he knows, are not that simple. Pause at each number:

Macbeth: *If it were done when 'tis done, (1) then 'twere well*
It were done quickly: (2) if the assassination
Could trammel up* the consequence, (3) and catch
With his surcease**, success; (4) that but this blow
Might be the be-all and the end-all – here;
But here, upon this bank and shoal*** of time,
We'ld jump**** the life to come. (5) But in these cases
We still have judgment here…   *1:7:1*

* bind up   ** completion   *** school   **** risk

Having major sense-units straddle lines, in this way, allows Shakespeare to introduce another variation into the iambic pentameter structure: it allows him to vary the *length* of his major sense-units; yet another way in which the spoken material begins to strain against the verse-form which contains it. A regular end-stopped line consists of the pentameter's ten syllables – the average length of a major spoken sense-unit in everyday speaking. When straddling the line, the major sense-units are still often made up of ten syllables; but often they will lean to either side of the average of ten, and may consist of twelve or fourteen syllables, or perhaps six or eight. You can see this in the major sense-units straddling lines in the Macbeth passage. Act these aloud and you will have a sense of how the length of each major sense-unit feels different to the regular ten-syllable pentameter:

…***then*** *'twere* ***well*** */ It were* ***done quick****-ly*… Only eight syllables, four strong stresses, four feet.

…***if*** *th'as-****as****-sin-****at****-ion / Could* ***tram****-mel* ***up*** *the* ***con****-sequ-****ence***… Fourteen syllables, seven strong stresses, seven feet.

*...and **catch** / With **his** sur-**cease**, suc-**cess**...* Eight syllables, four strong stresses, four feet.

The caesura

Pronounced: '*say-**zyu**-ra*' Plural: 'caesurae' or 'caesuras'

It will be obvious that if a major sense-unit flows through the end of one line and ends somewhere in the middle of the next, then a *new* major sense-unit necessarily begins right after; mid-line. And you may have noticed in the Macbeth passage above, that three of the breaks between major sense-units were marked variously with a colon, a semi-colon, and a full-stop.

Today, the word 'caesura' is most commonly used to refer to such obvious, more *complete* mid-line sense-breaks (*as noted earlier: page 92*). It is the caesura, in this sense of the word, that I wish to look at now.

Here are some further examples of caesurae from *Measure for Measure* and *Macbeth*.

Having been told by the highly esteemed Angelo that he will save her brother's life if she succumbs to his desires, Isabella soliloquises:

Isabella: *To whom should I complain? || Should I tell this*
Who would believe me? || O perilous mouths...   2:4:171

In a continuation of his speech above, Macbeth confronts the truth that natural Justice, or *karma*, will see the poison we serve to others, inevitably presented back for our own consumption. He then goes on to lay out all the *moral* reasons why he should not perform this deed against Duncan – a man to whom he is not only a kinsman, a subject and a host, but one who has so unimpeachably fulfilled his duties as a king:

Macbeth: *... This even-handed justice*
Commends th'ingredients of our poison'd chalice
To our own lips. || First, as I am his kinsman and his subject,
Strong both against the deed; || then as his host,
Who should against the murderer shut the door,
Not bear the knife myself. || Besides, this Duncan
Hath borne his faculties so meek, hath been
So clear in his great office...   1:7:10

As does any other mid-line sense-break, a caesura asks to be marked in the playing. But as regards performance, there are perhaps one or two considerations specific to caesurae that are worth drawing attention to.

Playing the caesura

Being the end of a major sense-unit, the section of a line *before* a caesura is going to be a form of pay-off, or conclusion to a thought which began in the previous line. I have highlighted the words an actor is likely to emphasise in these 'concluding' half-lines, to illustrate this point:

*To our **own lips**.* || ...

*Strong both **against** the **deed**;* || ...

*Not bear the **knife myself**.* || ...

And if we regard any speech as having continuously to build, then any sense-unit *following* a caesura needs to kick off at a higher level of intensity than the level reached at the end of the major unit just completed. It needs to inject fresh, and increased, energy into the 'journey' of the speech, driving it more inevitably towards its destined conclusion.

To illustrate this, I have isolated the openings of the major sense-units in the Macbeth passage which begin *after* a caesura. You will see that each of these opens at a higher level of charge than the one preceding. Again to help demonstrate the point more clearly, I have highlighted the words an actor is likely to emphasise as representing a 'step up' in his journey through the speech:

... || *He's here in **double trust**;*

... || *then as his **host***

... || ***Besides** this **Duncan***

The conclusion of one realisation opens up yet another realisation; one that is of even greater significance and moment to Macbeth than the one before.

And each new realisation comes to him in 'the gap'.

As you act any lines which have a caesura, you will find that you won't rush straight on to the second half of the line; you will find yourself naturally leaving a little gap. To have an experience of this, act these two lines:

*Strong both **against the deed**;* || *then as his host...*

*Not bear the knife **myself**!* || *Besides this Duncan...*

It is through this little gap that a new energy can flow into you; the energy required to launch you into the more highly charged sense-unit which follows it.

I'd like to give you the chance to try an exercise I have found very helpful in giving full value to caesurae.

Playing Caesurae: Interjecting thought bubbles – Macbeth
I have laid out the Macbeth speech again below, interspersed this time, not with questions, but with 'thought-bubbles' (in bold). These will draw attention to the nature of the fresh realisation, and energy, which is to enter in each gap.

Act the lines now, and when you come to a thought-bubble in a gap, take a pause; do not say the thought-bubble out loud, but read it, and take time truly to take in its significance. Feel the thought pulling the level of energy in you further up. Allow it to increase your level of horror at the outrage you have planned to perpetrate, and to impel you into the next sense-unit:

Macbeth: ... *This even-handed justice*
Commends th'ingredients of our poison'd chalice
To our own lips. || **(In the name of all that's holy!)** *He's here in double trust*
First as I am his kinsman and his subject,
Strong both against the deed; || **(And on top of the sacredness of those two**
bonds!) *then as his host,*
Who should against the murderer shut the door
Not bear the knife myself! || **(And on top of all of this again, and making it**
even worse!) *Besides, this Duncan*
Hath borne his faculties so meek, hath been
So clear in his great office...'

And now act Macbeth's lines again this time, allowing the gap at each caesura to be of a natural length, and feeling how the exercise has helped you map and actualise what each caesura asks for:

Macbeth: ... *This even-handed justice*
Commends th'ingredients of our poison'd chalice
To our own lips. || *He's here in double trust;*
First as I am his kinsman and his subject,
Strong both against the deed; || *then as his host,*
Who should against the murderer shut the door
Not bear the knife myself! || *Besides this Duncan*
Hath borne his faculties so meek
Hath been so clear in his great office...

Before applying this exercise to any other speech you may be working on, you will firstly need to look at each caesura in turn and take a few moments to create for yourself the thought-bubbles most likely to lift you up to the higher energy-level needed to launch you into the sense-unit which follows.

Why enjambements and the caesurae?

It is one thing to note the progressive use of enjambements and caesurae in the verse of Shakespeare's plays, but the questions remain: 'Why did he do this? And what is it telling the performer?' You are likely to come across differing explanations for some *specific* instances of enjambements and caesurae; but, I think, there are one or two general principles which are generally agreed on, and which can help guide, and be of use.

The structure of the verse gives a particular physical, external form to the (internal) intentions of any character. It provides a 'container' for whatever question, explanation or order the character wishes to put out into the world. But in its form, the verse will usually, also, embody the feelings that give rise to these intentions; and, importantly for this discussion, it will reflect the relative *unity within* the character, between these feelings and intentions.

This requires further explanation.

As a general principle, the greater the regularity of the line, the more balance, or unity pertains between the character's feeling, intention and his action. A character who is a 'speaker of regular verse' experiences a single feeling, or feelings, clearly. He then forms a perfectly appropriate, and unambiguous, intention in response to this feeling. Secure in this intention, he readily takes action, by creating an accurate, and effective, form to give utterance to this in the outside world – the spoken regular verse.

Strictly regular pentameters reflect a healthy balance between the *yin* and the *yang* within characters; a correspondence between how they *are* (what they *feel*), and the actions they perform in response to what they feel (what they *do*). Even if the feeling is turbulently passionate, 'regular verse-speakers' are *clear* about what it is they are feeling, and are clear, therefore, about what they wish to put out to the world, as a response to this feeling. They may be feeling confusion, but they will be clear about the source of their confusion, and can articulate this. This inner clarity and unity, therefore, is largely embodied in verse of a tidy, flowing articulateness; a verse in which, one at a time, each thought is laid out in an orderly and coherent manner and in which, by and large, there is 'one major sense-unit per end-stopped line'.

In the earlier plays of Shakespeare, and in plays written before him by other authors, characters, generally speaking, were unified within themselves, to the point often of being more 'types' than characters (as we think of characters in more modern drama). They tended to embody one key passion, virtue, obsession or vice etc.; and they usually demonstrated one clearly identifiable and unambiguous intention. Reflecting a change which was occurring in the way western man conceived of himself, some Shakespeare characters begin to be less single-minded, less confidently clear, about what they are feeling, thinking and doing. They experience conflict and contradiction within themselves. They begin more closely to represent what we now think of as more real, more *modern*, human beings.

When a character's feelings, thoughts, and actions are in alignment, it is as if the character has a strong and vivid sense of *who they are*. When feelings, motives and actions work less harmoniously together, or even contradict each other, then it is more difficult for a person to have such a clear and unified sense of this. It is difficult even to feel clear about *where*, or *in what*, a sense of self in fact resides: Am I my actions? My thoughts? My feelings? And if I am my feelings, *which* of my contradictory feelings is *most* me? Is the *real* me? The sense of self begins to shiver and fracture.

And as the vessel that is the character comes under the stress of such confusion and contradiction, so, in dynamic embodiment of this, the container of the verse they utter, can also come under strain. By no means always, but sometimes, the greater the strain in the character, the greater the strain on the iambic pentameters they speak.

Enjambements and caesurae embodying inner conflict – Shylock

Below is Shylock's speech from *The Merchant of Venice*, a play written around what might be termed the beginning of Shakespeare's middle period (1596-7). I have marked the points, mid-line, where a sentence ends, and a new one begins. I have also rendered in bold type the major sense-units which straddle the end of one line and run into the next: the two enjambements.

Jewish Shylock has been invited to dinner by the Christian Antonio. Jessica is his daughter:

> **Shylock:** *I am bid forth to supper, Jessica:*
> *There are my keys* || *But wherefore should I go?*
> *I am not bid for love;* || *they flatter me:*
> *But yet I'll go in hate,* **to feed upon**
> **The prodigal Christian.** || *Jessica, my girl,*
> **Look to my house.** || *I am right loath to go:*
> *There is some ill a-brewing towards my rest,*
> *For I did dream of money-bags to-night.*   2:5:11

It is clear that Shylock is in conflict. He wants to accept the dinner invitation and eat at a Christian's expense, but some other part of him feels he should not accept; and not just for one reason, but for two. Firstly, he is sure he is ationXX

not asked out of love; and secondly, he has had a presentiment of some ill that is to befall him. His conflicting thoughts can be patterned less neatly into regular verse, where the beginning and ending of lines coincide with the beginning and ending of a major sense-unit. You can sense the fracturing of his inner unity as he lurches between different feelings and intentions. It is as if there are two different characters within him. One is fearful and urges him to stay at home. The other wants to go so he can take something back from these Christians who have taken so much from him. Which is the self whose promptings he should trust and follow? This split inner-self is embodied in the many caesurae, in the splitting of the unity of the lines. What also helps to capture Shylock's inner disturbance is the strong contrast between the sudden flow of the centrally placed enjambements, and the shorter little shards of speech preceding them.

To have a sense of this, look back and act Shylock's words now. You will get a sense of his destabilisation, and of the two separate voices contending for control within him.

Caesurae and 'self-interruptions'

There is a particular, and not uncommon, circumstance in Shakespeare's verse which can lead to the occurrence of repeated enjambements, and major mid-line sense-breaks. In later plays, you will find some characters whose inner voices repeatedly *interrupt* the methodic flow of their own discourse. It is as if these characters are having to struggle to express themselves to their own satisfaction; as if they repeatedly experience the main thrust of what they are saying as not quite *enough*, as distressingly inadequate, fully to convey what they so obviously, and desperately, need to get across. In Shylock's speech we hear two conflicting voices take turns in their efforts to be heard; but in other speeches from later plays, it is as if the two voices are less prepared to queue and take turns. It is sometimes as if one inner voice impatiently *interrupts* another. Such 'self-interruptions' can, indeed, disrupt the orderliness of the regular end-stopped verse to such a degree that it feels that it might break down altogether.

Self-interruptions – Leontes

In *The Winter's Tale* (a very late play), King Leontes is in a psychotically disturbed state, and a significant portion of the verse he speaks reflects this. Below is a short speech of his: six of the nine lines contain a major sense-break, and there are three enjambments. Some of these 'infringements' of regular end-stopped verse are the result of the king disrupting the orderly presentation of his own discourse with repeated interjections. It is as if there is one person attempting to present his case in a coherent and adult manner while, at the same time, a wound-up and bitter side-kick cannot refrain from spitting interjections from the side.

I'd like you to take a few moments to examine this dense little passage, until you are clear as to what precisely Leontes is saying. Having done this, act the passage aloud, observing all the various sense-breaks in a highly exaggerated manner. (I have presented the interjections in bold.)

Believing her to be the product of his queen's adulterous relationship with his school-friend, Polixenes, the king has cast his baby daughter out to die. In this speech, he publicly repeats his accusation against the queen, and gives his judgement:

Leontes: ... *Your actions are my dreams;*
You had a bastard by Polixenes,
And I but dream'd it! || *As you were past all shame –*
Those of your fact are so – || *so past all truth:*
Which to deny concerns more than avails;* || *for as*
Thy brat hath been cast out, like to itself,**
No father owning it, || **which is, indeed,**
More criminal in thee than it, || *so thou*
Shalt feel our justice; || *in whose easiest passage*
Look for no less than death.   3:2:82

*and you make your denial that this is so, more important than will avail you of any good. *'concern'*: 'to be of importance'

** as befits it

With all the other irregularities (enjambements, caesurae, and different line lengths – there are two twelve-syllable lines), did you notice also, that on two occasions, the position of the sense-break is not around the middle of the line? On two occasions it is terminal *(lines 5 and 8)*. This off-centre positioning represents yet a further strain against the neatness and balance of the regular form of the verse.

To gain a sense, of the 'main' voice in the speech, as separate to the voice of the sniping interjector, I would like you, first of all, to speak out loud only the content of what the main voice is saying. Act this filleted version of the speech aloud a *few times*, so you have a strong grasp of the principal drift of what Leontes wishes to get across:

Leontes: *Your actions are my dreams;*
You had a bastard by Polixenes,
And I but dream'd it! As you were past all shame, –
so past all truth:

> *for as*
> *Thy brat hath been cast out, like to itself,*
> *No father owning it,*
>
> *so thou*
> *Shalt feel our justice; in whose easiest passage*
> *Look for no less than death.*

Now, here is the passage with the interruptions restored and placed between brackets. (Two of these interruptions are, indeed, bracketed in the first folio edition.) Act the passage aloud, remaining aware of the distinction between the main drift, and the various interjections. I think you will begin to sense how the distracted king's thoughts are tumbling, and layering, one on top of the other. It is as if his inner, interrupting side-kick feels the king is not quite succeeding to pack his utterances with sufficient evidence of just how unspeakable is the queen's crime; and so must throw in his own tuppence worth:

Leontes: *Your actions are my dreams;*
You had a bastard by Polixenes,
And I but dream'd it. As you were past all shame,
(Those of your fact are so) so past all truth:
(Which to deny concerns more than avails;) for as
Thy brat hath been cast out, like to itself,
No father owning it, (which is, indeed,
More criminal in thee than it), so thou
Shalt feel our justice, in whose easiest passage
Look for no less than death.

There are other Leontes' speeches where his self-interruptions are so frequent and frantic that they can make it quite difficult to work out exactly what he is saying; but I thought a passage somewhat less fragmented, and relatively simpler to understand, would better serve for purposes of illustration.

Another, vivid example of repeated self-interruption is provided by Hamlet's, *'Oh, that this too, too solid flesh would melt…'* soliloquy (1:2:129), and I will be examining this aspect of the speech in detail in the chapter dealing with 'Breathing the Verse' *(page 164)*.

But before moving on to these, I would like to make one general point about acting verse which is 'under strain'. It has been shown above that sometimes the greater the strain within some characters, the greater is the strain on the regularity of the iambic pentameters they speak. It is important, however, to emphasise, that when it comes to acting it, no matter how much strain the verse may be under, it must never be sensed to disintegrate altogether.

A sense must always be maintained of the underlying iambic pentameter structure, of there *being* an underlying iambic pentameter structure, which, even when tested by the severest of irregularities, manages, (even if just), to hold together.

It is the same with the form of any play as a whole. No matter how wildly chaotic or random the action of any play may seem at any given moment, if it is ultimately to satisfy an audience, it will always have an *underlying* structure which binds it all together, which endows it with a form; a form ultimately which gives it its meaning. And so it is with verse: if there is no container, or if the container sunders, then there can only be incoherence and meaninglessness.

Other verse forms

It has been noted in earlier pages that verse-lines shorter than the iambic pentameter tend to sound more consciously crafted, sound further from everyday speaking. This makes shorter verse-lines more appropriate for language that is indeed not intended to come across as everyday, but as deliberately wrought, and suiting to an out-of-the-ordinary purpose. Not unexpectedly, therefore, we see that Shakespeare, mostly uses line lengths shorter than the pentameter in his spells and songs, and in 'non-everyday' environments such as the magical fairy world of *A Midsummer Night's Dream*.

Here is the refrain from the witches' spell-making in *Macbeth*:

All Witches: *Double, double toil and trouble;*
Fire burn and cauldron bubble.   4:1:10

These lines are not made up of the five 'dee **dums**' that constitute an iambic pentameter. They are made up of four '**dum** dees' per line; four trochees. It is, therefore, a 'trochaic tetrameter':

*[**Doub**-le,] [**doub**-le] [**toil** and] [**troub**-le;]*
[dum dee] [dum dee] [dum dee] [dum dee]
trochee   trochee   trochee   trochee
1   2   3   4

*[**Fi**-re] [**burn** and] [**cauld**-ron] [**bub**-ble.]*
[dum dee] [dum dee] [dum dee] [dum dee]
trochee   trochee   trochee   trochee
1   2   3   4

With a spell such as this, the obviousness and regularity of the rhythm is part of its black-magical power, so one does not have to worry about over-emphasising it. It will be beaten out with whatever degree of incantatory deliberateness that is deemed appropriate in any particular production.

There are, however, other tetrameters where one might have to be a little more careful about banging out the rhythm too boldly. The structure of the lines in Puck's soliloquy in *A Midsummer Night's Dream* below might be analysed in different ways but, for me, one practical way is to regard them as being 'iambic tetrameters', i.e. consisting of four 'dee dums' – but where the 'dee' of most of the initial iambs is virtual, is silent.

Act Puck's lines and you will sense the virtual 'dee' (enclosed in round brackets), at the start of the first three lines; and find that, in the fourth line, the 'dee' of the opening iamb is *not* silent, but spoken (underlined): '*This flow-er's force…*')

Puck: *Through the forest have I gone*
But Athenian found I none
On whose eyes I might approve
This flower's force in stirring love…   2:2:65

*[(dee) **Through**]*	*[the **for-**]*	*[est **have**]*	*[I **gone**]*
[(dee) dum]	[dee dum]	[dee dum]	[dee dum]
iamb	iamb	iamb	iamb

*[(dee) **But**]*	*[A-**then-**]*	*[ian **found**]*	*[I **none**]*
[(dee) dum]	[dee dum]	[dee dum]	[dee dum]
iamb	iamb	iamb	iamb

*[(dee) **On**]*	*[whose **eyes**]*	*[I **might**]*	*[ap- **prove**]*
[(dee) dum]	[dee dum]	[dee dum]	[dee dum]
iamb	iamb	iamb	iamb

*[This **flow-**]*	*[er's **force**]*	*[in **stir-**]*	*[ring **love**]*…
[(dee) dum]	[dee dum]	[dee dum]	[dee dum]
iamb	iamb	iamb	iamb

Later, Puck and Oberon engage in a dialogue consisting also of iambic tetrameters (with many initial silent beats). Give yourself the experience of speaking this different type of verse. Perform Puck's lines aloud and feel how different it is to act these lines, compared to speaking an iambic pentameter, such as: *Oh, pardon me thou bleeding piece of earth*:

Puck: *Cap-tain of our fair-y band*
He-len-a is here at hand:
And the youth, mi-stook by me,
Plead-ing for a lov-er's fee.
Shall we their fond page-ant see?
Lord, what fools these mor-tals be!

Oberon: *Stand a-side. The noise they make*
Will cause De-met-ri-us to wake.   *3:2:110*

You will have noticed that even within this very much more 'verse-like' verse, Shakespeare, to provide relief to the 'jingliness', has introduced two irregular feet in Puck's speech. Can you identify where, and what, they are?

And staying in the world of *A Midsummer Night's Dream*, Bottom is performing the part of Pyramus in a play before the court, and shifts into verse consisting of two lines of only *two* feet ('dimiters') followed by one of three feet ('trimeters').

The dauntless knight has just come across the bloody mantle of his beloved Thisbe, and presumes her slain by a lion. Scan the lines and, with your pencil, bracket in what different feet you identify:

Pyramus: *But stay! O spite!*
But mark, poor knight,
What dreadful dole is here?
Eyes, do you see?
How can it be?
O dainty duck! O dear!   *5:1:265*

This is a good illustration of how, when human speech is crammed into lines shorter than the iambic pentameter, that the 'artificiality' of the verse can draw inappropriate attention to itself. Such tragic content squashed into such short rhyming lines can only produce a comic effect. This is a rare case where, in the service of comedy, part of one's job is to draw so much attention to the rhythm of the verse-form that it indeed comes across as of much more importance than the content. Act the lines of Pyramus; find out what fun it can be, consciously hamming-up the rhythm of such inappropriately short lines.

ACTING THE VERSE – Parts 1, 2 and 3 – Key points

– Clearly establish what each sentence and each word means, then identifying which utterances are orders, questions, explanations, or exclamations.

– Listen for any three-in-a-row weak beats you might be speaking, and decide if a strong beat has been dropped that needs to be restored; or if three consecutive weaks are what Shakespeare intended.

– Identify any other intended irregularities of rhythm, such as two- or three-in-a-row strong beats (both within a line or straddling two lines).

– Identify and play (no matter if only subliminally) the pivotal sense-breaks.

– Note how any initial, or terminal, sense-break might help you to 'back-up' what the line is trying to say.

– Sense the drive in each verse-line to the final word or words in the line; point these final words to the extent that supports what you want to get across. At the beginning of each line, have a sense of taking hold of the intention which launches you into it.

– Identify any irregularities of line: more or fewer than ten syllables, enjambements, caesurae.

– Establish in what sense, and to what degree, the line following the caesura asks to open at a higher level of charge. Allow new energy to enter in 'the gap' between the two half-lines.

– Decide how any irregularities of line or rhythm might be helping to reinforce the meaning of the lines and what they might be telling you about the inner state of the character in the moments of their uttering the lines.

CHAPTER TEN

RHYME

Most of the verse in Shakespeare's plays is 'blank' verse (unrhymed); but you will also come across a certain amount which is rhymed. In his earlier dramas there is much rhyme; rhyming becomes significantly less evident in the great plays of the middle period; then in some of the late, or latish plays (such as the 'romance' play, *Pericles* and the fairy-tale like, *All's Well That Ends Well)*, one again encounters many examples of rhyme.

Rhyming couplets

By far the most common rhyming device Shakespeare uses is the 'rhyming couplet'.

You have a rhyming 'couplet' when the word at the end of one line rhymes with the final word of the next. For example:

*Little Jack **Horner**,*
*Sat in his **corner**...*

An example from *All's Well That Ends Well*:

Countess: *My heart is heavy, and mine age is **weak**;*
*Grief would have tears and sorrow bids me **speak**.*   *3:4:41*

I will look now at some of the various ways Shakespeare uses rhyme in his plays.

Rhyme at the ends of speeches, scenes and plays

Within scenes written primarily in blank verse, a rhyming couplet is often used at the end of a speech, to lend it a concluding flourish and to help sum up, or 'nail home', one's final point.

Juliet suggesting to Romeo that it is perhaps time to leave her chamber:

Juliet: *Good night, good night. As sweet repose and rest*
Come to thy heart as that within my breast.   *2:2:123*

It can also be used to supply an extra pointing to a character's exit lines:

On leaving, Viola, in *Twelfth Night*, lets a besotted Olivia know that she will not be back to plead Orsino's suit:

Viola: *And so adieu, good madam, never more*
Will I my master's tears to you deplore.   3:1:163

Or a rhyming couplet can be used to sum up, and to stamp a final accent, on a whole scene.

In spite of the dangers, Antonio (*Twelfth Night*), determines to follow his beloved Sebastian to Orsino's court.

Antonio: *But come what may, I do adore thee so*
That danger shall seem sport, and I will go.   2:1:47

Or it will be used to bring an entire play to a satisfying close. A majority of Shakespeare plays conclude with a rhyming couplet (or two, or three). Here is the couplet which closes *Othello*:

Lodovico: *Myself will straight aboard, and to that state*
This heavy act with heavy heart relate.   5:2:368

Unfortunately, because of changes in pronunciation since Shakespeare's time, the couplet closing some of his plays no longer rhymes; with bathetic result:

The final lines of *King Lear*:

Edgar: *The weight of this sad time we must obey;*
Speak what we feel. Not what we ought to say.
The oldest hath borne most: we that are young
Shall never see so much, nor live so long.   5:3:322

Playing rhyme

You may come across varying approaches to the acting of rhyme, but to me, the most important and simple consideration is not to ignore it, or to attempt actively to 'bury', or 'smooth it out', in order to make lines sound less 'artificial', more 'naturalistic'. You will come across actors, or directors, who feel this is how rhyme should be approached. But it seems almost too obvious to state, that rhyme is *deliberate* on the part of a writer (just as the regular rhythms of verse are deliberate), and so are written to be honoured and used. If a performer does not acknowledge and to some extent *present* the rhyme in any lines he acts, it is a little bit as if someone in a musical came to a number and, instead of singing it, decided to just *say* the words of the song instead. A song's tune is deliberate and meant to be exploited. And imagine how disappointed a child would be if you recited 'Mary Had a Little Lamb' while deliberately trying to 'disappear' the rhyme. Try this: lean on the final word in each line of the 'Mary' poem as laid out below, exactly as you would if you were reciting the nursery rhyme in the usual way:

*Mary had a little **lamb***
*Its face was **white***
*As snow and every**where***
*That Mary went the **lamb***
*Was sure to **go**.*

Better to acknowledge and play the rhyme. Rhyme lends an extra musicality to the verse and (as will be shortly examined) it can also contribute to the expression of various types of heightened feeling. But if this musicality and heightened feeling are to be experienced, by both speaker and listener, then it must be *played*.

It has already been discussed how, when words are deliberately placed in opposition to each other, that the first word or phrase must be presented to the listeners in such a way that they expect some use is shortly going to be made of it; and that the second, opposing word or phrase must be played in such a way as to chime against the first. (*See Oppositions: page 19.*) In the Macbeth line below, for example, the words *'False face'* and *'hide'* must be set up so that the words *'false heart'* and *'know'* can be played against them. Act this line a couple of times doing just that, until you feel the set-up words, and the opposing words, are chiming one off the other:

Macbeth: ***False face*** *must HIDE what the* ***false heart*** *doth KNOW.*   1:7:83

As with playing oppositions, so with playing rhyme.

Playing rhyme 1 – Helena and Hermia

Here is a short exchange from *A Midsummer Night's Dream*: Helena is afraid that a confused and angry Hermia may lay violent hands upon her, for stealing Lysander's affection:

Helena: *Your hands than mine are quicker for a **fray**;*
*My legs are longer though to run **away**.*

Hermia: *I am amaz'd, and know not what to **say**.*   3:2:342

Here, Helena must 'set up' the word *'fray'* in the same way Macbeth needs to set up the first part of his opposition, *'False face'*. Having set up the word *'fray'*, she can then strike her rhyming word, *'away'*, against it. Then the confused Hermia must absolutely 'crown' Helena's preceding rhymes with the way she hits her *'say'*. Without overdoing it, her *'say'* must be presented as the cherry which tops this scene of comic confusions.

And so it is with all rhyme: the first element must be set up, and the second chimed against it. The fact that the climax of such a scene is locked into rhyme can be a large part of the fun for the audience; they shouldn't be cheated of it.

As with other aspects of the verse discussed, it is vital, when playing the rhyme, that you do not draw attention to it as seeming of more value than 'what you want to get across'. Any rhyme should be used as a means of pointing up the meaning of your question, order etc., together with the intentions and feelings which lie behind them.

Act Helena and Hermia's lines a few times now (on your own or with a partner), until you feel you are achieving what they ask in the playing: the *'away'* tops the *'fray'* and the *'say'* tops the *'away'*. This must be done in a manner that, as well as supporting the clarity of the young ladies' explanations, will help capture both Helena's keen resolution to avoid a scratched face, and Hermia's baffled astonishment:

Helena: *Your hands than mine are quicker for a fray;*
My legs are longer though to run away.

Hermia: *I am amaz'd, and know not what to say.*

But aside from helping to point up the surface meaning of any lines, rhyme asks to be acknowledged and played for a further reason. *Of itself,* rhyme is giving the listener information about the nature of the feelings and intentions that underlie and drive any lines in which it plays a part. Rhymes may represent, for example, the best means a character's heart can find to give appropriate shape to a love-sick longing. Using the rhymes in your playing, therefore, will help you to get in touch with this longing, as well as helping the audience to sense it. Rhymed lines may also arise from a *playful* intention, so in such an instance, if the rhymes are not played up, one against the other, an audience will have difficulty sensing the spirit of fun giving rise to them.

Rhyme in dialogue and within speeches

As well as rhyme being used to conclude speeches, scenes and plays, you will find speeches and extended stretches of dialogue which are composed entirely in rhyme.

A number of sections of *A Midsummer Night's Dream* are in rhyming verse, and as well as serving to capture the intensity of youthful first love, the rhyme lets us know we are in an elegantly confected world, where no conflict or confusion will scar too deeply, or remain unresolved. The play also provides some delicious examples of how rhyme can enhance the humorous element in a scene.

In one entirely rhymed scene, Lysander admits to Hermia that he has lost their way in the wood and makes the 'innocent' suggestion that they, therefore, lie down with *'one turf'* serving *'as pillow to us both'*. The strained and strongly rhyming 'niceness' with which they address each other, contrasts comically with the actual content of their conversation, the underlying sum of which might be distilled to: Lysander: *I want to do it with you right here.* Hermia: *In your dreams!*

And note the different, looser rhyming scheme used in Lysander's first four-line speech. Here the rhymes fall, not at the end of consecutive lines, but at the end of *alternate* lines. The alternating rhyme comes across as relatively less structured and formal than the tighter form of the rhyming couplet. One can imagine Lysander moving towards Hermia on these 'more casual' opening lines, as if he naturally *presumes* he and she will sleep side-by-side. This then prompts the shift into the 'I want to' / 'Well you can't' tension between the young lovers – a tension captured humorously by the shift into the over-polite but determined formality of the rhyming couplets:

Lysander: *Fair love, you faint with wand'ring in the **wood**;* a
And to speak troth, I have forgot our WAY: b
*We'll rest us, Hermia, if you think it **good**,* a
And tarry for the comfort of the DAY. b

Hermia: *Be it so, Lysander: find you out a **bed**;* c
*For I upon this bank will rest my **head**.* c

Lysander: *One turf shall serve as pillow for us BOTH;* d
One heart, one bed, two bosoms and one TROTH. d

Hermia: *Nay, good Lysander; for my sake, my **dear**,* e
*Lie further off yet, do not lie so **near**.* e

Lysander: *O, take the sense, sweet, of my innocence! etc.* f
2:2:34

Often, within one stretch of dialogue, there will be shift from prose, or blank verse, into rhyming verse. As with a shift from prose to blank verse, this will usually mark a shift in the character of the scene. It may represent a heightening in the scene's emotional stakes and temperature – into a more amorously charged situation, for example. Or it may reflect the lifting of a scene onto a more magical or mystical plane; or the movement into a more playful type of exchange, one, perhaps where the characters are using rhyme *self-consciously* as part of a contest of wit and wordplay.

In *A Midsummer Night's Dream*, Lysander proposes that Hermia comes to him in the woods the following night, so they can secretly wed. Hermia's heart-felt agreement shifts precipitately from a blank, to a rhymed verse, of almost hyperbolic fervour. If the play were a musical we can imagine Hermia's moment of breaking into rhyme as the moment when she bursts into her first big showstopper. For discussion and analysis, rhyming couplets are conventionally represented as: a,a; b,b; c,c etc.

Lysander: *And in the wood, a league without the town…*

…

There will I stay for thee.

Hermia: *My good Lysander!*		
I swear to thee, by Cupid's strongest bow,		
By his best arrow with the golden head,		
By the simplicity of Venus' **doves,**	a	
By that which knitteth souls and prospers **loves,**	a	
And by that fire which burn'd the Carthage QUEEN,		b
When the false Troyan under sail was SEEN,		b
By all the vows that ever men have **broke,**	c	
In number more than ever women **spoke,**	c	
In that same place thou hast appointed ME,		d
To-morrow truly will I meet with THEE.		d

1:1:165

Another occasion when the shift into rhyme comes close to the effect of a character breaking into song is found in *All's Well That Ends Well*. The aged Countess has just learned from her Steward that young Helena is passionately in love with her son. As the Steward exits, the Countess sees the love-sick Helena approach and, observing her, delivers a rhymed soliloquy pondering the inevitability and painfulness of youthful love. In distinct contrast to the prose she was speaking with the Steward, the rhymed verse pulls the soliloquy up into high relief. It creates the effect of its being a framed, self-contained set-piece; a quiet ruminative aria. For the opening of her speech, the Countess uses the looser alternating rhyme (as did Lysander at the opening of his scene with Hermia); this looser rhyming scheme feels appropriate for the more personal and exploratory opening lines during which the precise nature of the Countess' reaction to seeing the love-sick girl gradually forms. When the full clarity, and universality, of what she observes in Helena has come into a secure and tight, aphoristic focus, then the rhyming couplets begin:

Countess: *… Pray you leave me; stall this in you bosom; and I thank you for your honest care. I will speak with you anon.*

Exit Steward.   Helena is seen approaching.

*Even so it was with me when I was **young**:* a

If ever we are nature's, these are ours; this THORN b

*Doth to our rose of youth rightly **belong**;* a

Our blood to us, this to our blood is BORN; b

*It is the show and seal of nature's **truth**,* c

*Where love's strong passion is impress'd in **youth**...* c

1:3:123

Another passage from the same play provides an example where a shift into rhyme can elevate the nature of a discourse onto a plane other than the romantic, philosophical or passionate.

With the deployment of two consecutive rhyming couplets, the King brings to a determined conclusion, his argument against Helena's campaign to cure his sickness. As with rhyming proverbs and aphorisms, the King's rhyming imprints his words with the tenor of a final and incontrovertible truth. He asserts that Helena knows less than she thinks about his disease, and that she has no 'art' to cure it. But the confidence and determination in the King's couplets only drive Helena to push back with arguments ever more forceful – and all in equally determined couplets of her own. It is as if the rhyming now rivets the two characters together in an all-or-nothing contest. The stakes and tension in the scene are felt palpably to rise:

King: *Thou thought'st to help me; and such thanks I **give*** a

*As one near death to those that wish him **live**:* a

But what at full I know, thou know'st no PART, b

I knowing all my peril, thou no ART. b

Helena: *What I can do can do no hurt to **try**,* c

*Since you set up your rest 'gainst reme-**dy**.* c

He that of greatest works is finish-ER* d

Oft does them by the weakest minist-ER... d etc.

2:1:129

* God

A little later in the scene, Helena's words look like they have begun to sway the King. When the young woman senses this, see how she immediately moves to press her advantage. She first breaks in and shares with the King, not only a line, but for the first time also shares with him a rhyming couplet. With a radiantly manifest confidence, Helena moves to assure His Majesty that with her powers, she can cure him in no more than twenty-four hours. The young girl's rhyming elevates her words to the level of a powerfully persuasive, religio-pagan incantation:

King: *Are thou so confident? within what* **space**   a
Hopest thou my cure?

Helena: *The greatest grace* lending* **grace**,   a
Ere twice the horses of the sun shall BRING   b
Their fiery torcher his diurnal** RING,   b
Ere twice in murk and occidental **damp**   c
Moist Hesperus*** hath quench'd his sleepy **lamp**,   c
Or four and twenty times the pilot's GLASS   d
Hath told the thievish minutes how they PASS,   d
What is infirm from your sound parts shall **fly**,   e
Health shall live free and sickness freely **die**.   e

2:1:158

* God   **daily   *** the evening star

Sharing a couplet binds the King and Helena closely together in a ritual of persuasive enchantment. But such couplet-sharing can bind characters together in other ways. It might meld them together in the flush of first love, for example; or lock them in an altercation where one character tries to punch back, or 'trump', another by *consciously* rhyming the last word of his line, with the last word of the other's. Such an altercation might be deadly serious, or it can be playful, as in this exchange from *Romeo and Juliet*. In the first scene of the play, Romeo has been lamenting his beloved Rosaline's commitment to sexual abstinence:

Benvolio: *Then she hath sworn that she will still live* **chaste?**   a

Romeo: *She hath, and in that sparing makes huge* **waste**.   a

1:1:215

I'm sure you can sense how Romeo satisfyingly 'pings' his point home by consciously trumping Benvolio's *'chaste'* with his rhyming *'waste'*.

Rhymed songs and spells

Rhyme lends pointedness and memorability to words, but as we have seen in the King/Helena exchange above, when it is combined with regular rhythms, alliteration, and artful choice of words, rhyme can also 'raise' language to a height where it is experienced as more special, more potent, and much more mysterious than everyday language. As is true of most songs and spells in any context, therefore, Shakespeare's spells and songs are written in rhyme. It is especially true then that, just as with their rhythm, rhyme in spells should not be shirked by trying to play it down. Rhymes in songs will tend naturally to receive their appropriate degree of presentation, as the rhyming words will usually coincide with the end of a phrase of music.

Different rhyming schemes

Just as Shakespeare employs line lengths other than the pentameter, he uses rhyming schemes other than the couplet. You have already encountered the a,b; a,b scheme, in the opening lines of both Lysander, and the Countess, above. The Pyramus speech cited earlier as an example of verse with shorter line-lengths, provides an example of one of the other rhyming schemes used. Act these lines aloud and experience the silly and innocent pleasure they provide; the rhyming scheme is a,a,b; c,c,b:

The bold knight, Pyramus believes he has stumbled on evidence of his love's demise:

Pyramus: *But stay! O **spite!***	a
*But mark, poor **knight,***	a
What dreadful dole is HERE?	b
*Eyes, do you **see?***	c
*How can it **be?***	c
O dainty duck! O DEAR!	b

5:1:265

As with the insistent rhythm of these very short lines, (or indeed with the 'over-alliteration' they contain) one needn't be too wary about over-playing the rhymes.

Puck's little speech below comprises tetrameters (four feet) and has an unusual, and particularly 'noticeable', rhyming scheme: it comprises a couplet followed by no fewer than four consecutive lines which rhyme with one another (a,a; b,b,b,b):

Puck: *Captain of our fairy **band,***	a
*Helena is here at **hand.***	a
And the youth mistook by ME	b
Pleading for a lover's FEE.	b
Shall we their fond pageant SEE?	b
Lord what fools these mortals BE!	b

3:2:110

Overplaying, and drawing attention to, the short lines and rhymes in speeches such as those of Pyramus is part of the actor's job. The doggerel of such speeches provides an example where the dramatic verse is supposed to sound '*in*appropriate to purpose'. Puck's short lines and rhymes, on the other hand, provide an example where one must be careful *not* to overplay the rhyme; so as to *avoid* coming across as inappropriate to purpose – and not in a funny way. The actor playing Puck needs to be hyper-vigilant so as not to let the repeated rhyme and the 'dum dee dum' take over from the 'realness' of what he is saying, and the reality of his need to see it.

The same applies to the actor playing Oberon. Oberon continues the dialogue with Puck, still rhyming, and with the same short lines (tetrameters):

Oberon: *Stand aside: the noise they **make***	a
*Will cause Demetrius to **awake**.*	a

Puck: *Then will two at once woo **one**;*	b
*That must needs be sport al-**one**;*	b
*And those things do best please **me***	c
*That befall prepost'rous-**ly**.*	c

Enter Lysander and Helena.   *3:2:116*

Both characters' explanations, orders and questions need to be as sincerely and specifically motivated as any other line; this must remain their primary focus. The rhymes to some extent, however, need to be acknowledged, to be played 'as being there': they serve a purpose. The rhymes, and artificially short lines, the two share maintain the sense of the audience having access to a 'special' reality, very much 'other' than the everyday. They also help capture the close partnership between the two as co-conspirators, co-conjurers. Also, their condensed and highly-wrought rhyming exchange helps to create the sense of the tightening of a magical, and inescapable, knot of mischief around the unsuspecting pair of lovers, just about to enter.

RHYME – Key points
- Rhyme asks to be **played**; it does not ask to be smoothed over or 'disappeared' in the name of 'naturalness'.
- The first word of a rhyme requires to be 'set up' so that the word that rhymes with it can strike against it; can 'crown' or 'trump' it. This 'capping' must not be over-played; find a way for the rhyme to be essential to you in successfully conveying what you need to get across. Let clarity of feeling and intention be your guide as to how strongly to play it.
- A shift from prose, or unrhymed verse, into rhymed verse represents a shift in the character of a scene. The shift could represent a movement into more heightened feelings of joy, love, determination, conflict (playful or more serious), philosophical reflection, mystical conjuration etc. Find a way for the rhyme to become an essential element in how you manage to embody and convey this shift in the feelings in a scene. Find a way to **need** the rhyme.

CHAPTER ELEVEN

PRONUNCIATION

Words with apostrophes

On the page, an apostrophe is used to indicate that a part of a word is not to be pronounced when spoken. What are normally two separate words on the page, are often thereby, contracted to one. Familiar examples are: 'isn't' for 'is not'; 'don't' for 'do not'; 'we'll' for 'we will'; 'you'd' for 'you would'. When reading an edition of any Shakespeare play, you will come across many more apostrophes than you do in modern prose, or verse.

One of the most frequent uses Shakespeare makes of the apostrophe is to replace the 'e' in the 'ed' at the end words in the past-tense. Today the 'e' at the end of most past-tense words ending in 'ed' is not pronounced. E.g. 'Disappeared', 'sliced', 'cooked', 'blessed', 'borrowed', 'shattered'. In the case of words ending in 'd' or 't', and which have their past-tense form in '-ed' it is, of course, not possible to make the 'e' silent. In the following examples the final 'e' is pronounced: 'fretted', 'dreaded', 'bested', 'charted', 'flooded'. In Shakespeare's time, however, the 'e' could be either pronounced or silent, and to suit his rhythmic purposes, he will either ask for the 'e' to be pronounced, by allowing the 'e' to remain, or will replace the 'e' with an apostrophe, indicating that, in this instance, he does *not* want it to be pronounced.

In the line below, for example, where Hamlet addresses the ghost of his father, Shakespeare replaces the 'e' in the word 'damned' to indicate that he wants the word to be pronounced, not with two syllables, as it then acceptably could be, ('dam-ned'), but as one (as we pronounce it today):

Hamlet: *Be thou a spirit of health or goblin **damn'd**...*   1:4:40

In other circumstances, Shakespeare will want this same word to be pronounced as *two* syllables. In such an instance he will retain the 'e' in the '-ed'. Hamlet, in his very next scene, execrating Claudius:

Hamlet: *O villain, villain, smiling, **damned** villain!*   1:5:106

And a line from *Romeo and Juliet*:

Romeo: *O, Friar, the **damned** use that word in hell.*   3:3:47

Act Romeo's line aloud, first pronouncing the *'damned'* as Lady Macbeth does, as *one* syllable:

*O, Friar, the **damn'd** use that word in hell.*

Now act the line again, this time as Shakespeare intended, with *two* syllables:

*O, Friar, the **dam-ned** use that word in hell.*

Better? Speaking the word as *'dam-ned'* gives the line its ten syllables and restores the pentameter rhythms. This is the way Shakespeare heard the line and wants it acted and is why he, therefore, retains the 'e'.

There are many words where Shakespeare retains the 'e', but where today it would never be pronounced: *'damned'* is a perfect example. In such instances, some modern editors (not all) will place an accent over any such 'e' to alert the reader to the fact it should be pronounced, as in: 'damnèd', 'tirèd'.

Pronouncing the 'e' in past tense words – Richard III et al.

Below are examples where, in modern speech, we would not pronounce the 'e', but where, for the sake of the rhythm, Shakespeare lets us know, by retaining it, that he wants it pronounced.

Speak each line below aloud, firstly pronouncing the words in bold as we would today (*without* pronouncing the 'e'). Then speak the line again using the pronunciation that Shakespeare intended, i.e. with the 'e' pronounced. This will help impress on your awareness, the need to look out for, and pronounce, those retained 'e's'. It will also strengthen your understanding as to how Shakespeare's decision to retain final 'e's' is made for the same reason he sometimes replaces it with an apostrophe – to create his desired rhythm for the line. First *without* pronouncing the 'e'; then pronouncing it:

Richard the Third:

Richard: *I am **determin-ed** to play the villain.*   *1:1:30*

From Macbeth's speech to the phantom dagger:

Macbeth: *... Art thou but*
A dagger of the mind, a false creation,
*Proceeding from the heat **oppress-ed** brain*   *2:1:37*

From Antony's speech to the remains of Julius Caesar:

Antony: *Thou art the ruins of the noblest man*
*That ever **liv-ed** in the tide of times.*   *3:1:256*

A line from *A Midsummer Night's Dream*:

Egeus: *Happy be Theseus, our **renown-ed** Duke.*   *1:1:20*

I'm sure you found the lines more rhythmic and fully fleshed-out when acted as Shakespeare asks.

It is, of course, not only at the end of past tense words where Shakespeare uses the apostrophe; and not only will you regularly encounter instances where apostrophes contract a pair of words to one, there are numerous occasions when it is three words that they contract to one. Again, it is for the sake of achieving a particular rhythm that Shakespeare elects to do this. Surprisingly, it is not uncommon for performers to ignore such apostrophes.

Pronouncing words with an apostrophe – Lady Macbeth et al.

In the following short quotes from Lady Macbeth's, *'Come you spirits…'* speech, I have highlighted words that I have often heard spoken as if they did not include an apostrophe; the correct pronunciation is given after each quote.

Act each line aloud with the correct pronunciation until it comes easily and naturally. In some instances, because of the unfamiliarity of the contractions, achieving such naturalness may take a few attempts:

Lady Macbeth: … ***Thou'rt*** *mad to say it.*   1:5:31

'Thou'rt' does not have two syllables, as in *'thou-art';* but has *one* syllable: *'Thourt'.*

*Stop up **th'access** and passage to remorse…*   1:5:44
Not, 'the-ac-cess' (three syllables); but 'thac-cess' (two syllables).

            … *Come to my woman's breasts*
*And take my milk for gall, you **murth'ring** ministers…*   1:5:47
Not 'murth-er-ing' (three syllables); but 'murth-ring' (two syllables).

And some final practice with lines from other characters where, typically, the apostrophes can be neglected. Again, act each example until the pronunciation of the words with apostrophes feels comfortable to you:

Macbeth: *Mine eyes are made the fools **o'th'other** senses…*   2:2:44
Not 'o-the-other' (four syllables); but 'o-thoth-er' (three syllables).

Lysander: *Fair love, you faint with **wand'ring** in the wood.*   Dream 2:2:34
Not 'wand-er-ing'; but 'wand-ring' (two syllables).

Edmund: *Go to **th' creating** a whole tribe of fops*
Not 'Go to the creating'; but 'Go toth-creating'.   *Lear 1:2:14*

Keep acting the lines aloud:

Edmund: *Our father's love is to the bastard Edmund*
*As to **th' legitimate***   *Lear 1:2:17*
Not 'As-to-the-legitimate'; but 'As toth-legitimate'.

Hermione: *...hurried*
*Here, to this place, **i'th'open** air before*
I have got strength of limit...   *The Winter's Tale 3:2:104*
Not 'in the open air', or 'i' the open air'; but 'i-thopen air'.

Words stressed differently in Shakespeare's day

Some words in Shakespeare's time were stressed differently to the way we stress them today. Or in some cases, the same word could acceptably be stressed in alternative ways (as some English words are differently stressed in U.S. pronunciation than in the British. E.g. 'the-**a**-tre' vs. '**the**-a-tre'). Within a line of prose, the more modern pronunciation of a word can often be used, and a rhythm for the sentence still found that sounds '**right**'. In verse, however, if we use the modern pronunciation, the rhythm of the line will usually feel, and sound, 'wrong'.

The rhythm of a line at the opening of *A Midsummer Night's Dream* tells us that Shakespeare hears the word 'revenue' stressed as we would stress it today. Theseus laments that, just as a *'dowager'* (a propertied and/or titled widow), or a *'step-dame'* (step-mother), might live too long, and so hold off the time when a young man will come into his inherited *'revenue'*, so, the slow waning of the moon drags out the time until his marriage to Hippolyta:

Theseus: *She* lingers my desires,*
Like to a step-dame, or a dowager,
*Long withering out a young man's **rev-e-nue**.*   *1:1:4*

* the moon

The rhythm of a Lysander line later in the same scene, however, tells us that the word *'revenue'* should *not* have its main stress on the first syllable, as it does today; but should have it on the second syllable, as in: *'re-**ven**-ue'*.

Lysander informs Hermia of his wealthy aunt:

Lysander: *I have a widow aunt, a dowager,*
*Of great re-**ven**-ue...*   *1:1:157*

Act Lysander's lines, first pronouncing *'revenue'* the *modern* way, with a stress on the first syllable. Having done that, act it again, speaking *'revenue'* with the stress on the middle syllable.

His words flow better with the stress on the middle syllable ('re-**ven**-ue'), don't you find?

When a word is to be stressed differently to how it is today, in most editions, the editor will indicate the desired pronunciation, either by placing an accent over the appropriate syllable or syllables, as in 'revènue', or with the help of a footnote.

But when speaking a line such as Lysander's, you will often be able to sense yourself when a word asks to be stressed in a way other than you are used to, particularly as you become more attuned to the rhythm of Shakespeare's verse.

Here are a few more examples you are likely to come across, where using the modern pronunciation of a word will make a line feel, and sound, quite wrong.

Act each example twice, firstly pronouncing the hyphenated words the way you would today; then acting the line again, placing the stress on the syllable I have highlighted in bold. Acting the lines both ways will further develop your 'ear' for the integrity of the verse.

In *King Lear*, Edmund wonders why, as an illegitimate child, he should be called, '*base*':

Edmund: *... Wherefore* base?*
*When my dimensions are as well com-**pact**,*
My mind as generous, and my shape as true...   *1:2:6*

* why   * made up

Hamlet decries a mother, happy to marry so soon after her first husband's death:

Hamlet: *O God, a beast that wants dis-**course** of reason*
Would have mourn'd longer...   *1:2:50*

In *The Comedy of Errors*, Adriana believes (very mistakenly!) that the confused man she addresses is the husband who now only shows his more loveable sides to another woman:

Adriana: *Ay, ay, Antipholus, look strange and frown:*
*Some other mistress hath thy sweet a-**spects**.*   *2:2:101*

Keep pronouncing the words first the modern way, then as indicated.

Titania explains to Oberon what devastating events occur in the mortal world when he and she are in dissension:

Titania: *Therefore the moon, the governess of floods,*
Pale in her anger, washes all the air,
*That **rheum**-a-tic diseases do abound...*   *2:1:103*

Constance, in the play *King John,* begs access to a madness in which she might forget her grief:

Constance: *Preach some philosophy to make me mad,*
And thou shalt be can-on-ised, cardinal...   3:3:51

In *The Tempest,* Prospero explains to his daughter that, not long ago, he was the rightful Duke of Milan:

Prospero: *Twelve year since, Miranda, twelve year since*
Thy father was the Duke of Mil-an and
A prince of power.   1:2:53

In *Antony and Cleopatra,* the Egyptian queen protests she would rather hang than subject herself to the *'shouting varletry / Of censuring Rome...'*

Cleopatra: *...rather make*
My country's high py-ram-i-des my gibbet,
And hang me up in chains!   5:2:60

Rhymes that no longer rhyme

Apart from being stressed differently, or having variable stresses, many words in Shakespeare's time simply sounded quite differently to how we pronounce them today. There have, of course, been productions using what scholars believe to be 'original pronunciation', and one of the means scholars use to work out what original pronunciation might have been is to study the rhymes used in the verse of the period. Two words that clearly rhymed in Shakespeare's time (for example, *'love'* and *'prove'*) may not rhyme today, and so, by careful comparisons with the occurrence of the words in other contexts, it can be deduced how the words originally sounded. This means that some words that rhymed in 1600 will now no longer rhyme at all. Below are two Countess lines from *All's Well That Ends Well.* In Shakespeare's day the words, *'forgone'* and *'none'* would have rhymed, and, of course, today they do not.

The old Countess remembers that in her youth, as every young person was, she too was guilty of the *'fault'* of being painfully in love:

Countess: *By our remembrances of days foregone,*
Such were our faults, or then we thought them none.   1:3:129

In such a case, rather than suddenly introducing a single early seventeenth-century pronunciation to preserve the rhyme, most productions (rightly, I believe) will employ the contemporary pronunciation for both words.

Here, however, is Bertram in *All's Well That Ends Well,* summing up his argument as to why Diana should yield to his advances:

Bertram: ... *Say thou art mine, and **ever***
*My love as it begins shall so per**sever***. 4:2:36

In this case, if one were to pronounce 'persever' in the (unrhyming) way usual today ('**per**-sev-**ere**'), it would wreck the rhythm and sound of the line so painfully, as probably to raise a laugh. Try that:

*... Say thou art mine, and **ever***
*My love as it begins shall so **persever***.

I think you'll have got that in such a case, 'per-**se**-ver' is better.

Occasionally some fun is to be wrung out of 'rhymes that don't rhyme' today.

Here is Celia, in *As You Like It*, reciting aloud the closing lines of one of Orlando's (not entirely perfect) love poems to his beloved Rosalind:

Celia: *Heaven would that she these gifts should **have***
*And I to live and die her **slave***. 3:2:150

A commonly created joke in productions, and one I have used myself, is that Celia first pronounces '*slave*' to rhyme with '*have*' (understandably since the rest of the poem had been composed in rhyming couplets), then quickly corrects herself, and repeats the word '*slave*' the way we are used to hearing it today. This becomes a joke at the expense of Orlando's sincere, but somewhat inept, attempts at rhyming.

PRONUNCIATION – Key points

- To maintain the rhythms Shakespeare intended, the syllables which he frequently replaces with an apostrophe must not be sounded.

- When he wants it to be silent, Shakespeare replaces the 'e' in the '-ed' ending of past tense words with an apostrophe.

- Some words in Shakespeare's time were stressed differently to today, or could acceptably be stressed in alternative ways. Within a line of prose the more modern pronunciation of a word can often be used and a rhythm for the line still found that sounds 'right'. In verse, however, if we use the modern pronunciation, the rhythm of the line will usually feel, and sound, 'wrong'.

- Some words which rhymed in Shakespeare's time do not do so today, e.g. 'prove' and 'love'. Usually better to use the modern pronunciation rather than suddenly impose on the audience a strange-sounding sixteenth- or seventeenth-century pronunciation.

CHAPTER TWELVE

PLAYING SENSE-BREAKS IN PROSE AND PLAYING PARENTHESES

I have already suggested that 'making myself as clear as possible' should always be included as part of any objective. And in the chapter on 'Acting Shakespeare's Verse' it was discussed that one of the principal means to achieve this, was to reveal the 'architecture' of the language; to bring into relief the building-blocks out of which the verse-lines are constructed. These blocks, of course, are the major and minor sense-units. Described in that chapter, also, were exercises for helping one get in touch with the pivotal-breaks that separate the minor sense-units in a verse-line. Even though the various sense-units may be of a more variable length in prose than those in the verse, these exercises can be used, just as productively, to reveal the sense-architecture of any prose-passage, or line.

Swing-boating; clapping and stamping – Hamlet

Instead of swinging (or clapping and/or stamping) to mark the beginning of verse-lines, or pivotal breaks, you will, when working with prose, simply be swinging one way (or clapping/stamping) at the beginning of one sense-break, then swinging the other at the next. You will see that you can swing at either major or minor sense-breaks, or a combination of both.

And a reminder to fling the words forcefully against the walls of the room, and to send out the very *last word* of each sense-unit with as much energy as every other. *(For a full description of this exercise see page 96.)*

Read this beautiful passage of prose from *Hamlet*, and when you are clear as to its meaning, without thinking any more about it, speak it aloud:

> **Hamlet:** *What a piece of work is a man! how noble in reason! how infinite in faculty! in form and moving how express and admirable! in action how like an angel! in apprehension how like a god! the beauty of the world! the paragon of animals! And yet, to me, what is this quintessence of dust? man delights not me: no, nor woman neither, though by your smiling you seem to say so.*
>
> 2:2:303

Having acted it aloud, go through the passage again and, with your pencil, mark with a double upright line, every point where you decide there is a meaningful sense-break. Don't read any further until you have done this.

Below is the speech marked up as just one way of breaking the passage into its constituent sense-units. You may have marked in fewer, or perhaps more. (There can, and will always be, disagreements as to which size of sense-units this, or any other passage, might best be divided into. Such differences will not greatly diminish the effectiveness of the exercise.) So following either the scheme you have marked up for yourself above, and/or the version marked up below, swing-boat Hamlet's lines aloud. Really swing! As earlier, unless you have the piece by heart, you will be holding the text in one hand and swinging only one arm. I have marked in the first few 'lefts' and 'rights' to start you off:

> *(Swing right) What a piece of work is a man! (Left) how noble in reason!*
> *(Right) how infinite in faculty! (Left etc.) || in form and moving || how express*
> *and admirable! || in action || how like an angel! || in apprehension || how like*
> *a god! || the beauty of the world! || the paragon of animals! || And yet, to me,*
> *|| what is this quintessence of dust? || Man delights not me: || no, nor woman*
> *neither, || though by your smiling || you seem to say so.*

Now that you have vigorously 'swing-boated' the entire passage, act it again at what feels like an appropriate pace for getting your explanations across to Rosencrantz and Guildestern. You will feel much more engaged with, and in control of, the words. You will be clearer and more listenable-to.

By way of illustrating how far you can go breaking any speech or line down into its constituent sense-units, I have laid out below a breakdown of the Hamlet piece which is even more detailed than the version offered above. Speak it aloud again, this time, replacing the swings with hand claps and/or foot stamps. A reminder: the claps and stamps must not be 'on' a word. They come as a percussive punctuation *inserted between* each pair of sense-units. (And remember that if you are at risk of disturbing others, instead of stamping or clapping at every break, you can lightly tap your pencil or finger on your desk, or press your foot into the floor. Or you might want to invent your own discreet version of the exercise.)

> *(Clap and stamp) What a piece of work (Clap and stamp) is a man! || (Clap*
> *and stamp) how noble || (Clap and stamp etc.) in reason! || how infinite ||*
> *in faculty! || in form || and moving || how express || and admirable! || in action*
> *|| how like an angel! || in apprehension || how like a god! || the beauty || of the*
> *world! || the paragon || of animals! || And yet, || to me, || what is this quintessence*
> *|| of dust? || man delights not me: || no, || nor woman neither, || though || by your*
> *smiling || you seem to say so.*

Now, let go of the clapping and foot stamps and, again, deliver the passage more naturally, allowing the trace of the exercise to do its work.

Experiencing the emptiness – Shylock

Apart from swinging/clapping/stamping, another highly effective exercise you can use to connect to, and to reveal the architecture of any line or passage is one I call, 'Experiencing the emptiness'. (This is another exercise which can be applied quite as effectively to verse, as to prose.)

You can get to know this exercise using the prose passage below from *The Merchant of Venice*. As you did with the Hamlet speech, I want you first to read it for meaning. Then, without pondering over it, speak it aloud.

Shylock explains why he might be deemed justified in wanting revenge on Antonio:

Shylock: *He hath disgraced me, and hindered me half a million; laughed at my losses, mocked at my gains, scorned my nation, thwarted my bargains, cooled my friends, heated mine enemies; and what's his reason? I am a Jew. Hath not a Jew eyes? hath not a Jew hands, organs, dimensions, senses, affections, passions? fed with the same food, hurt with the same weapons, subject to the same diseases, healed by the same means, warmed and cooled by the same winter and summer, as a Christian is?*   3:1:49

Having acted it aloud, go through the segment again, and mark in every sense-break you think it useful to identify.

With your sense-breaks marked up, act the passage again. This time, however, rather than bringing your sense-breaks into relief by swinging or stamping etc., leave instead a large gap of silence between each of them; and in that silence…wait. *Keeping alert, and totally connected to whomever you are addressing,* relax, and fully experience the 'emptiness', the 'no-man's land', the 'vacuum' of the silence. And do not hang on to the energy of the previous phrase – let it go entirely. Keep a sense of the vacuum in your awareness, and wait for the next sense-unit to 'occur' to you. Even if it takes five, ten, twenty or more seconds, wait until the words of the next half-line 'bubble', or 'body forth', out of the void, all of their own accord; until they spontaneously rise up *out of* the experience of the 'felt emptiness'. Have a go at this now. As well as achieving clearly discernible results, this exercise can be immensely calming, and focussing, to do.

Having experienced the silence in each of your sense-breaks, act the passage again, but at a more 'normal' pace. You and any listener will feel, and appreciate, the difference.

As a last illustration of the amount of detail you can profitably go into with this exercise, below is the Shylock piece again, divided up into its smaller sense-units. This time you need only clap your hands together smartly between each sense-unit:

(Clap) He hath disgraced me, (Clap) and hindered me (Clap) half a million; (Clap) laughed (Clap etc.) at my losses, || mocked || at my gains, || scorned || my nation, || thwarted || my bargains, || cooled || my friends, || heated || mine enemies; || and what's his reason? || I am a Jew. || Hath not a Jew || eyes? || hath not a Jew || hands, || organs, || dimensions, || senses, || affections, || passions? || fed || with the same food, || hurt || with the same weapons, || subject || to the same diseases, || healed || by the same means, || warmed || and cooled || by the same winter || and summer, || as a Christian is?

Playing parentheses, or 'non-essential' sense-units

Another productive way to get in touch with the meaning-architecture of any sentence (in prose or verse) is to separate its 'essential' sense-units from its parentheses, or 'non-essential' sense-units.

'Parentheses' (singular: 'parenthesis') are qualifying words, or phrases, which are 'stuck into' any sentence, in order to add extra information or detail. A parenthesis usually occurs in the text between commas, or brackets, as in: 'John (the man we met last night) has sent a note.' Or, 'John, the man we met last night, has sent a note.' You can see that if we read, or speak, this sentence leaving out the words between the brackets, or commas, that the sentence still makes complete sense. It will still make its main point: *'John has sent a note.'* The parenthesis (in this instance, *'the man we met last night'*) may be of great interest, but is *not essential* in order for the main element of the sentence, on its own, to make complete sense. This 'main' element of the sentence, I refer to as its 'spine'.

And to pre-empt any possible confusion, parentheses can occur as readily in sentences which are questions, orders, or explanations. To illustrate:

Explanation: *'John (the man we met last night) has sent a note.'*

Order: *'Tell John (the man we met last night) to send a note.'*

Question: *'Was it John (the man we met last night) who sent the note?'*

And for the purposes of this discussion, and the exercise to follow, I will use the term 'parenthesis' more loosely than it normally may be. I will use it to refer to any sense-unit within a sentence which is not *absolutely* essential to its central point, to its spine. And I am aware that there may be disagreement as to what I suggest is an essential, or a non-essential, sense-unit in the examples I will use. But in order for you to learn how to apply, and get the benefit of, the exercises here, there is no need for any full agreement on this matter. Whatever term one attaches to them, all words and phrases which 'add detail' in the course of a sentence can usefully be 'singled and separated out'; can be treated as if they *were* parentheses.

Playing the spine of the sentence – Antony and Calpurnia

I would like to take you through an exercise I often use and which invariably yields noticeable results.

First of all, speak aloud the few lines from *Julius Caesar* below.

Mark Antony assures the Roman people that he would never wish to wrong the honourable men responsible for Caesar's assassination:

Antony:　　… *I rather choose*
To wrong the dead, to wrong myself and you,
Than I will wrong such honourable men.　　　　　　　　3:2:126

Here is the 'spine' of Antony's utterance separated out:

Spine:　　… *I rather choose*
To wrong the dead,
Than I will wrong such honourable men.

The parenthesis here is: *'to wrong myself and you'.*

Delivering the sentence without the parenthesis in this way, you will have found that it is still perfectly playable and makes complete sense. Act this spine a few times again, now, until you feel you have fully connected to its meaning, and are communicating it solidly to the listener.

Having done that, go back and act Antony's sentence again – this time complete. As you do this, make it part of your objective that, without having to concentrate too hard, the audience should 'get' which bit of your sentence is the spine of what you are saying, and which is the parenthesis.

Such single, short parentheses as those above are relatively straightforward to make clear to the listener, but Shakespeare offers us frequent challenges with his longer, and with his 'multiple' parentheses.

Next is a section of another speech from Julius Caesar with, again, a single but *longer* parenthesis. Firstly, deliver this sentence complete. Then act the spine a few times, till you feel it is under your belt, and that you are communicating its meaning clearly.

Calpurnia tells her husband, Caesar, that a messenger has brought news about the ominous signs of disaster that have been seen, over and above the ones they already know of:

Calpurnia: *... There is one within,*
Besides the things that we have heard and seen,
Recounts most horrid sights seen by the watch.   2:2:14

The spine: *... There is one within,*
Recounts most horrid sights seen by the watch.

Parenthesis: *Besides the things that we have heard and seen,*

You can again see that the parenthesis provides detail *extra* to the principal explanation Calpurnia wishes to convey.

And now, remaining very clear about your 'back-bone' explanation, bring back the parenthesis, and perform the sentence complete:

Calpurnia: *... There is one within,*
Besides the things that we have heard and seen,
Recounts most horrid sights seen by the watch.

You will sense how, for a listener, you are now distinguishing more clearly between the primary, and the secondary, strands of the sentence.

Playing multiple parentheses – Titania

Calpurnia's sentence contains quite a long, but still only a single, parenthesis. It is extremely common, however, for Shakespeare to create sentences which contain any number of parentheses. And when acting any such sentences, one has consciously to work to ensure that the meaning is not 'drowned' or 'buried' under the plethora of its various parentheses.

The following are some further lines of Titania's from *A Midsummer Night's Dream,* for you to use as practice with multiple parentheses. These lines are particularly fun to play the spine-game with.

Firstly, read the complete sentence until you fully understand it; then (again without peeking ahead), bracket in each of the sense-units you regard as not being *absolutely* essential to Titania's main point; be ruthless. The units not enclosed in brackets will give you your spine.

Titania is telling Oberon that ever since the beginning of mid-summer, no matter where she and her fairies have gathered to perform their ring-dances (*'ringlets'*), he has never failed to cause a disruption:

Titania: *And never, since the middle summer's spring,*
Met we on hill, in dale, forest or mead*,
By pavèd fountain or by rushy brook
Or in the beachèd margent** of the sea,
To dance our ringlets to the whistling wind,
But with thy brawls thou hast disturb'd our sport   2:1:82

* meadow   ** edge

You may not have been as ruthless as I am going to be with this passage.
I have stripped Titania's sentence to its barest bones, regarding even the
smallest added detail as a separate and non-essential sense-unit. For example, I have identified the small sense-unit, *'on hill'* as a separate parenthesis
from, *'in dale'*, *'forest'* as a separate parenthesis from *'or mead'* etc.. There
may be disagreement as to what is definitely essential, or non-essential, to
Titania's main point here, but for this exercise to do its work total agreement is not a condition. As I have broken this passage down, there are ten
parentheses:

Titania: *And never, **(since the middle summer's spring,)***
*Met we **(on hill,) (in dale,) (forest) (or mead)***
(By pavèd fountain) (or by rushy brook)
(Or in the beachèd margent of the sea,)
*To dance our ringlets **(to the whistling wind,)***
*But **(with thy brawls)** thou hast disturb'd our sport.*

Act the spine now – *a number of times* – until this, the 'meat' of the sentence
is 'in you':

The spine:
And never,
Met we
To dance our ringlets
But
thou hast disturb'd our sport

And now, maintaining the spine at the fore-front of what you want to
communicate, start reintroducing, *one at a time*, each of the omitted
parentheses, as laid out below:

And never, since the middle summer's spring,
Met we
To dance our ringlets
But
thou hast disturb'd our sport.

> *And never, since the middle summer's spring,*
> *Met we on hill,*
> *To dance our ringlets*
> *But*
> *thou hast disturb'd our sport.*

Keep prioritising the spine:

> *And never, since the middle summer's spring,*
> *Met we on hill, in dale,*
> *To dance our ringlets*
> *But*
> *thou hast disturb'd our sport.*

> *And never, since the middle summer's spring,*
> *Met we on hill, in dale, forest,*
> *To dance our ringlets*
> *But*
> *thou hast disturb'd our sport.*

> *And never, since the middle summer's spring,*
> *Met we on hill, in dale, forest, or mead,*
> *To dance our ringlets*
> *But*
> *thou hast disturb'd our sport.*

> *And never, since the middle summer's spring,*
> *Met we on hill, in dale, forest, or mead,*
> *By pavèd fountain,*
> *To dance our ringlets*
> *But*
> *thou hast disturb'd our sport.*

And so on; keep delivering the line until you have re-introduced all ten parentheses.

By the time you have re-introduced every parenthesis, you will find that you are conveying the content of what you are saying much more easefully and graphically to Oberon and the audience. And with the experience of playing this game with the speeches examined here, and with other speeches you care to look at, you will soon find yourself 'instinctively' sensing, and separating out, the spine from the non-essential parentheses, and giving each its appropriate emphasis and value.

PLAYING SENSE-BREAKS IN PROSE
and PLAYING PARENTHESES – Key points

– To some degree, all sense-breaks in verse, or prose, ask to be acknowledged and marked.

– Exercises to help get in touch with sense-breaks are 'Swing-boating' (Page 96), 'Clapping and/or stamping'(Page 97), and 'Experiencing the emptiness'.

– An exercise to help develop your skill in playing parentheses, especially double and multiple-parentheses is 'Playing the spine' (Page 135).

CHAPTER THIRTEEN

ADJECTIVES AND ADVERBS

There is a degree of overlap between the subject of 'non-essential sense-units' and the subject of this chapter. I believe, however, that the 'playing of adjectives and adverbs' is of such importance as to warrant a separate discussion. For anyone who might remain a tad fuzzy about exactly what adjectives and adverbs are, a quick explanation is in order.

Adjectives

An adjective is a word which describes a particular quality of a noun. A 'noun' is a word for a 'thing', 'person' or a 'place': 'sky', 'girl', 'Seattle', 'tree', 'soup', 'love', 'Patrick', 'programme' and 'Saint Teresa' are nouns.

In these sentences the adjectives are in italics: The sky was *dark*. The girl is *angry*. This tree is *older*. Wisconsin is *wet*. The soup is *delicious*. His love was *limitless*. Patrick was *happiest*. The sea was *green*.

An adjective is a single word; but a phrase made up of two or more words can also function as an adjective; for example: Harry is a *happily married* man... That was a *hard-to-understand* lecture... I saw a *down-on-his-luck* financier begging in the street... Shakespeare is particularly fond of such adjective-phrases.

And often a noun can be placed next to another noun to serve the same describing purpose as an adjective. Some instances:

'*bus* ticket' ... '*household* word' ... '*tongue* twister' ... '*bottle* opener' ... '*party* pooper' ... '*concert* pianist' ...

Similarly, not just a single noun, but a whole 'noun-phrase', can be placed next to a noun in order to provide information about the person, or thing, it attaches to. A few examples:

Alex, *the fastest runner in the world*, arrives at nine... Mandy, *that laugh-a-minute party-girl*, has been kidnapped by bandits... Arthur Walsingham, *composer of so many unforgettable quartets*, has recently sued his grandmother.

Adverbs

An 'adverb' is a word which can offer information, not about a noun, but variously about a 'verb', about an adjective, or, indeed, about another adverb.

A verb is the term used for an 'action word'. 'Go' is a verb, as are the words 'eat', 'burn', 'hurry', 'cogitate' and 'swim'.

Here is an example of an adverb giving information about a verb:'Robert ran eagerly towards the gang-plank.' In this sentence, 'ran' is obviously the action word, the verb; 'eagerly' is the word (the adverb) giving more information *about* the verb. Two more examples:

Don't eat your food so *quickly*. ... Ellis *gladly* agreed to leave the firm...

Adverbs usually do end in 'ly', but not always; for example: 'Do work *hard*', 'Sit up *straight*', 'Don't arrive *late*', 'Oh, *very* nice!'.

And here is an example of an adverb adding information to an *adjective:* 'Angie felt *decidedly* grumpy.'

...and adding information to an *adjective-phrase*: 'Harry is a *deliriously* unhappily married man.'

And, lastly, a few examples of adverbs providing information about other adverbs: *Suspiciously* willingly, the funeral director agreed to the price... Kate arrived *terribly* late... *Very* slowly does it.

Acting adjectives and adverbs

From this point on, anything discussed relating to adjectives can be regarded as applying equally to the adverbs, adjective- and noun-phrases etc. just discussed.

I find, the principal problem in the playing of adjectives, or adverbs etc., is that they often come across as if there is 'nothing underneath' them. This particularly seems to be the case when they stand immediately next to the word, or phrase, about which they are giving information: as in, 'horrid *deed*' or 'vaulting *ambition*'. In such adjective/noun pairings, it is often the case that the adjective becomes 'absorbed' into the noun, as if it had no apparent value or meaning of its own. The adjective (or adverb) and the noun are run together, as if they were one word.

But when adjectives etc. are played with a genuine understanding of their precise meaning, and when they are played with a considered awareness of why the character has selected these *particular* adjectives to go with these *particular* nouns – then the vibrancy, 'preciseness', and general truthfulness of a line or speech, will be greatly enhanced.

The 'Playing the spine' exercise described in the preceding chapter *(see page 135)* can be adapted, and applied, with immediate results to the playing of adjectives and adverbs etc. This adapted version of the exercise I refer to (with no great access of imagination), as 'Omitting the adjectives etc.'. A proper use of this exercise can help the actor to discover a source, a 'felt necessity' within, for each and every adjective, adverb etc. their character employs.

Omitting the adjectives etc. – Henry V et al.

The first part of this exercise is to single out all the adjectives, adverbs, describing nouns or phrases etc. in whatever sentence, or speech, you are working on, and to underline (or circle) them. Then, deliver the line(s) whilst leaving out every word, or phrase you have circled or underlined. As an easy start to the practice, I will start you off with a short phrase containing a single adjective:

Henry: *We few, we **happy** few...*   *Henry V 4:3:62*

Deliver this phrase as written. Then deliver it, *omitting* the adjective, *'happy'*. It becomes,

'We few, we few...'

As you did in the 'Playing the spine' exercise, repeat this phrase until you feel wholly connected to it.

The second part of the exercise is then to deliver the line again, this time with the omitted adjective restored. You will feel you are now giving more value to *'happy'*, that the word occurs to you more in the moment when you speak it.

Deliver this line of Juliet in which she urges the horses which draw the chariot of the sun across the sky to get a move on – so that the dark of night can provide cover for Romeo's arrival in her chamber:

Juliet: *Gallop **apace**, you **fiery-footed** steeds...*   *3:2:1*

Then act it without the adverb (*'apace'*), and without the adjective-phrase (*'fiery-footed'*).

Gallop, you steeds...

Then restoring only the adverb:

Gallop apace, you steeds...

Then restoring as well, the first part of the adjective-phrase:

Gallop apace, you footed steeds...

And finally the line complete:

Gallop apace, you fiery-footed steeds...

Sense how, when the words have their place back, that they have become more important to you. They feel more deliberately, and specifically, selected by the character. You may also begin to feel that when you do say the words, *'fiery-footed', 'happy'*, etc., in this more 'chosen' way, that the specific meaning the words have will begin to 'work' *you*. They will begin to connect to, tap into that part within you from which these words arise when you speak them spontaneously in the context of your real life.

Apply this exercise now to the few lines below from further on in Juliet's speech.

Underline, or circle, every adjective, adverb, adjective-phrase etc.; then act the line omitting everything you have circled or underlined; then deliver the line re-introducing the dropped words of phrases, *one by one*. (Be sure to break the adjective-phrase, *'black-brow'd'* into two, as you did with *'fiery-footed'* in Juliet's earlier line.)

Juliet: *Come, gentle night, come, loving, black-brow'd night,*
Give me my Romeo...   *3:2:20*

A terrific speech to practise this game with is the opening of Richard the Third's *'Now is the winter...'* speech (1:1:1). In its first thirteen lines, there are no fewer than fifteen describing words.

> ### ADJECTIVES AND ADVERBS – Key points
> — Adjectives and adjective-phrases are used to describe a person or a thing.
> — Adverbs and adverb-phrases are used variously to give information about a verb, ('doing' word), an adjective, or another adverb.
> — When adjectives etc. are played with their precise meaning, and with an awareness of why the character has chosen to use them, then the vibrancy, 'preciseness', and general truthfulness of a line, or speech, will be greatly enhanced.
> — To ensure you are not running adjectives etc. together with the elements they describe (as if they were one longer word), use the 'Omitting the adjectives etc.' exercise: Identify, then underline or circle every adjective, adverb, adjective-phrase etc.; act the line omitting everything you have circled or underlined; then deliver the line re-introducing, one at a time, the omitted words or phrases.

CHAPTER FOURTEEN

SHORT LINES

You may have noticed many examples of lines in verse dialogue, and even in verse speeches, that are significantly shorter than the full pentameter. For discussion purposes such short lines can be grouped into two different types: 'free-standing' short lines; and 'shared' short lines.

Shared lines, and free-standing lines

In dialogue, different characters may 'share' a verse-line between them. One delivers the first part of a pentameter, and the other completes it by delivering the second half. In the lines below, Puck tells Oberon he will fly around the globe to search for a flower, the juice of which will put a spell on Titania. To draw attention to them, I will highlight the half-lines:

Puck: *I'll put a girdle round about the earth*
In forty minutes.

Oberon: ***Having once this juice***
I'll watch Titania when she is asleep,
And drop the liquor of it in her eyes…   *2:1:175*

In such a case, if you put the two short lines together, you have the equivalent of a single, and regular, verse-line:

*In **for**-ty **min**-utes. **Hav**-ing **once** this **juice**…*

In most contemporary Shakespeare editions, short lines that are deemed to be shared are visually, and helpfully, indicated by their placing on the page. How the Puck/Oberon lines were first presented above is how you will find them laid in a modern edition.

A short line deemed *not* shared, but 'free-standing' is placed on its own, next to the left margin, or next to its character-title, as in this Marulluls (sometimes spelt 'Murellus') example from *Julius Caesar*:

Flavius: *… Disrobe the images,*
If you do find them decked with ceremonies*.

*symbols of pomp

Murullus: *May we do so?*
You know it is the feast of Lupercal. 1:1:67

In some instances there can be debate as to whether a line is free-standing, or is intended to be shared. In the original seventeenth-century Quarto and Folio editions of the plays, short lines were sometimes not printed as separate lines, but were often tagged on to the end of the preceding full line, as in:

Puck: *I'll put a girdle, round about the earth, in forty minutes...*

Or each short line was printed one below the other, next to the left margin or character title. Here are a few short lines shared by Macbeth and Lady Macbeth as they will appear in most contemporary editions:

Macbeth: *... My dearest love,*
Duncan comes here tonight.

Lady Macbeth: *And when goes hence?*

Macbeth: *Tomorrow as he purposes.*

Lady Macbeth: *O, never*
Shall sun that morrow see! 1:5:58

But in the original editions, this is how these lines are laid out:

Macbeth: *My dearest love,*
Duncan comes here tonight.

Lady Macbeth: *And when goes hence?*

Macbeth: *Tomorrow, as he purposes.*

Lady Macbeth: *O never,*
Shall sun that morrow see!

In the instances above it is relatively straightforward to establish that these are indeed shared lines. But there are occasions, for example, where there are *three* short lines in a row, and this results in a decision having to be made as to which line is the one meant to be free-standing, and which are the two short lines meant to be shared. Because of this, you will find that in various modern editions certain short passages have been laid out differently on the page by different editors.

Fascinating as I find it, a more detailed discussion of this issue is beyond the scope of this book. In most circumstances, students/actors will be relying on the research and scholarship of the editor of whichever edition they are using, and that will usually serve them well. (But thanks to the marvels of the age, anyone wishing to compare how lines are laid out in a modern text, with how they appear in a first edition, can now view the original folios and quartos on the internet. Extraordinary. Simply search, 'Shakespeare Facsimile'.)

The pertinent questions to be asked regarding short lines are: 'To what end did Shakespeare write them?' and 'What do they indicate, if anything, in terms of performance?' (Short lines increase from 35 in *A Midsummer Night's Dream* (1595-6), to 355 in *The Winter's Tale* (1610-11)). As with other aspects of the verse, there are instances where the reason is fairly clear, and others where there is room for debate. But with a little thought, it can usually be established which particular dramatic, or rhetorical, effect the short lines are intended to achieve. Being aware of the intended effects means that you can endeavour to support them in performance.

I have already cited the Murullus examples of a short line occurring just before a full verse-line. Short lines in this position will often constitute an address, or an introductory phrase, that invites attention from another character (and by extension, from the audience); and they are to be used as such. Modern equivalents would be: 'Hang on a minute!', 'Are you sure!', 'Ladies and gentlemen', 'Guess what!' or 'Where do I begin?' An example from *Antony and Cleopatra*:

Enobarbus: *I will **tell** you.* (Three missing feet)
The barge she sat in, like a burnish'd throne,
Burn'd on the water...   2:2:190

And from *Pericles*:

Pericles: *Great **King**,* (Four feet short)
Few love to hear the sins they love to act...   1:1:92

And on occasions, a short line will occur before a speech which opens a scene, so getting the new scene off to an impactful start. In *Julius Caesar*, Brutus, on entering, addresses himself to an offstage Lucius :

Brutus: *What **Luc**-ius, **ho**!* (Three missing feet)
I cannot by the progress of the stars...   2:1:1

More regularly, a short line will provide a final flourish crowning the *end* of a speech. Not infrequently, it will crown the end of a speech which finishes a scene. Such short lines serve to round off a scene in somewhat the same way as the addition of one or two snappy, 'add-on' chords can serve to round off a piece of music. Also, the *content* of such short, scene-closing lines will sometimes point to the possibility of further dramatic action. They can, therefore, be played charged with the appropriate energetic intent.

Here is Parolles promising future goings-on, as he closes a scene from *All's Well That Ends Well*:

Parolles: *There's place and means for every man alive.*
*I'll **af**-ter **them**.* (Three missing feet)   4:3:328

At the Duke's palace, Orlando, who lives in poverty under the thumb of his brother, has just fallen for Rosalind. A courtier then tells him to quit the palace, since said tyrannical duke has taken against him. As does Parolles' short line above, Orlando's short line not only ends his speech, it ends a scene, so affording it a closing accent; and, again, it gives promise of future action; in this instance, of a romantic nature:

Orlando: *Thus must I from the smoke into the smother,*
From tyrant Duke unto a tyrant brother.
*But **heav**-en-ly **Ros**-a-**lind!*** (Two missing feet)   1:2:277

On occasion, short lines are interjected between another's complete verse-lines, as in this exchange:

Brutus: *Is not tomorrow boy, the first of March?*

Lucius: *I **know not**, Sir.*

Brutus: *Look in the calendar and bring me word.*

Lucius: *I **will**, Sir.*

Brutus: *The exhalations whizzing in the air…*   2:1:40

Here, I think, the quick, functional interjections of Lucius can be considered as lines running, as it were, in a dimension parallel to the verse of Brutus, and not essentially impinging on its integrity or flow. Another such example is a short interjection of Leontes in *The Winter's Tale*. The temporarily delusional monarch has just accused Antigonus of sending his outraged wife, Paulina, to beleaguer him:

Antigonus: *I did not, Sir,*
These lords, my noble fellows, if they please,
Can clear me in't.

Lords: *We can: my royal liege,*
He is not guilty of her coming hither.

Leontes: *You're **li**-ars **all!*** (Three missing feet)

A Lord: *Beseech your highness, give us better credit…*   2:3:141

Akin to an extra syllable slipped into an otherwise regular line of verse, Leontes' interjection here is like a stone hurled into the steadily flowing river of the men's verse. It has impact, but does not essentially disrupt the current's onward movement. The fact that the men's verse resists the impact, and carries on regardless, in a way reinforces the power of its forward momentum.

Playing shared lines – Juliet et al.

The general principle for playing *shared* lines is that there should be *no* pause between the lines, thus maintaining the rhythm and onward progress of the verse. In the exchange below, the actors need to work together to achieve this:

Romeo: *I would I were thy bird.*

Juliet: *Sweet, so would I...* 2:2:182

In somewhat the same way as playing the first element of a shared opposition *(see page 20)*, Romeo needs to deliver his half of the line as a 'feed' for Juliet's He must maintain a strong intention and pulse through his words, serving up the stress on the word *'bird'* with sufficient muscle that Juliet can pick up his beat and run with it to the end of this perfect iambic pentameter:

*I **would** I **were** thy **bird**. Sweet, **so** would **I**...*

Try this out now by acting these two half-lines as if they were one. As Romeo, work to pass the baton to Juliet. As Juliet, take the baton up and onward run.

Here is another exchange from *All's Well That Ends Well* which contains a number of shared lines. The Countess strives to have the low-born, Helena, admit that she is deeply, and inappropriately, in love with the Countess' son, Bertram:

Countess: *... Tell me truly.*

Helena: *Good madam, pardon me!*

Countess: *Do you love my son?*

Helena: *Your pardon, noble mistress.*

Countess: *Love you my son?*

Helena: *Do not you love him, madam?*

Countess: *Go not about; my love hath in't a bond*,*
Whereof the world takes note: come, come, disclose
The state of your affection; for your passions
Have to the full appeach'd.**

Helena: *Then, I confess,*
Here on my knee, before high heaven and you,
That before you, and next unto high heaven,
I love your son...   1:3:180

* mother/son bond   ** stood evidence against you

These shared lines indicate that the characters are seriously connecting in their exchanges, even if connecting in strong resistance to one another. A relentless pressure played in the Countess' questioning will provide Helena with something hard to hit against, something substantial against which to lob back her desperate evasions.

Act these lines now as single lines, as if the words, both of Helena and the Countess, were spoken by yourself. The break between the half-lines is the equivalent of the central pivot in a full verse-line. On either side of this point, both actors needs to press their short line hard against the other – like jousters in a tournament:

Tell me truly. ‖ *Good madam, pardon me!*

Do you love my son? ‖ *Your pardon, noble mistress*

Love you my son? ‖ *Do not you love him, madam?*

You will have sensed that the dramatic build to Helena's falling vanquished to her knees would not be as pacey and electric if it comprised an exchange of *whole* verse-lines.

The Macbeth passage referred to above provides another example of shared lines creating an intense connectedness between characters, and resulting in a powerful forward momentum – in this case a headlong rush into the killing of a king:

Macbeth: *My dearest love,*
Duncan comes here tonight.

Lady Macbeth: *And when goes hence?*

Macbeth: *Tomorrow as he purposes.*

Lady Macbeth: *O, never*
Shall sun that morrow see!   1:5:58

And here is an example of lines not merely split in two, but divided into even smaller parts. Macbeth has just killed Duncan:

Macbeth: *I have done the deed. Didst thou not hear a noise?*

Lady Macbeth: *I heard the owl scream, and the crickets cry.*
Did not you speak?

Macbeth: *When?*

Lady Macbeth: *Now.*

Macbeth: *As I descended?*

Lady Macbeth: *Ay.* 2:2:14

Written as one continuous (albeit irregular) iambic pentameter, the shared line becomes:

*Did **not** you **speak**? **When**? **Now**. As **I** de-**scend**-ed?*

It is clear that Shakespeare chose to share the line variously between the two characters, in order to convey how tightly they are locked together in their need of what the other has to say, so capturing the breathless tension of their situation. How each actor can contribute to realising this effect is by energetically picking up on cues, and preserving the relentless forward pulse of verse.

Short lines and pauses

When a short line occurs within an exchange, or in the course of a speech, it can often be an indication that the 'empty' section of the incomplete line is meant to represent a pause. Such pauses may indicate a moment, or a few moments, of silence, intended to create a dramatic effect. Or, it may indicate that the pause is intended to be filled by some stage action, or business; or it is meant to allow for the entrance of a character or characters. The standard view is that any such pause in the verse should approximate to the time it would have taken to speak the missing feet.

In the following exchange, a messenger has just been struck down by Cleopatra for informing her that Antony is married: she reiterates her question to the terrified man:

Cleopatra: *Is he **mar**-ried?* (three missing feet)
I cannot hate thee worser than I do. 2:5:89

It is easy to imagine the tension created in this three-foot pause: an enraged Cleopatra awaits her response, and the messenger stands torn between the fear of giving insult to the queen by refusing to answer, and the terror of what might befall him if he repeats his news.

Sometimes when it comes to performance, a decision might have to be made as to whether a free-standing short line simply represents a short preamble of the *'I will tell you...'* variety; or whether it is indicating a pause. In the speech below Helena struggles to tell her beloved, but reluctant, Bertram what it is she wants before he leaves for the wars in Italy:

Bertram: *... What would you have?*

Helena: *Something, and scarce so much: nothing indeed*
I would not tell you what I would, my lord.
Faith, **yes:** (four missing feet)
Strangers and foes do sunder and not kiss.   2:5:82

Is Helena's *'Faith yes...'* a short, attention-asking phrase opening a speech with no pause indicated? Or should a four-foot pause follow it: an agonising silence in which Bertram impatiently waits, and Helen searches for the courage to reveal what she so greatly desires? Of the two options, I prefer the agonising pause; but either works.

Another line in *All's Well That Ends Well* offers an example where missing feet in a line allow for an entrance. Helena has cured the King of his mortal illness, and her reward is the pick of the young bachelors at the court:

King: *...a second time receive*
The confirmation of my promis'd gift,
Which **but** *at-***tends** *thy* **nam**-*ing.* (two missing feet)

Enter three of four lords.

Fair maid, send forth thine eye. This youthful parcel
Of noble bachelors stand at my bestowing...   2:3:49

Pauses other than short-line pauses

It is true that, more than in most modern plays, the current of a Shakespeare drama is carried in the spoken words, and that the entire play can be regarded as a single, continuous poem. Because of this, it has been suggested that, apart from the pauses following short free-standing lines, there should be no pauses, at any time, in the course of a scene; and that the short-line pauses *strictly* should last no longer than it would take to speak the missing feet. Some even advocate that the 'no-pause' principle should apply, not only between lines, but between scenes, so that, without pause, the beat of the opening line of one scene should pick up the beat from the concluding line of the scene before. The benefits of keeping the current of a speech, and of a production, uninterruptedly flowing, of course, cannot be denied; but in reality, most productions will have pauses of varying lengths, and in places other than after short lines. I would agree that actors or directors need carefully to weigh up the value of any pauses they consider inserting; but so long as a pause contributes truthfully to the clarity and impact of a scene, it needn't, in my view, mar the production's onward flow. It is a different matter if pauses are inserted for indulgent reasons, such as to draw attention to an actor's 'great depth and sensitivity', or to a director's 'concept' or 'cleverness'. So long as a palpable connection, and tension, between characters is maintained, the dramatic current of the drama can not only be held in suspense within a pause, its charge can build dramatically (like flood waters swelling behind a dam), before rushing onwards, now with increased attention-holding power.

For instance, I can imagine a highly effective pause being inserted before, and after, the final three words in Leontes' speech below from *The Winter's Tale*. King Leontes commands the upright lord, Antigonus, to pick up the baby his queen has just borne, and abandon it in some far-off place, to live or die (I have written in the two potential pauses):

Leontes: *... I do in justice charge thee,*
On thy soul's peril and thy body's torture,
That thou commend it* strangely to some place
Where chance may nurse or end it. (Long pause) *Take it up.*

(Very long pause)

Antigonus: *I swear to do this...*   *2:3:179*

* the baby

Some purists may raise an eyebrow but, for me, these pauses could greatly reinforce, rather than diminish, what is the dramatic turning-point of this wonderful scene. In the pauses the audience could be made to hold its breath as Antigonus struggles between two impossible choices: to obey and abandon an innocent baby to almost certain death, or to disobey, bringing upon his head the murderous wrath of the maddened King.

SHORT LINES – Key points

– There are 'free-standing' short lines, and there are 'shared' short lines.

– Free-standing short lines opening scenes, or speeches, will often constitute an address, or an introductory phrase, that calls for attention from another character – and by extension, from the audience. Modern equivalents would be: 'Are you kidding!', 'Ladies and gentlemen'; or 'Where do I begin?'

– Short, scene-ending lines often provide a distilled summing-up, and **gathering**-up, of the action and feeling that has been generated by the scenes they conclude. They ask therefore to be played with the consciousness of this dramatic purpose.

– Actors sharing verse-lines need to play them as they would a tennis match, each energetically picking up on cues, so maintaining the forward rhythmic pulse of the pentameter.

– Often when a short line occurs within an exchange, or in the course of a speech, it can be an indication that the 'empty' section of the incomplete line is meant to represent a short silence. Such a silence may indicate a dramatic pause. Or, it may indicate that the break in the line is intended to be filled by some stage business, or the entrance of a character or characters. The standard view is that any such pause in the verse should approximate to the time that would have been taken up by speaking the missing feet.

CHAPTER FIFTEEN

BREATHING THE VERSE

There are a number of physical problems actors or students may have as regards how they use their breath and voice. For example, their breathing may be too shallow; or they may have tensions in the neck, jaw, chest etc. which reduce resonance, and restrict free and full breathing etc. Such difficulties can diminish the effectiveness (and one's own enjoyment) of *any* acting; but I believe they can get in the way more, and more obviously, when it comes to acting Shakespeare. This means, of course, that relieving any breath and vocal limitations will pay great dividends when it comes to acting the lines; and with some effort and application these can be significantly reduced, if not eliminated. The means to begin sorting such technical difficulties, however, are beyond the brief of this book.

The two principal breathing problems which are appropriate to be discussed in the present context are:

- Taking breaths in the 'wrong' place.
- Attempting to say too many lines on one breath.

To take a breath somewhere in the middle of a sense-unit, for example, might often and very obviously be a 'wrong place', as it is likely to obscure what the line was written to convey. A student I was teaching recently was inserting a breath at a very odd place when acting his version of an Angelo speech from *Measure for Measure*. Act these few lines now, and take a small breath where I have marked it ('||'):

Angelo: *… What, do I love her,*
That I desire to hear || her speak again,
And feast upon her eyes? …   2:2:177

You can sense that breaking up the sense-unit with a breath in this way, obviously reduces the clarity of the line's meaning, as well as interfering with the pulse of the verse.

And this introduces my guiding principle in this area – a principle in line with those I have proposed might guide decisions in a number of other areas of acting Shakespeare's language. It is:

Breathe the line, A) in a manner that will best help to convey the particular explanations, orders etc. that the lines contain; and, B) in a manner which does not inappropriately distort the containing form of the verse. (And, of course, these two considerations often amount to the same thing.)

The most fruitful way to use the breathing to help convey the explanations etc. in any lines, is to ensure that it is working in support of a meaningful presentation of the sense-units of which they consist. A new intake of breath can charge up a new sense-unit, and bring it into purposeful relief; but I'm not suggesting that an intake is necessary, or advisable, before *every* sense-unit, major or minor. To experience the truth of this, I would like you to try doing just that in the following exercise.

Practice with breathing the verse 1 – Antipholus

Here, again, is the opening of the consistently end-stopped Antipholus' speech, from the early *Comedy of Errors*. Act it aloud, and as you do, take a breath at every point I have marked:

Antipholus: *Go bear it to the Centaur,* || *where we host,*
|| *And stay there, Dromio,* || *till I come to thee.*
|| *Within this hour* || *it will be dinner-time:*
|| *Till that,* || *I'll view the manners of the town,*
Peruse the traders, || *gaze upon the buildings...*   1:2:9

I don't imagine breathing at every minor sense-break in this way was a particularly happy experience. However, since each line in this passage contains a discrete *major* sense-block, the passage provides an example where a breath (perhaps only a small top-up) *might possibly* be taken to fuel each line. Have a go at that and see how it compares to breathing before every minor sense-unit; the breaths are marked:

Antipholus: || *Go bear it to the Centaur, where we host,*
|| *And stay there, Dromio, till I come to thee.*
|| *Within this hour it will be dinner-time:*
|| *Till that, I'll view the manners of the town,*
|| *Peruse the traders, gaze upon the buildings,*
|| *And then return and sleep within mine inn,*
|| *For with long travel I am stiff and weary.*

How does that feel to you? It would not be how I would act the passage myself, but I don't think it would sound *wholly* strange to hear it breathed in that way. As a scheme, it certainly helps to separate, and present, the major sense-units (and consequently the verse-lines), all in a way that is helpful for the listener.

But, even when we are strictly observing the principle of 'what most will help convey the meaning', I don't say there is ever only one 'correct' answer as to how a passage should be breathed. As was the case with scanning the verse, you will encounter different interpreters confidently proposing different schemes. As another step towards developing an awareness of what, *for you*, might constitute an effective breathing pattern in any speech, I want you to act again four of Antipholus' lines. This time add a tiny top-up breath where I have marked them in the middle of two of the lines. You may have to act the speech with this scheme two or three times before you really know how it would feel to breathe it that way as part of a performance. Work to make where you take the breaths as meaningful to yourself as possible:

‖ *Within this hour it will be dinner-time:*
‖ *Till that,* ‖ *I'll view the manners of the town,*
‖ *Peruse the traders,* ‖ *gaze upon the buildings,*
‖ *And then return and sleep within mine inn...*

How did that feel? Did you feel the two mid-line breaths helped you to convey what you were explaining? Perhaps one felt of more potential use than the other in this regard. Or perhaps you felt both simply got in the way?

I can very well hear an actor wanting to sustain the last three of Antipholus' lines on just one breath. Try this two or three times:

‖ *Within this hour it will be dinner-time:*
‖ *Till that, I'll view the manners of the town,*
Peruse the traders, gaze upon the buildings,
And then return and sleep within mine inn...

How did that feel? Did you miss the breaths? If you record yourself, how does it sound when you listen back?

Some directors/teachers recommend combing through all your lines and speeches and working out in advance where you are going to take each and every breath. To do this with a number of speeches certainly is a good exercise, by way of developing a sense generally of what makes effective breathing in any speech you might encounter. But, neither as a director or teacher, do I overly draw the attention of actors or students to how they are breathing a passage in the early stages of preparation. Instead, I listen to how they are acting a passage, and 'talk breathing' only if they are tending to run out of breath, or if the way they are breathing the lines fights against their meaning; or against what the verse is asking. Then, I set about establishing with them, a breathing scheme which is comfortably within their current ability, honours the verse, and serves to get across the explanations etc. of which the speech is made.

It should be pointed out that, as with scansions, once a certain stage of preparation and rehearsal has passed, when feelings and intentions start to do their work, the actor's instinct often takes over, and most of an effective and natural-seeming breathing pattern emerges of its own accord. When actors are one-hundred-percent sure of what they are saying, and are in touch with the underlying feelings and intentions, then they will tend naturally to breathe in a pattern that is in support of it. And this pattern may be quite different to the way they pre-planned their breaths in early rehearsal – at a point when they were still simply 'saying' the lines, without the full charge of feeling and intent. 'How we feel', and 'what we consequently intend', is naturally going to be reflected in the way we breathe in our utterances. Having said that, with certain speeches or passages, and at whatever stage of rehearsal, raw instinct can let us down, and a meaningful, natural-feeling way to breathe may not come readily at all. For that reason, it is useful to have the principles outlined above to refer to, by way of troubleshooting when breathing is causing a problem.

As I did in the section on scanning the lines, what I can best do here, therefore, is examine a few more short passages and, on the basis of our principles, propose various breathing schemes that I think could 'work'. I will also offer you the opportunity to try out some breathing schemes of your own: this will help build a basis from which you can confidently resolve any future breathing confusions you may encounter.

Practice with breathing the verse 2 – Prince Hal

Below is a passage from *Henry the Fourth, Part One*. The play is not one of Shakespeare's earliest plays but, as regards its verse, the ends of sense-units still tend to coincide with the ends of lines. Also, in this particular speech, there are no instances of a major sense-unit, or a sentence, beginning in the middle of a line (i.e. there are no caesurae). The end-stopped verse in a speech such as this does make it easier for an appropriate way to breathe to suggest itself; but you may sense that compared to the Antipholus speech from the earlier *Comedy of Errors*, there is already, in Hal's speech, a little more flow from one line to the next. For me, therefore, there is more scope as to how the speech might be breathed.

As always, make sure you understand what every word and line means in Hal's speech, then act them aloud. Often (perhaps usually), 'wrong breathing' is a result of not being absolutely clear what one is explaining, ordering etc.

When you have fully grasped the meaning, act the passage, primarily with the intention of making clear the explanations of which they consist. Don't plan the breath in any way – allow where you breathe to occur naturally, as a means of helping you communicate the content.

Having done this, act the passage again, this time being aware of where you are tending to take a breath. In everyday circumstances we don't usually have to think about where we take breaths when we speak. Even when acting, a student or actor may rarely think about, or be aware of, how they are breathing in a speech. So you may have to act some parts two or three times until where you are breathing becomes quite clear to you. When you have succeeded in identifying the points where you are taking breaths, I want you to mark these in the text. Doing this exercise with Hal's speech (and one other to follow) will greatly help to develop your sensitivity to your breathing when it comes to acting any other lines or speeches: you will become aware if it is supporting, or undermining, the clearest and most effective delivery of the speech or lines.

Hal is attempting to convince his father, King Henry, that he will change his dissolute ways and prove himself worthy to be his son: he will fight to the death the much-celebrated young rebel, Harry Percy:

Prince Hal: *I will redeem all this on Percy's head*
And in the closing of some glorious day
Be bold to tell you that I am your son;
When I will wear a garment all of blood,
And stain my favours in a bloody mask,
Which, wash'd away, shall scour my shame with it:
And that shall be the day, whene'er it lights,
That this same child of honour and renown,
This gallant Hotspur, this all-praised knight,
And your unthought-of Harry chance to meet.   *3:2:132*

Look at the marks you have made. Did you breathe at the start of each line? Or were there occasions where one breath took you from one line into the next? Were there any instances where you took a breath in the middle of a line?

Even when sense-units obediently coincide with the beginning of new verse-lines, there are times when, I think, one might carry a breath through the end of one line and into the beginning of the next.

As with the end-stopped Antipholus' speech, I reckon one could *just about* perform Hal's speech taking a breath for each new line. Is this what you did? Particularly with a speech in which one senses a greater flow between the lines (even when end-stopped), it can easily begin to sound a bit plonky and monotonous to have the breath always coinciding with the beginnings of lines.

Below is one possible scheme for the Hal passage which breaks up the possible plonkiness of breathing at the beginning of every line, and which I can imagine hearing in a theatre. Act it this way and see how it feels to you.

Prince Hal: || *I will redeem all this on Percy's head*
|| *And in the closing of some glorious day*
Be bold to tell you that I am your son;
|| *When I will wear a garment all of blood,*
|| *And stain my favours in a bloody mask,*
Which, wash'd away, shall scour my shame with it:
|| *And that shall be the day, whene'er it lights,*
That this same child of honour and renown,
|| *This gallant Hotspur,* || *this all-praised knight,*
And your unthought-of Harry chance to meet.

How was that? How does it feel compared to the way you first breathed it, if it is different?

Act these two further variations below. For now, commit fully to the versions below as you act them:

|| *And stain my favours in a bloody mask,*
|| *Which,* || *wash'd away, shall scour my shame with it:*
|| *And that shall be the day,* || *whene'er it lights,*
|| *That this same child of honour and renown,*
|| *This gallant Hotspur,* || *this all-praised knight,*
And your unthought-of Harry chance to meet.

How did that feel/sound to you? And now try this version:

|| *And stain my favours in a bloody mask,*
Which, || *wash'd away,* || *shall scour my shame with it:*
|| *And that shall be the day,* || *whene'er it lights,*
|| *That this same child of honour and renown,*
This gallant Hotspur, this all-praised knight,
And your unthought-of Harry chance to meet.

Does sustaining the final three lines on one breath, help or hinder the effectiveness of Hal's argument to his father? Are there breaths you would add or subtract in either of the versions, by way of making real for yourself, and for the audience, just how passionate is Hal's need to convince the king?

Breathing irregular lines 1 – Lady Macbeth et al.

One view on breathing Shakespeare's verse you may hear, or read about, is that you should indeed take a breath at the end (which means really at the beginning) of every verse-line (even if it is an almost subliminally fast and small one). Related to this view is another, that you should never take a breath in the middle of a line. I would not go along with either of these stipulations, even as regards the acting of the most regular, end-stopped verse. But particularly in the case of Shakespeare's later, more irregular passages, I believe that one should not try to impose such a rigid breathing protocol. There are many, many instances, where to do this, to me, would feel unnatural and disruptive.

The examples so far have been pretty regular, end-stopped passages where, to some extent at least, the breath can follow the verse-lines. But, as has been explored, in his later works, Shakespeare's line-lengths become more varied, and there are many more instances where lines are not end-stopped, but straddle the start of the following line (enjambements); and there are many more instances where new major sense-units, and often whole new sentences, boldly begin mid-line (caesurae).

For me, the breathing can often *go with* such irregularities; it can *support* them. This will sometimes mean breathing in the middle of lines, and not taking a new breath at the beginning of lines.

For instance, no matter how I might imagine any of the characters' nature or inner state, I would find it very strange to breathe at the beginning of each line in any of the short passages below. Similarly, I would find it odd *not* to take a breath before the beginnings of the sentences which start in the middle of a line. But test this for yourself and see how it feels to you.

In these snippets, I want you to take a breath at the start of each of the lines; and *not* to take a breath in the middle of any line, even where a new sentence begins there.

Lady Macbeth assures her husband that if she has anything to do with it, the next morning's light will never shine on King Duncan's planned departure from their castle:

Lady Macbeth: *... O, never*
|| *Shall sun that morrow see!*
|| *Your face, my Thane, is as a book, where men*
|| *May read strange matters...*   1:5:60

In *A Midsummer Night's Dream*, Theseus is to marry Hippolyta at the next new moon, and he laments how slowly the time is passing till then:

Theseus: *…four happy days bring in*
|| *Another moon: but O, methinks, how slow*
|| *This old moon wanes!..*   *1:1:2*

In *Measure for Measure*, Angelo asks if it is possible that one's senses might be aroused more by a woman of modesty than by one of easy virtue (*'lightness'*):

Angelo: *… || Can it be*
|| *That modesty may more betray our sense*
|| *Than woman's lightness? O, let her brother live!*   *2:2:168*

How did that feel for you?

I think, if the line is not end-stopped, it is often better *not* to breathe at the end of that line, but to let the same breath support the sense-block right through into the next line, and to its natural end, wherever that may be. It will usually be somewhere in the middle of the second line, but may even go on to the very end of that line, or even flow through to somewhere in the line after that.

And if a major new sense-block, or new sentence, begins in the middle of a line, then usually it will deserve a new breath; so as 'to gather up' the energy for it and see it on its way.

Because Shakespeare often places key words at the ends of lines, some commentators express concern that if line endings and beginnings are not emphasised by being separated by a breath, then such key words will lose their vital pointing, so reducing the clarity of the line and the verse. But even though you may breathe through the end of a line straight into the next, key end-line words can still be 'brought out' to the extent that is thought necessary. *(For a full discussion and exercises on 'Playing line endings' see page 90.)*

Below are suggestions for a breathing pattern for the various snippets above which, I feel, better supports what each character wishes to get across. Act each set of lines again using this scheme, and as you do, experiment with how, even when breathing through the end of one line into the next, you can still point up (as lightly or as heavily as you like) any end-line words you may wish to. As an aid, I have highlighted the key end-line words:

Lady Macbeth: *… O, **never***
Shall sun that morrow see!
|| *Your face, my Thane, is as a book, where **men***
May read strange matters…

Theseus: *… four happy days **brings in***
*Another moon: || but O, methinks, how **slow***
This old moon wanes! …

Angelo: *Can it* **be**
That modesty may more betray our **sense**
Than woman's lightness? …

Breathing irregular lines 2 – Edmund

Read the lines below where, in *King Lear*, Edmund asks why, as 'illegitimate', he should be considered '*base*', since, after all, he was conceived in the fire of nature and lust, and not within 'the law', in a passionless, merely fop-producing marriage bed:

Edmund: *… Why brand they us*
With base? with baseness? bastardy? base, base?
Who, in the lusty stealth of nature, take
More composition and fierce quality
Than doth, within a dull, stale, tired bed,
Go to th' creating a whole tribe of fops
Got 'tween asleep and wake?   2:1:9

The passage comprises one long sentence (a question), and students often become confused as to what is the most effective way to breathe it.

Edmund's second line is broken up into five small sections (*'With base? with baseness? bastardy? base, base?'*) and it is understandable if actors or students are unsure whether they should support the complete line on one breath, or breathe before all, or only before some, of these small units.

Act this half- and full line, taking a breath where marked:

|| *Why brand they us*
With base? || *with baseness?* || *bastardy?* || *base,* || *base?*

On the one hand, this might be thought to break the line up so much that the onward flow of the pentameter could be destroyed. On the other hand, injecting the line with fresh energising intakes in this way could be appreciated as capturing well Edmund's embittered struggle to comprehend how the world perceives him.

Try this other scheme:

|| *Why brand they us*
With base? || *with baseness? bastardy?* || *base, base?*

And now compare: go back and act the lines with the previous scheme, and then again with the scheme directly above. Do they feel they are much of a muchness; or does one feel better to you? If one feels better, can you identify the reason for that? You may not be able to articulate the reason, but still feel clear that one is better, and that is fine. You are just setting out to develop an 'informed feel' for which breathing-scheme, to you, is most effective in any given passage.

Now play the complete Edmund passage with the breathing plan laid out below; the last five lines are marked to be acted on a single breath:

> ... || *Why brand they us*
> *With base?* || *with baseness? bastardy?* || *base, base?*
> || *Who, in the lusty stealth of nature, take*
> *More composition and fierce quality*
> *Than doth, within a dull, stale, tired bed,*
> *Go to th' creating a whole tribe of fops*
> *Got 'tween asleep and wake?*

How did this feel? Did you miss having a breath between each of the five units in the second line? Was it effortful for you to act the five line passage on one breath? Did you run out of breath completely? Even if you could sustain the last five lines on one breath, were there any breaths you would like to have taken for the sake of conveying more clearly what you want to get across?

When the problem of running out of breath occurs, one does have to stop and look carefully at the text in order to make some decisions. Having examined the text, you may decide that the passage would indeed be better *not* sustained on a single breath. Or you may become convinced that the problem passage does indeed deserve to be sustained on one breath, (that is, on the basis of the guiding principles) and decide therefore, to achieve this by taking a much fuller breath at its outset. If your conclusion is that one breath would better support the line, you may have to concede that, for now, your lungs aren't quite up to that challenge, and will need, therefore, to identify the point, or points, at which to breathe, which won't overly interfere with conveying your meaning.

It can be a challenge to deliver these five Edmund lines on one breath, without it being, and coming across as, effortful; but with some basic breath-work and a warm-up, it can be achieved. For a long time, I bought into the idea that acting large numbers of lines on one breath in this way was always going to be an exciting thing to pull off; that it would keep the energy building in an unbroken stream; and I would usually encourage acting the five lines of Edmund's in this way. But now, although a one-breath delivery can be perfectly fine and sound impressive, I feel that, for an audience, one or two breaths along the way can help shape the meaning, and generally invigorate, a long passage such as this.

I would like you now to look at the same passage with the breathing pattern I have marked up below. You will see that there are a few instances where, again, I have marked a breath, or breaths, in the course of a single line; and instances where I feel it is better to let one breath take you through the end of one line into the next. Act the passage this way now:

> ... || *Why brand they us*
> *With base?* || *with baseness? bastardy?* || *base, base?*
> || *Who, in the lusty stealth of nature,* || *take*
> *More composition and fierce quality*
> *Than doth,* || *within a dull, stale, tired bed,*
> || *Go to th' creating a whole tribe of fops*
> *Got 'tween asleep and wake*

How do you respond to breathing the lines with this scheme?

Breathing irregular lines 3 – Hamlet

Offering you one further opportunity to extend your 'breathing know-how', following is a section from one of Hamlet's speeches. (This is the speech I referred to earlier, on *page 109*, which provides a further, and terrific, opportunity to experience 'self-interruptions'.) It is irregular in several respects: there are a number of enjambements; there are a number of lines with eleven or twelve syllables; there are a number of deviations from the strict iambic rhythm; and there are many occasions when a new major sense-unit begins in the middle of a line. Hamlet repeatedly interrupts the flow of his own explanations by interjecting other smaller explanations, or orders. I count no fewer than nine separate interjections to the main sentence. It is a speech where the most appropriate breathing may not fall in to place until the actor has started to access the inner turmoil that wracks the young prince; but even then, some conscious thought may well be called for before an optimum scheme can be decided on.

First of all, read Hamlet's lines till you are clear what they all mean; then, without thinking at all about your breathing, act the passage aloud with the aim of clearly getting across the various (mostly) explanations which make it up. As you act it then a second time, become aware of where you are taking breaths; even the small, near-subliminal ones. As with the earlier Hal speech, you may have to act a section two or three times before you become quite sure about this. When you are clear as to the points where you are tending to breathe, mark them in the text.

Hamlet tries to come to terms with the reality that less than two months after his beloved father has died, his mother has married his dead father's brother:

Hamlet: ... *Why, she* would hang on him***
As if increase of appetite had grown
By what it fed on; and yet, within a month –
Let me not think on't! – Frailty, thy name is woman! –
A little month, or ere those shoes were old
With which she followed my poor father's body
Like Niobe, all tears – why she, even she
(O God! a beast that wants discourse of reason
Would have mourn'd longer) married with my uncle;
My father's brother, but no more like my father
Than I to Hercules – within a month –
Ere*** yet the salt of most unrighteous tears
Had left the flushing in her galled eyes,
She married!   *1:2:143*

* his mother   ** his father   *** before

In a passage such as this one, Shakespeare creates a meaningful tension between the pentameter verse form, and the various irregularities that he creates to strain and stretch it from within. And I believe it is generally preferable not to resist such irregularities by trying to breathe such passages as if they were rhythmically regular and neatly end-stopped. The breathing can be used to *back up, to intensify* the intended irregularities, so that the strain they create within the pentameter form might be felt more powerfully. *Within* a single line, therefore, one or two short breaths might be taken before each of the small, but discrete, sense-units it may contain; and on occasions, one long breath can be taken to support a major sense-unit through an enjambement.

By saying that it can be effective for the breathing to 'go with' any irregularities a line may contain, I am not suggesting that the pentameter aspect of any line should, therefore, be ignored. As well as breathing with the irregularities, you still can make use of all the other knowledge of verse acquired so far: you can give value to the strong beats and bear in mind that each line tends to drive towards the last word or words.

Before you act these lines, it might be helpful to note (if you haven't already), that for all the number of words and phrases, the essential content of this passage can be distilled to one main explanation, followed by a shorter version of that explanation. Here is that explanation, and its repetition, separated out from the full text:

> ... *Why, she would hang on him*
> *As if increase of appetite had grown*
> *By what it fed on; and yet, within a month...*
> *...she...married with my uncle...*
> *...within a month...*
> *... She married!*

The words above represent the spine of the passage; everything else represents an interruption with a non-essential sense-unit. In a speech such as this, where so many separate new sense-units interrupt the main sentence, I think it is particularly advisable separately to breathe in, if not all, then many of the interjected sense-units. When a unit is breathed in separately in this way, it will be clearer to an audience that it *is* indeed its own unit-of-sense: one that is separate from the sense-units making up the main explanation, and one which is separate also from all the other sense-units which interrupt the main explanation. *(For a full discussion on playing the spine and non-essential sense-units see the chapter on 'Playing parentheses', page 134.)*

But you must test this out for yourself. Act the lines again a few times, using the breathing scheme laid out below. As an aid to your also acknowledging the pentameter lines, I have highlighted the key line-ending words. I seem to be asking a lot here, but don't think too much about it in advance; simply act the lines breathing where marked, and point up (lightly or otherwise) the highlighted words at the end of each line:

Hamlet: ... || *Why, she would hang on **him***
*As if increase of appetite had **grown***
By what it fed on; || *and yet, within a **month** –*
|| *Let me not think on't –* || *frailty, thy name is **woman!** –*
|| *A little month,* || *or ere those shoes were **old***
*With which she followed my poor father's **body***
|| *Like Niobe,* || *all tears –* || *why she,* || *even **she***
|| *(O God! a beast that wants discourse of **reason***
Would have mourn'd longer) || *married with my **uncle;***
|| *My father's brother,* || *but no more like my **father***
Than I to Hercules – || *Within a **month,***
|| *Ere yet the salt of most unrighteous **tears***
*Had left the flushing in her galled **eyes,***
*She **married!***

How was it? How does that compare with how you first delivered the passage when not thinking about the breathing? Do the lines feel *too* broken up to you now? Are there any pairs or groups of sense-units you would prefer to do on one breath? Have another go and see if there is anything you would prefer to adjust for yourself.

For further consideration, here are a few of the lines marked to be played on one breath. See how you feel delivering them this way:

‖ *A little month, or ere those shoes were old*
With which she followed my poor father's body
Like Niobe, all tears —

Better or not so good? If not so good, which breath(s) did you miss?

And at the end of the speech, would it flow better not to take a breath before '*She married…*' Try that:

‖ *Ere yet the salt of most unrighteous tears*
Had left the flushing in her galled eyes,
She married!

Good? Or do you miss the breath?

Separately breathing a large number of the many and varied interruptions will make the speech easier to follow, but also, the erratic pattern of shifts between the shorter breaths taken to support the interjections, and the longer breaths needed to support the enjambements and longer sense-units, will serve to connect the actor with the Prince's inner turbulence and distress; and help to capture it for the audience.

> **BREATHING THE VERSE** – Key points
> — Best to start by knowing fully what any speech means, then, without thinking about how you are breathing it, act it, with the sole aim of clearly getting across the various explanations, orders etc.
> — Become aware, A) of where you are tending to breathe, B) if you are running out of breath at any point, C) if the way you are breathing is fighting against the meanings, or intentions of the lines, or D) is fighting too much against what the verse is asking. Then, you can set about confirming a breathing pattern which ensures that the length of each breath is comfortably within your current ability, and which, while honouring the verse, serves best to get across the explanations, questions etc. of which the speech is made.
> — Consider if your breathing might most effectively serve any speech or line by 'going with' any irregularities it may contain, by breathing mid-line, or sustaining breaths from one line to the next.

CHAPTER SIXTEEN

ACTING SHAKESPEARE'S PROSE

Shakespeare's plays are written (mostly) either in iambic pentameters, or in non-verse: that is, prose. Unlike verse, prose is not written in lines of a fixed length, and its rhythms are more random. Overall there is significantly more verse in the plays than prose, and different plays comprise very different proportions of each. In some plays the writing will shift between one and the other, within a single scene.

The two questions that understandably arise regarding Shakespeare's prose, therefore, are, A) why does he sometimes write in prose as opposed to verse, and vice versa, B) what are the considerations when it comes to acting prose, as distinct from acting verse?

At this point in the book, you may not be fully surprised to discover that one encounters widely differing answers to these questions. I recently read two completely contradictory pieces of advice in the same hour: one said that prose should be delivered much more quickly than verse, the other that it should be delivered more slowly. One said the delivery of prose was generally considered easier to master than that of verse; the other proposed it was the other way around. It is best you become your own judge; and this is what I will endeavour to help you do in this chapter.

Why verse? Why prose?

Some scholars and commentators have attempted to come up with a single reason for 'Why verse? Why prose', but to my knowledge, no-one has put forward a completely convincing 'fits-all' explanation. Most agree that there are certain types of discourse for which Shakespeare generally uses prose; but most agree also, that there is no single type of discourse for which he *exclusively* uses prose.

I remember being told, when I was at secondary school, that prose was the language spoken by Shakespeare's lower-status characters, such as peasants and clowns. And explanations one often hears for 'why verse?' is that characters speak in verse when what they are saying comes more 'from the heart', when they are being true to their truest selves; or when they are in a state of heightened emotion; or when they are delivering truthfully penetrating and elevated observations. There are many instances which will, indeed, support such explanations. But then one observes Richard the Third, and Iago in *Othello*, routinely employing verse when they are at their most insincere and manipulative; so talking decidedly *not* from their heart. And there are many instances of upper-class characters expressing heartfelt emotion, or elevated thoughts, in a prose more poetic and highly-structured than a lot of Shakespeare's verse. An example is Hamlet's *'What a piece of work is a man...'* speech cited earlier *(page 131)*. Some scholars argue that the reason Shakespeare wrote some of his most elevated and elaborately wrought passages in prose was for no other reason than to demonstrate what he believed prose was capable of as a literary form: in Shakespeare's time, only the composition of successful verse represented literary seriousness and excellence.

There is some truth in the 'lower orders speak in prose' proposition. In *Henry the Sixth Part 2*, the rebelling 'lower-orders' consistently speak in prose, while their 'betters' speak in verse. The tradesmen (*'rude mechanicals'*) in *A Midsummer Night's Dream* converse in prose. In the opening scene of *Julius Caesar*, the verse spoken by the tribunes, Flavius and Murullus, is insistently interspersed with the prose spoken by the tradesmen they address. Do we deduce that Flavius and Murullus speak verse because they are in a heightened and heartfelt state of outrage against the commoners' enthusiasm for Caesar; or do tribunes speak verse, simply by virtue of being tribunes (albeit 'tribunes of the people', encharged officially with maintaining republican values)?

Prose

> **Second Commoner:** ... *I am, indeed, sir, a surgeon to old shoes; when they are in great danger, I recover them. As proper men as ever trod upon neat's* leather have gone upon my handiwork.*

> * cow's

Verse

> **Flavius:** *But wherefore art not in thy shop today? Why dost thou lead these men about the streets?*

Prose

> **Second Commoner:** *Truly, sir, to wear out their shoes, to get myself into more work. But, indeed, sir, we make holiday, to see Caesar and to rejoice in his triumph.*

Verse

Murellus: *Wherefore rejoice? What conquest brings he home?*
What tributaries follow him to Rome,
To grace in captive bonds his chariot-wheels?
You blocks, you stones, you worse than senseless things! ...   *1:1:24*

There are, however, many exceptions to the commoner/upper-class indicator. The lowly shepherd, Corin, in *As You Like It*, often speaks in verse, and to suggest he is a verse speaker because his discourse is from his heart, is to imply that other prose-speaking, lower-status characters do not speak from the heart.

As regards the 'from the heart/not from the heart' argument: prose is, indeed, often the register of language employed on occasions when someone is 'not talking from the heart', but from the *head*, in the sense that their discourse is of a practical nature. It is often the medium, therefore, for organisational or domestic talk. Prose, too, is often the medium when characters are not talking from their heart, but from their groin, and so is the medium preferred by those enjoying talk of a bawdy or risqué character.

And prose is indeed often talked by characters not speaking from their heart, in that they are eager to project a false version of their selves by being, for example, pretentious or pedantic. Polonius in *Hamlet* provides an entertaining example:

Polonius: *The best actors in the world, either for tragedy, comedy, history,*
pastoral, pastoral-comical, historical-pastoral, tragical-historical, tragical-comical-
historical-pastoral, scene individable, or poem unlimited: Seneca cannot be too
heavy, nor Plautus too light. For the law of writ and the liberty, these are the only
men.   *2:2:395*

Prose is also the medium for 'head-based' humour, such as satire and the canny observations and witticisms of the clown characters; or for witty exchanges amongst characters other than clowns. In *Julius Caesar*, Casca speaks prose to deliver his sardonic description of how the people offered Caesar a crown. In *Much Ado About Nothing*, prose is the weapon of choice for the witty sparring between Benedick and Beatrice. In *As You Like It* the bouts of clever talk between the young ladies, Rosalind and Celia, are likewise in prose. And once characters retreat into, or pretend to retreat into, a deranged mind, they express their insanity in prose. In her sleep-walking scene, Lady Macbeth expresses her torment in prose; and as King Lear lurches erratically in and out of madness on the heath, so he lurches madly between prose and verse. When Edgar impersonates 'poor Tom', the madman, he gibbers in prose; then reverts to verse in his heartfelt asides and soliloquies.

Shifts between verse and prose

As can occur in the course of one of King Lear's mad outpourings, there can be more than one shift between prose and verse within any single scene. In most cases, and with a little thought and know-how, a dramatic purpose for each can usually be identified. Having said this, in certain instances, the attempt to pin down a rationale to justify *every* shift within a scene can be challenging. In order to make decisions as to what Shakespeare wants us to deduce from such switches, I believe we must assess each one on its individual merits and see how we get on.

As a general guide, it is true to say that a shift from prose to verse, or the other way round, usually will reflect a shift in a scene's emotional depth or temperature; it can be an indication that the utterances of the speaker, or speakers, in the scene are, in some way, now coming more from the heart than the head, or the other way round.

Towards the end of the first scene of *All's Well That Ends Well*, for example, Helena delivers a heartfelt verse soliloquy concerning her hopeless love for Bertram, then quickly switches to prose with Parolles, in a series of witty and bawdy *double entendres* woven around the subject of virginity:

Verse

> **Helena:**   *…withal, full oft we see*
> *Cold wisdom waiting on superfluous folly.*

Short lines of salutation

> **Parolles:** *Save you fair queen!*
>
> **Helena:** *And you, monarch!*
>
> **Parolles:** *No.*
>
> **Helena:** *And no.*

Prose

> **Parolles:** *Are you meditating on virginity?*

Helena: *Ay, You have some stain of soldier in you; let me ask you a question. Man is an enemy to virginity: how may we barricado it against him? Etc.*

1:1:102

In the following passage from earlier in the same scene, there is a sudden shift, this time from prose to verse. The court is assembled to see the young Count Bertram off to the royal court in Paris. Speaking prose, the Countess and Lafeu (an old retainer), have been catching up on news, and discussing the rights and wrongs of the grieving process. As soon as the Countess then begins addressing her parting advice, and heartfelt blessing, to her wayward son, she speaks in verse:

Prose

> **Lafeu:** *Moderate lamentation is the right of the dead, excessive grief the enemy to the living.*

> **Countess:** *If the living be enemy to the grief, the excess makes it soon mortal.*

> **Bertram:** *Madam, I desire your holy wishes.*

> **Lafeu:** *How understand we that?*

Verse

> **Countess:** *Be thou blest, Bertram, and succeed thy father*
> *In manners, as in shape! thy blood and virtue*
> *Contend for empire in thee, and thy goodness*
> *Share with thy birthright! Love all, trust a few,*
> *Do wrong to none…*
>
> *1:1:51*

In *Twelfth Night*, Viola is stunned into verse when her rival in love, Olivia, unveils her heart-stoppingly beautiful features:

Prose

> **Olivia:** (unveiling) *Look you, Sir, such a one I was this present. Is't not well done?*

> **Viola:** *Excellently done; if God did all.*

> **Olivia:** *'Tis in grain, sir; 'twill endure wind and weather.*

Verse

Viola: *'Tis beauty truly blent*, whose red and white
Nature's own sweet and cunning hand laid on...*   1:5:237

* blended

Acting prose

The first thing to establish on the subject of acting Shakespeare's prose is that, although it is not composed in fixed rhythm or in fixed line-lengths, it is often constructed just as carefully as verse. It is often also, as rich in the rhetorical and poetic devices that Shakespeare deploys in his verse. Because of this, I would propose that, to a great extent, the guidelines for acting Shakespeare's prose are the same as those for acting verse.

A prose-sentence is always going to be constructed from the same sense-units that comprise a sentence in verse. These units, and the breaks that separate them, need to be identified and presented with just as much pointedness and clarity as when acting verse.

Similarly, any poetic or rhetorical devices used in prose ask to be acknowledged, and played, with as much conscious presentation as when they occur in verse. For example, the oppositions around which so much prose is shaped need to be pointed up and played off, one against the other. Any assonance or alliteration needs equally to be acknowledged, relished and used. Images need to be explained as concretely as in verse. A sentence spoken to a personification needs to be addressed just as connectedly to that personification. And although the rhythm of prose is not fixed, it is very highly controlled, and demands to be identified and honoured with as much attention as the rhythm of the verse.

As the principles for playing sense-breaks and parentheses are as applicable to Shakespeare's verse, as to his prose, I have discussed these in a chapter immediately following that dealing with the acting of verse. *(See 'Playing sense-breaks in prose' etc. page 131.)*

In this section, therefore, the focus will be on identifying and playing aspects of the architecture of Shakespeare's language *over and above* those achieved by playing the individual sense-units, parentheses and so on. What I wish to do is draw your attention to some of the more common structures, or patterns, into which Shakespeare *groups* his sense-breaks. These patterns Shakespeare uses as much in verse as he does in prose; but rather than discussing the same topic under two different headings, I will discuss it once here and occasionally remind you that it is just as important to identify, and play, the patterns in any verse that you approach.

Identifying poetic devices in prose – Hamlet

The following prose exchange between Hamlet and Ophelia, offers itself as one very good example of just how finely wrought Shakespeare's prose can be. Before examining any structural devices that the passages contain, I would like to examine it by way of illustrating that all the rhetorical/poetical devices Shakespeare uses in his verse, he deploys as plentifully in his prose. It has been my experience, that when approaching the acting of Shakespeare's prose for the first time, most do not expect to find the same wealth of poetic devices as they may take for granted they will encounter in his verse. They may not, therefore, set out to identify and take advantage of them.

Read through the exchange below between Hamlet and Ophelia, and mark with your pencil, any *oppositions* you come across. When you have done this, I would like you then to mark up as many examples of *alliteration* that you can find. No glancing ahead:

Hamlet: *If thou dost marry, I'll give thee this plague for thy dowry: be thou as chaste as ice, as pure as snow, thou shalt not escape calumny*. Get thee to a nunnery, go: farewell. Or, if thou wilt needs marry, marry a fool; for wise men know well enough what monsters you make of them. To a nunnery, go, and quickly too. Farewell.*

Ophelia: *O heavenly powers, restore him!*

Hamlet: *I have heard of your paintings too, well enough: God has given you one face, and you make yourselves another: you jig, you amble, and you lisp, and nick-name God's creatures, and make your wantonness your ignorance. Go to, I'll no more on't; it hath made me mad. I say, we will have no more marriages: those that are married already, all but one, shall live; the rest shall keep as they are. To a nunnery, go.* Exit   *3:1:135*

* defamation

Here are some of the oppositions I identify *(For a full exploration of playing oppositions, see Chapter 2)*:

> **God** *has* GIVEN *you* **ONE FACE**, *and* **you** MAKE *yourselves* **ANOTHER**...
> ...*and make your* **wantonness** *your* **ignorance**...
> ... *If thou* **dost marry**..., *Or, if thou* **wilt needs marry**...
> ... *marry* **a fool**; *for* **wise men** *know well enough*...
> ... *all but* **one**, *shall* LIVE; *the* **rest** *shall* KEEP AS THEY ARE

Examples of alliteration I found are these 's' and 'c' sounds:

> ...*be thou as* **ch**a**s**te *as* **i**ce, *as pure as* **s**now, *thou* **sh**alt *not es-*ca**pe** **c**alumny...

And these 'm' sounds:

*...for wise **men** know well enough what **monsters** you **make** of them...it hath made **me** mad...I say we will have no **more** marriages: those that are **married** already...*

As with verse, relishing any alliteration or assonance, and giving due pointing to the oppositions, will help significantly to release the power of a speech.

Structural devices in prose

Once one looks closely at any Shakespeare's passage in prose, all sorts of simple, and more subtle, structural patterns begin to disclose themselves: patterns which are not as artificial as might at first appear. These structures are among those which English speakers (and perhaps speakers of all languages) regularly and spontaneously employ to organise their sense-units when talking in everyday life; especially when in more formal or emotionally heightened situations. Shakespeare simply takes these common structures and deploys them in a more concentrated and artful way.

Because versions of these structures are commonly used by all of us in real life, you will tend to exploit many of them in your playing *instinctively*; without first having to tease them out and analyse them. It is nonetheless important *consciously* to be familiar with what these structures are, so you can be sure you are indeed recognising, and taking full advantage of them.

Possibly the most common structural devices to be found in Shakespeare's writing (prose or verse) are what I call 'see-saws' and 'triads'.

See-saws

In the section on 'Playing the pivotal sense-breaks' *(page 93)*, I suggested that most lines of verse consist of two minor sense-units, which, see-saw-like, pivot around a mid-line sense-break. In prose also, see-saw structures are explanations, questions or orders consisting of two halves which pivot around a central sense-break. The difference between a verse and a prose see-saw is that in the case of prose, the two halves of the see-saw do not have to be of a length to fit into a ten-syllable line; they can be shorter, or sometimes quite a bit longer. Here are a few example lines from our Hamlet speeches which may be regarded as see-saws. Act these lines and, as an exercise, 'over-emphasise' the sense of the utterance being bi-partite:

Or, if thou wilt needs marry, || marry a fool;

If thou dost marry, || I'll give thee this plague for thy dowry:

God has given you one face, || and you make yourselves another...

When acting such prose see-saws, the pivotal sense-breaks ask to be marked as clearly as do the sense-breaks in any line of verse.

Triads

The 'triad' is another of the main structural devices Shakespeare employs, both in verse and in prose. As with a see-saw, the difference when a triad occurs in prose, as opposed to verse, is that it does not need to conform to the strictures of the iambic pentameter line.

In everyday discourse, in jokes, in political speeches, in comedians' routines, in stories, in songs etc., it is very common for words, or sense-units, or events, or persons, or ideas, to be presented in groups of three. These groupings I refer to as 'triads'. The 'triad' structure is readily observed in these examples:

'Get ready! Get set! Go!'

'Paddy the Englishman, Paddy the Scotsman and Paddy the Irishman went into a pub; says Paddy the Englishman etc…'

'A maiden fair to see,
The pearl of minstrelsey,
A bud of blushing beauty…'
(Song from Gilbert and Sullivan's *H.M.S. Pinafore.*)

'Location! Location! Location!' (It wouldn't be as catchy if there were two or four 'Locations!', would it?)

Three is the minimum number with which you can create a sense of any utterance or events building to a climactic point or 'payoff'. In any situation where you hear someone say 'Get ready! Get set! Go!', the second order, ('Get set!') will usually be delivered with an energy which is manifestly building on the energy with which the first order (the 'Get ready!') has been delivered. On hearing the 'Get set!', there will be a sense of anticipation of the explosion, or release of energy, which will come with the delivery of the third section (Go!).

In the classic Paddy joke there will be a 'headline' or 'set-up statement': 'Paddy the Englishman, Paddy the Scotsman and Paddy the Irishman went into a pub…'. This is then followed by a triad of events: whatever the first Paddy does or says lays the base, or foundation for the little story. What the second Paddy does or says creates a sense of something building, a sense of suspense or anticipation, as to what the third Paddy is going to do. What the third Paddy then goes on to do, or say, provides the pay-off, or punch-line, to the joke.

One reason a triad has power for us is because it embodies the dynamic manifest in all life forms – human, vegetable, animal or cosmological: birth (base statement), growth (building energy) and death (final release of the building energy).

Here are two examples of triads from Hamlet's speeches:

(1) *be thou as chaste as ice,* (2) *as pure as snow,* (3) *thou shalt not escape calumny…*

(1) *you jig,* (2) *you amble,* (3) *and you lisp…*

In order to allow these groupings of three to do their rhetorical work – so helping to make the prince's argument clear, energetic and memorable – the actor needs to be guided by the 'Ready! Get set! Go!' principle: the first unit of the triad is the *base*, second is the *build*, and third is the *blast-off.* The energy of the second part needs to build on that of the first, and the third asks to be played with a concluding, 'pay-off' emphasis.

Above I referred to the first line of a Paddy joke as the 'headline' or 'set-up' statement.

Headlines

In a speech, a 'headline' is the statement of an issue that is to be discussed, explored or otherwise elaborated on. There is normally an *overall* headline at the opening of any soliloquy, for example, which introduces the topic that the speech will explore as a whole. Examples of such soliloquy-opening headlines would be:

Hamlet: *To be or not to be; that is the question…*   3:1:58

Brutus ponders the means of preventing Caesar from becoming a dictator:

Brutus: *It must be by his death…*   2:1:10

Macbeth ponders the threat represented to him by Banquo:

Macbeth: *… To be thus is nothing,*
But to be safely thus. Our fears in Banquo
Stick deep…   3:1:47

I always regard a headline as equivalent to the statement of a musical subject, or theme, at the beginning of a symphonic movement, which (as with the headline) will go on to be developed and explored. And to avoid any confusion about a headline representing the 'statement' of a subject: it will indeed often be an explanation. But a headline might just as readily be 'stated' in the form of a question. Here are the opening lines of two speeches from *Measure for Measure*:

Angelo: *What's this? What's this? Is this her fault or mine?*   2:2:162

Isabella: *To whom should I complain?*   2:4:171

And a line opening a speech from *Twelfth Night*:

Viola: *I left no ring with her: what means this lady?*   2:2:16

But in the course of any speech, there are usually also some *subsidiary* headlines which introduce a secondary, related subject to be elaborated on in the course of the speech.

These two explanations from Hamlet's speeches constitute headline statements:

If thou dost marry, I'll give thee this plague for thy dowry...

...and he goes on to explain what dowry he will give.

I have heard of your paintings too, well enough...

...and he goes on to explain what he means by *'paintings'*.

This is a subsidiary headline:

I say, we will have no more marriages...

...and he goes on to qualify.

What you want to achieve by your delivery of such headlines is to grab any listener's attention. You want them to understand that what you are introducing is a subject that is important, and one on which, immediately and interestingly, you intend to elaborate.

Refrains

What I refer to as 'refrains' are phrases or sentences (or phrases or sentences that are similar to one another) which recur within a speech or exchange. Such refrains function somewhat as do recurring choruses, or repeated motifs, in a song or piece of music. Hamlet's speeches include a repeated refrain:

Get thee to a nunnery, go: farewell.

To a nunnery, go, and quickly too. Farewell.

Go to, I'll none of it. It hath made me mad.

To a nunnery, go.

Stanzas

If you regard Hamlet's two small speeches as effectively one speech with a pretty much ignored interruption from Ophelia, then we can say that the speech is in four sections, or stanzas; and that each section, or stanza, is capped with a version of the same refrain: *Get thee to a nunnery, go: farewell...* With its four stanzas and refrains, the speech takes on the form almost of a traditional folk-song. (Although the more commonly used word is 'verse', I use 'stanza' here, to avoid any confusion with 'verse' as I have been using it so far, to refer to Shakespeare's writing in iambic pentameters.)

To honour the stanza form in one's playing, the level to which the energy rises in each one, must be higher than that reached in the one before. The speech, thereby, will rise in four waves, the second, third and fourth bigger than the one before. Likewise, the refrain which crowns each wave must be delivered with more charge and intention than the refrain that precedes it. Here is the speech laid out in traditional 'ballad form':

STANZA ONE

If thou dost marry, I'll give thee this plague for thy dowry: be thou as chaste as ice, as pure as snow, thou shalt not escape calumny.

Refrain:

Get thee to a nunnery, go: farewell.

STANZA TWO

Or, if thou wilt needs marry, marry a fool; for wise men know well enough what monsters you make of them.

Refrain:

To a nunnery, go, and quickly too. Farewell.

(Ophelia: *O heavenly powers, restore him!*)

STANZA THREE

I have heard of your paintings too, well enough; God has given you one face, and you make yourselves another: you jig, you amble, and you lisp, and nick-name God's creatures, and make your wantonness your ignorance.

Refrain:

Go to, I'll no more on't; it hath made me mad.

STANZA FOUR

I say, we will have no more marriages: those that are married already, all but one, shall live; the rest shall keep as they are.

Refrain:

To a nunnery, go.

So, in his two short speeches, Hamlet employs all of the main structural devices so far described. He structures his argument in a series of four verses, each one comprising an introductory headline, a subsequent combination of either see-saws or triads, and a closing refrain.

Before going on to examine the structures of Hamlet's speeches in more detail, I should point out that, although most prose speeches contain some, or all, of the above ways to pattern the sense-units in a speech, some speeches allow for different interpretations as to which sense-units are part of which device. For example, there may be disagreement as to whether a group of four sense-units comprises two see-saws, or should be thought of as a headline followed by a triad. Usually, but by no means always, one particular structural arrangement will suggest itself as the better one; by 'better' here I mean, 'which better reveals the meaning of the question, explanation etc. I wish to get across'. The only reason the structural analysis of a speech is productive is that, more than anything else, an understanding of how the sense-units are grouped, will instruct the performer as to how the speech might be delivered with optimum meaning and impact. So, however you conclude that any set of sense-units should be structurally grouped, you must, when you act them, *use* the groupings you decide on. You must point up, *reveal* your groupings in such a way that they support your objective in delivering the content of the lines.

To me, Hamlet's first stanza breaks down into three sub-sections: a headline (which is, in itself, a see-saw); a triad; and a refrain (which is, in itself, another triad). Such a structural breakdown can be difficult to follow when expressed in words, but laid out graphically, it becomes clear:

Headline (a see-saw):

(A) *If thou dost marry,* (B) *I'll give thee this plague for thy dowry:*

Triad:

(1) *be thou as chaste as ice,*

(2) *as pure as snow,*

(3) *thou shalt not escape calumny.*

Refrain (a triad):

(1) *Get thee to a nunnery,*

(2) *go:*

(3) *farewell.*

Mapped out on the page in this way, one begins to see just how highly structured this little stanza is.

Following is one way of structuring the second stanza:

Triad:

(1) *Or, if thou wilt needs marry,*

(2) *marry a fool;*

(3) *for wise men know well enough what monsters you make of them.*

Second refrain (a triad):

(1) *To a nunnery, go,*

(2) *and quickly too.*

(3) *Farewell.*

An alternative structure into which the sense-units of this stanza might be grouped is a long see-saw, as in:

See-saw: (A) *Or, if thou wilt needs marry, marry a fool;* (B) *for wise men know well enough what monsters you make of them.*

And each of the two halves of this see-saw could, themselves, be thought of as a see-saw:

(See-saw 1) (A) *Or, if thou wilt needs marry,* (B) *marry a fool;*

(See-saw 2) (A) *for wise men know well enough* (B) *what monsters you make of them.*

Deliver this sentence, firstly as laid out immediately above: as a long *see-saw* consisting of two see-saws. When you have done that, act it as a *triad*, as laid out again below. Alternate between one way of acting it and the other, thoroughly playing up the structure of each, till you can feel the difference between them; the difference may not feel huge, but it will be there.

Triad:

(1) *Or, if thou wilt needs marry,*

(2) *marry a fool;*

(3) *for wise men know well enough what monsters you make of them*

Which one feels better as regards getting across what you want Ophelia to understand?

Speaking out the structural units – Hamlet

A terrific exercise for getting solidly to grips with the structure of a passage, is not only to act the words, but also to speak aloud the titles, numbers and letters which indicate the various structures. When you act the passage again *without* speaking numbers and letters etc., you will experience the trace of the exercise noticeably informing your delivery; it really works.

As well as the main text in the passage below, speak out loudly and clearly, *all* the titles, numbers, and so on, which I have highlighted in bold. Do this at least two or three times:

STANZA ONE

See-saw:

(A) *If thou dost marry,* **(B)** *I'll give thee this plague for thy dowry:*

Triad:

One: *be thou as chaste as ice,*

Two: *as pure as snow,*

Three: *thou shalt not escape calumny.*

Refrain:

One: *Get thee to a nunnery,*

Two: *go:*

Three: *farewell.*

Having spoken out the units, act the text on its own (below). You will feel more engaged with the structure and meaning of the line:

If thou dost marry, I'll give thee this plague for thy dowry: be thou as chaste as ice, as pure as snow, thou shalt not escape calumny. Get thee to a nunnery, go: farewell.

Other exercises useful for the playing of see-saws and triads are the 'Swing-boating' and 'Stamping and clapping' exercises described earlier for getting to grips with sense-breaks. To apply Swing-boating to see-saws and triads, you vigorously swing your upper body and outstretched arms to one side as you speak one part of the structure, then swing equally vigorously to the other side as you speak another; as in:

(Swing one way) *Or, if thou wilt needs marry,* (Swing the other) *marry a fool...*

To apply 'Clapping and stamping', you simply clap, stamp, or both, *in the gaps between* each unit:

(Clap/stamp) *be thou as chaste as ice,* (Clap/stamp) *as pure as snow,* (Clap/stamp) *thou shalt not escape calumny.*

(For a full description of Swing-boating and Clapping and stamping, see pages 96 - 97.)

Below now is one way of breaking down Hamlet's next two stanzas. Slowly look over them until you have fully understood the logic of how I have structured them:

STANZA THREE

Headline:

I have heard of your paintings too, well enough:

See-saw:

(A) *God has given you one face,* (B) *and you make yourselves another;*

Triad:

(1) (A triad) (1) *you jig,* (2) *you amble,* (3) *and you lisp*

(2) *and nick-name God's creatures,*

(3) *and make your wantonness your ignorance.*

Third refrain (a triad):

(1) *Go to,*

(2) *I'll no more on't;*

(3) *it hath made me mad.*

STANZA FOUR

Headline:

I say, we will have no more marriages:

Triad:

(1) *those that are married already,*

(2) *all but one, shall live;*

(3) *the rest shall keep as they are.*

Final refrain:

To a nunnery, go.

You will notice that the first line of the first triad in stanza three, is marked as a triad in itself (set out in bold):

Triad:

(1) (A triad) (1) ***you jig,*** (2) ***you amble,*** (3) ***and you lisp***

(2) *and nick-name God's creatures,*

(3) *and make your wantonness your ignorance.*

I would like now to offer you a little practice in identifying structural devices on your own.

Playing stanzas, headlines, see-saws etc. – Benedick

In the prose passage below from *Much Ado About Nothing*, Benedick is outraged by the fact that his young friend-in-arms, Claudio, (who always laughed at the follies of other men smitten by love), has himself, (ever since he fell for Hero,) gone more soppy and poetic than the best of them.

Read the passage concentrating solely on any stanzas, headlines, triads, see-saws, or refrains that present themselves to you. As you spot them, mark them with your pencil. This is a wonderful high-comedy speech which is mostly very easy to understand and will well reward giving it your attention. (Don't worry if you cannot quite follow the little bit about the oyster; it *is* obscure):

Benedick: *I do much wonder that one man, seeing how much another man is a fool when he dedicates his behaviours to love, will, after he hath laughed at such shallow follies in others, become the argument of his own scorn by failing in love: and such a man is Claudio. I have known when there was no music with him but the drum and the fife; and now had he rather hear the tabour and the pipe*; I have known when he would have walked ten mile a-foot to see a good armour; and now will he lie ten nights awake, carving the fashion of a new doublet. He was wont to speak plain and to the purpose, like an honest man and a soldier; and now is he turned orthography; his words are a very fantastical banquet, just so many strange dishes. May I be so converted and see with these eyes? I cannot tell; I think not: I will not be sworn, but love may transform me to an oyster; but I'll take my oath on it, till he have made an oyster of me, he shall never make me such a fool. One woman is fair, yet I am well; another is wise, yet I am well; another virtuous, yet I am well; but till all graces be in one woman, one woman shall not come in my grace. Rich she shall be, that's certain; wise, or I'll none; virtuous, or I'll never cheapen her; fair, or I'll never look on her; mild, or come not near me; noble, or not I for an angel; of good discourse, an excellent musician, and her hair shall be of what colour it please God.*   2:3:6

* *tabour and the pipe:* the music of clowns and shepherds; *'tabour':* little drum

How did you get on? It is choc-a-bloc, isn't it, with the basic devices I have been talking about?

Did you get that the passage comprises three distinct sections, three 'stanzas', which, in a way, means that the speech is, in itself, a large triad? Here are the headlines which I see as opening each stanza; you can see that each introduces a new (albeit related) theme:

STANZA ONE

Headline:

I do much wonder that one man, seeing how much another man is a fool when he dedicates his behaviours to love etc.

STANZA TWO

Headline:

May I be so converted and see with these eyes? Etc.

STANZA THREE

Headline:

Rich she shall be, that's certain etc.

As with any triad, these three stanzas need to be played with the 'Ready! Steady! Go!' dynamic. The energy level at the start of the second stanza needs to pick up from the level at which the first left off and build; the third needs to take off at the energy level at which the second left off, and build to the end of the speech.

But before giving you the opportunity to do that, I would like to look at how Shakespeare has patterned the sense-units *within* each of these stanzas.

The first element to be noted in stanza one is the headline to the overall speech; most unambiguously, Benedick spells out what it is that so mystifies him:

STANZA ONE

Headline:

I do much wonder that one man, seeing how much another man is a fool when he dedicates his behaviours to love, will, after he hath laughed at such shallow follies in others, become the argument of his own scorn by failing in love: and such a man is Claudio.

Having explained the source of his astonishment in this headline, Benedick now goes on to explain what he is talking about in further detail. One way of viewing this sentence (and, I think, some others) is as a triad.

Firstly, take a little time to look at the sentence as laid out below. You will notice that the first two parts of the triad are see-saws; and that the third part is itself another triad. When it makes complete sense to you, act the lines, making the structures exaggeratedly clear (this time, no need to speak out the titles or letters etc.):

Part one of the triad:

See-saw:

(1) (A) *I have known when there was no music with him*

  (B) *but the drum and the fife;*

(2) (A) *and now had he rather hear the tabour*

  (B) *and the pipe:*

Part two of the triad:

See-saw:

(1)   (A) *I have known when he would have walked ten mile a-foot*

(B) *to see a good armour;*

(2)   (A) *and now will he lie ten nights awake*

(B) *carving the fashion of a new doublet.*

Part three of the triad:

See-saw:

(1)   (A) *He was wont to speak plain and to the purpose,*

(B) *like an honest man and a soldier;*

(2)   (1) *and now is he turned orthography;*

(2) *his words are a very fantastical banquet,*

(3) *just so many strange dishes.*

Take a look at the second section of part three (immediately above). You will
see that Shakespeare has made it, not yet another see-saw, but a triad. Making
it a triad, as opposed to a see-saw, provides Benedick with an extra build to
his climax. Within itself, this last triad builds up to, and then explodes on
the word, *'dishes'*; making this word the pay-off point to which this whole
first stanza builds. In the layout of the lines below, I have represented the
sense of a build by highlighting, in increasingly large bold print, the words
an actor is likely to use as 'steps' to climb towards the climactic, final word
of this verse:

Part three of the triad:

(1) **See-saw:**   (A) *He was wont to speak plain and to the* **purpose,**

(B) *like an honest man and a* **soldier;**

(2) **Triad:**   (1) *and now is he turned* **orthography;**

(2) *his words are a very fantastical* **banquet,**

(3) *just so many strange* **dishes.**

Just as it is important with speeches composed in verse, when you achieve an internal climax such as this, you must hang on to the energy and begin the next section *on top* of the point of energy you have already reached.

Benedick must, 'stay with', or 'hold on to' the level of energy attained on the word *'dishes'*, as he moves into the line opening the next stanza:

May I be so converted and see with these eyes?

The energy on the words *'I'* and *'see'* in this line, therefore, will be slightly higher than the level attained on *'dishes'*. It is as if the word, *'I'* is the first step on the flight rising *up* and away from the landing Benedick has reached on *'dishes'*.

To present this point in visual form:

*…just so many strange **dishes.***

*May **I** be so converted and **see** with these eyes?*

Obviously you cannot overdo this 'topping' and building, or you will rise so high, so quickly, that you will have nowhere to go. But any speech does need continually to build towards a pay-off point (be this only from one to two, on a scale of ten).

Another element to note in this speech is the refrain effect of the two *'I have known'* and the *'he was wont'*, together with the three *'now'*. As Benedick spells out for himself the details of Claudio's transformation, he will become increasingly convinced in his outrage, and so each repetition of these elements will come from a place of higher charge. Act the lines with this in mind:

*I have known when there was no music with him
but the drum and the fife;*

***and now** had he rather hear the tabour
and the pipe:*

***I have known** when he would have walked ten mile a-foot
to see a good armour;*

***and now** will he lie ten nights awake,
carving the fashion of a new doublet.*

***He was wont** to speak plain and to the purpose,
like an honest man and a soldier;*

***and now** is he turned orthography;
his words are a very fantastical banquet,
just so many strange dishes.*

Laid out graphically below is one way of breaking down the architecture of Benedick's *next two* stanzas. Is it similar or different to the patterns you discerned when combing through the speech yourself?

STANZA TWO

Headline:

May I be so converted and see with these eyes?

See-saw: (A) *I cannot tell;* (B) *I think not:*

See-saw: (A) *I will not be sworn, but love may transform me to an oyster;* (B) *but I'll take my oath on it, till he have made an oyster of me, he shall never make me such a fool.*

Triad:

(1) **See-saw:** (A) *One woman is fair,* (B) **Refrain:** *yet I am well;*

(2) **See-saw:** (A) *another is wise,* (B) **Refrain:** *yet I am well;*

(3) **See-saw:** (A) *another virtuous,* (B) **Refrain:** *yet I am well;*

Climactic pay-off line:

See-saw: (A) *but till all graces be in one woman,* (B) *one woman shall not come in my grace.*

STANZA THREE

See-saw: (A) *Rich she shall be,* (B) *that's certain;*

See-saw: (A) *wise,* (B) *or I'll none;*

See-saw: (A) *virtuous,* (B) *or I'll never cheapen her;*

See-saw: (A) *fair,* (B) *or I'll never look on her;*

See-saw: (A) *mild,* (B) *or come not near me;*

See-saw: (A) *noble,* (B) *or not I for an angel;*

(All of these 'B's might also, of course, be considered another type of refrain.)

Climactic triad:

(1) *of good discourse,*

(2) *an excellent musician,*

(3) **See-saw:** (A) *and her hair shall be* (B) *of what colour it please God.*

The six consecutive, slowly-building see-saws above (in a way one triad on top of another) form what is often, and appropriately, referred to as a 'ladder'. With any such ladder within a speech, each rung (no matter how subtly) must bring the speaker from one level of energy to a higher one. In this instance, Benedick uses each rung gradually to build up the energy which peaks with his final triad – the last part of which I have identified as a final see-saw. I can imagine Benedick exploiting the pivot of this final, climactic see-saw, by holding in it a long pause; a pause during which he struggles to identify what, for him, is the perfect hair-colour for this ideal woman:

(A) *and her hair shall be* **Long pause** (B) *of what colour it please God.*

Or possibly:

(A) *and her hair* **Long pause** (B) *shall be of what colour it please God.*

A note on see-saws

Note that in every see-saw there will usually be one word, or occasionally two, on either side of the central pivot which ask to be given a 'priority stress'. It is as if the weight on each side of the see-saw is anchored in these key stressed words. Hitting these balancing key words with appropriate emphasis, therefore, will ensure a line's see-saw structure is received unambiguously by any listeners; so helping to reveal to them its meaning. Act the three separate see-saw lines below, putting due stress on the words in bold; this will bring you more actively behind the built-in, swing-boat dynamic of each line: 'on the one side, *this*; on the other side, *that*'.

(A) *I have known when there was no* **music** *with him* (B) *but the* **drum** *and the* **fife***;*

(A) *One woman is* **fair***,* (B) *yet I am* **well***…*

(A) *I* **cannot tell***;* (B) *I* **think not***…*

As you apply any know-how gained in this chapter to any lines or speeches (prose or verse) you may be working on, do not be concerned if the piece doesn't seem to break down precisely into *only* the categories introduced here. My intention here has been to familiarise you with the principle types of groupings Shakespeare most regularly tends to use; understanding these principal structural devices will equip you to identify others, and to create other ways of grouping sense-units that seem useful to you.

Rhythm in prose

As much as the structures in prose are highly wrought, the rhythms are strongly defined. While committing his prose to the page, Shakespeare, I feel sure, heard these rhythms as loudly and clearly as he did when composing his verse. The most obvious remark to make about the rhythm of the prose is that it is less regular than the 'dee-dum, dee-dum' of the verse. The other remark commonly made is that one needs to stress fewer words or syllables when speaking prose. Generally speaking both these remarks are true.

What is the appropriate rhythm for any prose-line or passage, however, will largely tend to sort itself out once, A) (as always) you are clear as to the exact meaning of each question, explanation or order in the piece, and when you make communicating these your main priority; when B) you have identified, and are using, the particular structures (stanzas, headlines, triads etc.) to help give meaningful shape to these questions, orders etc.; when, C) you appropriately stress the key words which balance see-saws; and D) when you are aware of, and use, any poetic or rhetorical devices (images, oppositions, personifications etc.) so as further to enhance the communication of your meanings. Once these factors are in place you will tend naturally to give appropriate stress to the appropriate words. And one thing I then would add about stressing such appropriate words is: don't be shy about it. Hit them.

PROSE – Key points

Verse versus prose

- Overall there is significantly more verse in the plays than prose, and different plays comprise very different proportions of each.

- Prose is rich in all of the poetic and structural devices found in verse.

- There is a broad tendency for prose to be spoken by 'lower-status' characters, and verse by the 'higher-orders'; but there are many exceptions to this.

- Again, there are many exceptions to this, but verse is used when characters speak more from the heart and less from the head. Prose, therefore, is generally the medium for satire, witty or bawdy exchanges, and the observations of clowns; for the expression of insanity, real or feigned; for organisational talk; for pretentious or pedantic utterances.

- As a general guide, any shift between prose and verse usually will reflect a shift in a scene's emotional depth or temperature; will be an indication that the utterances of a speaker, or speakers, are in some way, now coming more from the heart, than the head, or vice versa.

Playing the structural devices of prose and verse

To reveal the meaning architecture of prose (or verse) you need to identify and play, not just the sense-units, and the sense-breaks, but the patterns into which Shakespeare groups his sense-units, namely:

- Stanzas (ensure that each takes off at a level of charge greater than where the previous one left off.

- Headlines (use them clearly to proclaim the theme about to be developed).

- See-saws (decide which words anchor the balancing weight on each side).

- Triads (be sure to act them with the 'base, build, blast off' dynamic; and to decide on what word or words each one reaches its climax).

- Refrains.

CHAPTER SEVENTEEN

SOLO SPEECHES

There are a number of different types of speeches in Shakespeare. Most are delivered by one character to another onstage character, and are delivered in response to something that has just been said or done to them. There are, however, quite a number of speeches in Shakespeare's plays which are *not* delivered to another character on stage. I will refer to these as 'solo speeches'. In their turn, solo speeches can be divided into two rough categories: 1) epilogues and prologues and, 2) soliloquies.

Prologues

Prologues are delivered just before a play begins – or before a new act of a play begins – by personages usually bearing the name of Prologue or Chorus (the different titles indicate no difference in purpose). Occasionally Shakespeare makes a Prologue figure a personification: the Prologue in Henry the Fourth, Part Two, he calls 'Rumour'; and the figure linking Acts Three and Four in *The Winter's Tale* is called, 'Time'.

Functioning as narrators, prologue figures provide background information to the play. Or, in between acts, they, for example, update the audience on what has been going on since the end of the previous act; or provide an outline of what the coming act contains. Whatever their title, prologue figures take no part in the action of the play, or acts, they introduce, and their speeches are spoken directly to the public, *acknowledged as an audience* (often respectfully referred to as *'gentles'*).

As well as being a narrator, chorus figures serve somewhat as the company's warm-up, or link-person, with the spectators, typically begging their indulgence towards any shortcomings of which the players may be guilty. They also express the hope the audience will employ their own thoughts and imaginations to fill in any aspects of the story that the company is not equipped, or may fail, to furnish. As such, a good Prologue needs to have sufficient presence to establish an immediate rapport with the public, and to make his or her speech sufficiently clear and interesting to create a sense of pleasurable anticipation of what is to follow.

Here are the first lines of the opening prologue to *Romeo and Juliet*. The lines explain to the public where the play is set, and inform them of the ancient *'grudge'* that has always existed between the great families of Capulet and Montague, and which recently has broken out in open hostilities:

Chorus: *Two households, both alike in dignity,*
In fair Verona, where we lay our scene,
From ancient grudge, break to new mutiny...

And here are the closing lines which assure the audience that if they lend the players a patient ear, they will work to better themselves in any area where they are deemed to be inadequate:

...if you with patient ears attend,
What here shall miss, our toil shall strive to mend.*

* not measure up

The following are some lines from the Prologue to *Henry the Fifth*. The Chorus entreats the audience to use its imagination to 'suppose' that the theatre walls contain two great kingdoms, divided by a narrow channel. He urges them to fill in with their 'thoughts' any other elements the players cannot physically represent:

Prologue: *... And let us...*
On your imaginary forces work.
Suppose within the girdle of these walls
Are now confined two mighty monarchies,
Whose high upreared and abutting fronts
The perilous narrow ocean parts asunder:
Piece out our imperfections with your thoughts...

...

Think when we talk of horses, that you see them
Printing their proud hoofs i' th' receiving earth...

What might be considered an exception to the principle that prologue figures take no part in a play's action, is the opening speech of *Richard the Third*. This great solo speech is exceptional in that it functions both as a type of prologue to the play, and as a soliloquy. While very much 'in character', disfigured Richard acts as narrator to his own story, bringing the public up to date with both the great public events just passed, and letting them in on the plots that he has already laid:

Richard: *Now is the winter of our discontent*
Made glorious summer by this son of York...

...

And therefore, since I cannot prove a lover,
To entertain these fair well-spoken days,
I am determined to prove a villain
And hate the idle pleasures of these days.
Plots have I laid, inductions* dangerous...   *1:1:1*

*initial preparations

It would be hard to imagine Richard directing the bulk of this speech anywhere but to the house.

Epilogues

Epilogues are spoken at a play's conclusion, mostly by a member of the company who 'steps out of character' and addresses the audience directly, as an audience. Their main purpose is to invite the public's forgiveness for any shortcomings the company may have displayed in their playing, and to invite them to join their hands, in appreciative applause, for the parts the audience have enjoyed.

Here are some lines from the epilogue to *A Midsummer Night's Dream*:

Puck: *Gentles, do not reprehend:*
If you pardon, we will mend...

... So, good night unto you all.
Give me your hands, if we be friends,
And Robin shall restore amends.   *5:1:415*

(In *Henry the Fifth*, it is, exceptionally, not a character from the main action who speaks the Epilogue, but the Chorus, and before inviting them to show their appreciation, he also offers the audience the bonus of a broad outline of the events which unfolded *after* those enacted in the play.)

Soliloquies

Whilst not being addressed to another onstage character, soliloquies are delivered by characters who remain 'in character', and who speak as, and about, themselves.

A soliloquy can occur in very different circumstances.

For example, the term can refer to a speech delivered by a character who is alone on stage, or...

...to a speech where the speaker is deemed to be out of the hearing of other characters who are onstage...

...to a speech which, if the speaker is not careful, is in danger of being overheard...

...to a speech where the character *believes* he is alone, but is in fact being overheard, and...

...some commentators argue that Hamlet delivers his *'To be or not to be...'* soliloquy *pretending* to believe he is alone, but is, in fact, in full knowledge that he is being listened to. Such a speech is sometimes referred to as a 'feigned soliloquy'.

Key questions to ask when acting a soliloquy

In most plays, characters' lines and speeches are spoken as reactions to something that has just happened to them. Mostly, this 'thing' that has happened is something some other character has just said or done. And this is how most plays proceed: character A says or does something to character B, and the audience wonder what character B is going to do as a result; character B is then witnessed to do what he or she does, and as a result character A, or possibly another character, does something else which, in turn...and so on.

From this point of view, soliloquies are best regarded as being no different from any other speeches, or lines, in a play. As far as possible they should be thought of as being another essential 'link' in the ongoing chain of 'actions' and 'reactions' that makes up the play. It is better *not* to regard them as 'interludes' where nothing actually 'happens', where the flow of time and forward movement of the play 'freeze' for a while, as the character offers a peep-hole into his pre-existing private thoughts.

It is more profitable to hold:

- that any soliloquy is a speech delivered in *reaction* to some event in the play's story (on-stage or off) which has stimulated new feelings, or strongly reinforces existing feelings, within the character

- that, by its end, the soliloquy has brought the character to a *new understanding* of these new, or reinforced, feelings which, if acted upon, will create further dramatic action

- that by the end of a soliloquy, an audience should, therefore, be curious as to what the character might go on to do as a consequence of this new understanding; and, indeed, the speech will often offer an explicit, or implicit, idea as to what action he or she intends to take.

In order to get an initial, *overall* handle on any soliloquy, therefore, it is useful to ask some particular questions regarding the beginning of the speech; and some questions regarding its conclusion. Having established answers to these 'top and tail' questions, one will be better equipped to find appropriate answers to questions regarding the 'in-between sections of the speech'; what we might refer to as the 'body' of the speech.

Questions to ask about the beginning of a soliloquy:

> *Q. To what event is this speech a reaction?*
>
> *Q. What feelings are stimulated, or re-enforced, in the character by this event?*
>
> *Q. What is the need – created in response to these feelings – which impels the character to launch into the speech?*

Deciding on answers to the first two questions will link the soliloquy into the play's flow of cause and effect. Playing it as a reaction, prevents the soliloquy from becoming a static pool of contemplation, ring-fenced off from the rest of the play's action.

In many instances, the event which triggers a soliloquy is abundantly obvious; but with certain others, identifying an event might call for a little thought and imagination. I will now look for answers to the first two of these initial questions in respect of a few well-known solo speeches.

To what event is this speech a reaction? What feelings are stimulated or re-enforced in the character by this event?

A speech of Viola's from *Twelfth Night* provides a good example of a soliloquy where the event that 'causes' it is perfectly evident. Viola (disguised as a boy) is on her way back from an interview with the Lady Olivia. Malvolio overtakes her and 'returns' a ring which he says Viola has brought to Olivia as a token of the love the Count Orsino has for her (Orsino is Viola's master). When Malvolio exits, Viola opens her soliloquy with the words:

Viola: *I left no ring with her…* 2:2:16

In this instance the answer to our first question is that Viola's soliloquy is in immediate reaction to the extraordinary event of Olivia's steward, Malvolio, 'returning' a ring which she has not given to anyone. An answer to the second question might be that the *feeling* created in Viola by the event is something such as 'confused astonishment'. So the energy with which Viola launches into her speech must be witnessed by the audience to connect directly to what has just happened. Even if, after Malvolio has exited, the actor holds a long pause before beginning (I'm not necessarily recommending this!), Viola's speech must still connect, and 'bounce off', this event; even as one speech bounces off another in a stretch of dialogue. And the feeling that fuels the speech must be experienced by the actor, and perceived by the audience, as springing up in direct consequence of the experience of this event. This may seem staringly obvious, but how often have I seen an actor 'let go' of the energy created by the 'stimulating event', and begin a soliloquy as if from an energetic clean slate; making it almost a stand-alone 'set-piece'.

Having finalised arrangements with Rosencrantz and Guildenstern to dispatch the troublesome young Hamlet off to England (and to his death), and seen Polonius off to eavesdrop on the Prince's interview with his mother, Claudius is left alone and immediately launches into his marvellous soliloquy:

Claudius: *O, my offence is rank, it smells to heaven;*
It hath the primal eldest curse upon't,
A brother's murther! ...   3:3:36

It is true that, ultimately, the event Claudius is reacting to, is his own gaining of the throne through the murder of his brother; but there has, however, been a specific triggering-event – even though it does not occur in the scene of which the soliloquy is a part.

The trigger occurs in the previous 'play-scene,' when Claudius witnesses a near-exact dramatisation of his murder of his brother. It would be productive for the actor to imagine that Claudius has not yet had the opportunity to be alone to deal with the powerful invasion of guilt and self-disgust which the play has triggered in him – and that, therefore, he is carrying, and just manages to contain, until the others leave; at which point, almost overwhelmed by the feelings triggered in the scene before, Claudius almost bursts into his soliloquy (*'O, my offence is rank!'*). Performed this way, the speech does not come across as a speech dealing with a guilt Claudius has been carrying around for some time, and which could equally well have been delivered at some other point in the play. His soliloquy becomes tightly bound into the play's sequence of actions. Of course, what might function as a secondary, *reinforcing* trigger for his soliloquy is the fact that, unbeknownst to the two young courtiers, Claudius is arranging for the, now dangerous, Hamlet to be murdered also.

Soliloquies which open scenes

But what of cases where the character wanders on to the stage when no-one else is there, and starts to deliver a soliloquy; when we have not seen anyone do or say anything to the character to trigger a reaction?

Act 1 Scene 7 of *Macbeth* begins with our hero entering alone and opening a soliloquy with these lines:

Macbeth: *If it were done when 'tis done, then 'twere well*
It were done quickly... 1:7:1

The *'it'* he refers to here is the murder of King Duncan; he has planned to carry out this deed later that night. But the question is: To whom, or what, can Macbeth be reacting since he has just entered alone, and starts speaking, apparently 'out of nowhere'? At the end of his soliloquy, Lady Macbeth enters in search of her husband, and we learn that what has happened just before Macbeth entered, is that he has suddenly risen and hurried away from the banquet that is being given in Duncan's honour (Lady Macbeth: *Why have you left the chamber!* 1:7:29). So we can imagine that it is something almost overpowering that Macbeth is reacting to, if it causes him suddenly to stand in front of the king and the other guests, and rush out of the dining-chamber. It would be useful and reasonable, therefore, to suggest that the feeling in Macbeth as he launches into his speech is a confusion of guilt, horror and fear about the murder he is about to commit. But it will be even more helpful for an actor to imagine a specific 'event' that triggered this tidal upsurge of confused feeling. One might imagine that Duncan has said, or done, something in particular at the table which suddenly makes Macbeth see the king in his full humanity and goodness; and that this, specifically, is what has triggered his desperate need to rush from the table. Or perhaps one might imagine that Macbeth has been attempting to suppress his terror about the possible consequences of what he has agreed to do, but that, at a certain moment, the pressure simply becomes too much, and there is sudden dam-burst of the feelings within him.

So even a soliloquy which opens a scene is best regarded as a reaction to a specific event; and to an event, ideally, that has just, or recently, happened.

So having established (through an act of informed imagination or otherwise) exactly what the character is reacting to, and what this has made them feel, one can go on to ask, Question 3:

What is the need – created in response to these feelings – which impels the character to launch into the speech?

Other ways of asking this question are, 'What is the character hoping to achieve by setting out into the speech?', 'What makes the speech necessary for the character?' or 'What is the character's *objective* for the speech?' *(For a definition and detailed discussion of objectives see 'Objectives': page 1.)*

Students and actors are often taken aback if I ask them what the objective of any soliloquy is. They know that lines delivered to other characters must have an objective; but because 'there is no-one else listening', it doesn't occur to them that, in the same way, a soliloquy could, or should, have an objective.

They are, however, usually highly relieved to learn that it is not only possible, but *essential*, to identify an objective to motivate what they are saying.

Often the first objective they then offer, is something along the lines of; 'to express my frustration'; or, 'to let the audience know what I am feeling'. I will suggest they pity the poor audience who have paid their money, not to see actors slosh about in a static slough of 'thought' or 'feeling', but to see the actors… 'act'. The audience wants to see the character 'doing something which has a purpose', and to wonder whether that purpose will be achieved; and then be led to wonder what will happen as a consequence of that purpose being achieved or not. Anything else is not drama.

In an attempt then to find a more active motivation, something they are *doing*, they will sometimes look heavenward, or somewhere else away from the text, and begin surmising, almost free-associating, attempting to pluck an apt objective out of the air. The more they do this, the more 'abstract' and less relevant to the speech the suggestions usually become. And so often the active objective they seek is stated right there, clearly and concretely, *within* the text; frequently it is spelt out in the first or second line. So I always advise seeking the evidence for what the objective may be *within the text*; in particular, within the first few lines.

Here is the first line of Viola's speech complete:

Viola: *I left no ring with her: what means this Lady?*

With the first half of this line we have established that Viola feels confused (*'I left no ring with her…'*). She feels confused by the Lady Olivia 'returning' a ring that she has not given her. Her objective, however, is not to 'to express her confusion'. The second half of her first line plainly declares what her objective is: Viola needs to find a *resolution* to her confusion by working out what Olivia could mean by doing such an unexpected thing. That is her immediate and active objective. And it is explicitly stated: *'What means this lady?'*

Here are the opening, love-tormented lines of the Gaoler's Daughter from *Two Noble Kinsmen*. The girl is head over heels in love with a nobleman held in the prison where her father is the keeper:

Gaoler's Daughter: *Why should I love this gentleman? 'Tis odds*
He never will affect* me. I am base,
My father the mean keeper of his prison,
And he a prince.   2:4:1

* love

As with Viola, the need awoken in the Gaoler's daughter by the 'triggering-event', is precisely what so many other characters have as an objective for their soliloquies. By launching into her speech, the Gaoler's Daughter can be understood to be attempting to 'get a handle on' her turbulent, but as yet, secret feelings of desire and love.

Trying to get a handle on the situation

As we all do when we talk over some difficult situation with a friend, the young girl hopes that by 'talking it out' and getting her situation absolutely clarified in her head, that it might bring her to some tolerable accommodation with it; might reveal to her how best to go forward into the rest of her day, and the rest of her life.

The balancing of mind and feeling in soliloquies

An audience will give a soliloquy their attention if they experience a character doing what Viola and the Gaoler's Daughter are endeavouring to do; that is, to forge a fruitful, forward-looking relationship between the feeling roused by the 'triggering-event', and the 'thinking' that the character creatively brings to bear on that feeling.

The journey of many soliloquies can be regarded as a process of re-balancing of thought and feeling; head and heart; masculine and feminine; *yin* and *yang*. The stimulating event plunges the character (male or female) into an unsettling swelling of, as yet, 'unravelled' emotion; a troubling excess of the feminine, of 'yin'. The character's instinct then (as it is in any healthy human being) is to initiate a more balanced intercourse between the *yin* and *yang*, between the 'feeling' and 'thinking'; an intercourse from which will be conceived (all going well) the basis for new and fruitful action. Were I to spell out what a character's thoughts are by the end of a great number of soliloquies, it might go something like this: 'Now that I have taken time to tease out, look at and think about this stew of feeling inside myself, I have increased clarity about what it all means, and I am clear as to what can or cannot be done about it.'

Soliloquy as 'process of enlightenment'

I repeatedly find myself pointing out that a soliloquy is much more a *mental* process than an *emotional* event; more an *intellectually driven* journey, than a delving into *feeling*. So a more useful way to regard a soliloquy is, not as an 'expression of feeling', but as a 'process of enlightenment' or 'intellectual discovery'.

A clear illustration of this principle in action is provided by Angelo's soliloquy in *Measure for Measure*. When novitiate nun, Isabella, comes pleading for the life of the brother whom Angelo has recently condemned to death, Angelo is beset by a torrent of lustful desires for the young woman. Once again the character's problem, and what he wants to achieve, his objective, is explicitly stated in his very first lines:

Angelo: *What's this? What's this? Is this her fault or mine?*
The tempter or the tempted, who sins most? Ha?
Not she: nor doth she tempt: but it is I...   2:2:162

The need to come to some understanding about the new feelings flaring up in him is an almost life-or-death situation for Angelo – a man, heretofore, so frozen in his sexual feelings, and so proud to be. The character is not musing philosophically for the sake of it. His serious and immediate intent, his objective, is to confirm exactly what these powerful feelings are; then to establish who is to be held sinfully responsible for them. If the actor plays the speech in this way, as an urgent need for enlightenment, then the audience will wish to 'stick with it', in order to find out what conclusion the character reaches, and what action, if any, he or she will take as result of having reached it.

Hamlet, too, makes it very clear with the opening line of his *'To be...'* soliloquy what it is he is endeavouring to work out:

Hamlet: *To be or not to be, that is the question...*

As a consequence of the recent upheavals in his life, *'all the uses of this world'* now seem *'flat and unprofitable'* to the young prince. He wishes, therefore, to weigh up the pros and cons of the two main courses of action he might take in response to such dark feelings. He can stay alive and face all the suffering life brings or, he can depart this life forever by committing *'self-slaughter'.* To reach a decision about which is the better choice provides the speech with a most profound and urgent objective. Hamlet is not indulging a quiet and objective philosophical speculation on existence, which he might have had at any time. The young man pressingly needs to achieve 'enlightenment' regarding the deeply troubling distress that he feels; and to know what might be the best action to take as a result.

Having discussed the most useful questions to ask concerning the beginning of a soliloquy, I will now examine what is most useful to ask about the conclusion.

Questions to ask about the conclusion of the soliloquy:

Q. *What new* understanding *does the character come to, as a result of completing the soliloquy?*

Q. *What is the new* feeling *the character shifts into as a result of this new understanding?*

Q. *What will the character* do *as a result of this new understanding, and new feeling?*

Just as the objective of a soliloquy is often stated in its first lines, often the conclusion the character reaches, and the subsequent action they propose, are both stated, or implied, in its closing lines.

At the end of the Gaoler's Daughter's speech, the young girl lets us know exactly what decision she has reached concerning the beautiful nobleman shut up in her father's prison:

Gaoler's Daughter: ... *Say I ventur'd*
To set him free? What says the law then?
Thus much for law or kindred! I will do it,
And this night, or tomorrow, he shall love me.   *2:4:30*

By the end of his *'If it were done…'* speech, Macbeth has come to understand the full horror of the murder he has planned to carry out. And he also now understands the vanity (in both senses of the word) of his own motivation in planning to murder the gracious Duncan. His motivation is a *'vaulting ambition'* which inevitably over-reaches itself and sends the perpetrator hurtling earthward, as if over the other side of a high wall he or she has determinedly scaled:

Macbeth: ... *I have no spur*
To prick the sides of my intent, but only
Vaulting ambition, which o'er leaps itself
And falls on t'other…   *1:7:25*

Then, almost immediately after Lady Macbeth enters looking for her husband, we find out what Macbeth intends to *do* as a result of the clear understanding and feeling to which the speech has taken him:

Macbeth: *We will proceed no further in this business…*   *1:7:31*

A clear, if short-lived, (as it turns out) resolution.

At the end of his *'To be…'* speech, the clear understanding Hamlet reaches is that the reason most people turn away from the *'self-slaughter'* option is because:

…the dread of something after death …
        …puzzles* the will,
And makes us rather bear those ills we have
Than fly to others that we know not of …   *3:1:78*

* baffles

And, to conclude, Hamlet expands his understanding of why people avoid *'self-slaughter'* into a general understanding of how the impulse towards great enterprise can be extinguished by thinking too much about what might lie ahead:

> *And thus the native hue of resolution*
> *Is sicklied o'er with the pale cast of thought,*
> *And enterprises of great pith and moment,*
> *…lose the name of action.*   3:1:84

This understanding is where the soliloquy 'takes him'. It is the 'new thing' that is born out of the speech. And we can imagine that the feelings resulting from this new insight are a bitter frustration and self-disgust with his own inability to stop thinking, and his consequent failure to act; and a feeling, therefore, of being forever trapped in a life he finds so unbearable. We might now well wonder where this realisation leaves the Prince, in terms of any further action he might perform in the play. As we discover, it is sometimes his decisions not to act (as in this soliloquy) which constitute his actions.

There are instances where it may seem that a character does not arrive at any new insight, feeling or course of action by the end of a soliloquy; where they appear, from the outset, already to know how they feel and see the situation in which they find themselves. But examined more closely, most speeches can be understood to involve a development towards some new or deepened feeling or insight.

The last lines in Helena's speech in *All's Well* tell us very specifically what the young girl intends to do as a consequence of hearing that Bertram will not come back to his home in France while she remains there:

> **Helena:**   *… Come, night; end, day!*
> *For with the dark, poor thief, I'll steal away.*   3:2:128

But by the third line of her speech, Helena has already leapt instinctively to the idea of leaving:

> *Nothing in France until he has not wife!*
> *Then thou shalt have none, Rossillion, none in France…*   3:2:100

The speech, however, still constitutes (and asks to be played as) a journey: one towards a hugely *more urgent, more horrified*, understanding of what her *not* leaving might imply; namely, the death of her beloved Bertram in the foreign wars. It is this understanding, reached in the course of the speech, which copper-fastens Helena's motivation to leave.

And now, before going on to look at questions to be asked about the 'middle' or 'body' of soliloquies, it is the appropriate time to look at that 'overall' question which invariably crops up with those first approaching the performance of a soliloquy:

Q. *To whom or what am I addressing this speech?*

Addressees in soliloquies

'I'm not sure where to put it all!' This is a cry I hear regularly from students, or from actors who have before only performed in 'naturalistic' plays, plays in which lines are comfortably and reliably directed by one character to another.

There is a fairly widespread view today that there is no choice as to where soliloquies should be directed: they must *all* be addressed directly to the audience. There is, however, another hotly argued view that, apart from prologues and epilogues (and a few other speeches from early comedies), Shakespeare did not intend *any* of his soliloquies to be addressed to the public, and that, in his time, they never were; that the character spoke their soliloquies 'to themselves'. It appears that the 'to the public' mode of delivery was introduced in the late seventeenth century, as a way to overcome what the more 'realistic' conventions of Restoration theatre had come to view as the ludicrous practice of characters 'talking to themselves aloud'. Over the centuries since then, fashion as to which mode was dominant in productions has fluctuated. In the late nineteenth, and first half of the twentieth century, 'self-address' prevailed, with 'audience address' enjoying a comeback in the sixties. Audiences and critics alike were startled by this 'new' practice, many liking the effect, but others, including, for example, John Gielgud, expressing nothing like enthusiasm for it.

Whether or not it was how Shakespeare expected his soliloquies to be performed, this 'to the audience' style of delivery can 'work'. I, by no means, believe, however, that it is the most effective way to act *all* soliloquies; or even all sections of those soliloquies which can appropriately be directed *primarily* to the public. What I can most helpfully achieve here, is to explain what I believe are the possible options, and to suggest which options, to my sensibility, are best suited to which circumstances, and to which type of speeches.

There are instances where, I think, there can be little debate as to whether the audience is intended to be the addressee of a soliloquy; where they are 'the external other'.

Addressing Solo Speeches to the audience

In most naturalistic plays of today, the audience would be startled if a character suddenly turned and addressed his or herself directly to the public. But this is precisely what some characters in Shakespeare frequently are meant to do.

Within the mode of addressing soliloquies to the audience, I think it is helpful to identify two 'poles': the pole of what might be termed, 'Intimate Audience Address' and the pole of 'Formal Audience Address'. I believe it is productive to regard all audience-addressed speeches, or sections of speeches, as existing at some point on a 'sliding scale' between these two.

In cases where directors, actors and theatre companies do employ audience address, there will be diverging views as to whether the 'Formal' or 'Intimate' pole is more appropriate in which instance.

Addressing the audience – Intimate Mode

In the Intimate Mode of address, characters have more freedom as to how they may interact with the audience. In this mode, they can openly acknowledge, and chummily eye-ball, the house *as a whole*; or sometimes have fun eyeballing, pointing, or gesturing, to individual members, as if they were their best friends. As well as making a decision as to whether a character will address the playgoers individually, or as a collective, the actor must also decide on the particular quality and intensity of the relationship his or her character will have with them.

As a rule, the more broadly comic and clown characters can have the cosier relationship with the audience; and the more *needy* relationship. These characters more manifestly *need* something from their audience; and precisely what that is has to be established by the actor, and made clear to the audience. Is it approval the character needs; or admiration; applause; a shocked reaction; or help to solve a problem? And how do they go about getting their need fulfilled: blusteringly, shyly, slyly, arrogantly? What the need is, and how they go about attempting to have it fulfilled will, to a large extent, define and reveal the character of these comic personages to the audience.

In *The Two Gentlemen of Verona,* it would be hard to imagine the solo speeches of the clown character, Launce, being directed anywhere apart from to the public. In one speech Launce enters to tell of a highly disturbing incident involving his dog, Crab. Crab has just stolen a leg of poultry (*'capon's leg'*) from Mistress Silvia's platter, then gone on to relieve himself against a gentlewoman's skirts. Rather than see the dog punished, Launce claims the offence was of his own doing, and gamely endures a whipping:

> **Launce:** ... *I was sent to deliver him* as a present to Mistress Silvia from my master, and I came no sooner into the dining chamber but he steps me to her trencher** and steals her capon's leg. O, 'tis a foul thing when a cur cannot keep himself in all companies!* ...   4:4:6

* the dog   * plate

Here Launce even refers *directly* to the presence of the audience when he says, *'You shall judge'*, inviting them to assess for themselves whether or not Crab would have been hanged if Launce had not intervened:

> ... *If I had not had more wit than he, to take a fault upon me that he did, I think verily he had been hanged for't. Sure as I live, he had suffered for't.* ***You shall judge...***

The Two Gentlemen of Verona is an early romantic comedy, and Launce's appeal to the audience is an example of the few Shakespeare speeches which do serve as an entertaining 'set piece' or interlude from the main action. Launce could, to some extent, be considered to be 'processing' for himself the incidents he describes; but he is not so needful of 'getting a handle' on his situation as characters are in most other soliloquies. The clown seems pretty clear about his feelings in relation to his mutt's misdemeanours. However, he must still have an objective; and in speeches such as this of Launce, the objective will be identified primarily *in relationship to the audience*. Launce could be said to be driven by a great need to gain the understanding and sympathy of his listeners. And the 'tone' used in his endeavour to gain the public's understanding will differ according to how the actor defines the character's relationship to them. Does he view them as likely to understand and sympathise readily? Or is his view of life that people generally never really fully understand him. (Whichever tone an actor playing Launce decides to adopt, he must always remember that his hope of achieving his objective of 'winning sympathetic understanding', will depend primarily on the clarity of his explanations and questions. The *line-by-line* intention, therefore, will be 'to get across by explaining to the audience' the great service he has performed for his mutt, and the cruel punishment he endured on his behalf.)

The speeches of the rogue Autolycus in *The Winter's Tale*, offer another good example of where a character's objective can be defined in terms of what they want from the spectators. With no need to 'get a handle' on his feelings – he is more than delighted with his feelings – his objective is unambiguously and joyfully to have the spectators see what an extraordinary chap he is! He has sold all his pedlar's wares at the sheep-shearing festivities, so enabling him to spot whose purses were worth the pinching. And pinch them he did. He can play off the house as a whole, or when the humour takes him (and given that the lighting conditions allow), can boast to any one of the individuals that make it up.

> **Autolycus:** *Ha, ha! what a fool Honesty is! and Trust, his sworn brother, a very simple gentleman! I have sold all my trumpery; not a counterfeit stone, not a ribbon, glass, pomander, brooch, table-book, ballad, knife, tape, glove, shoe-tie, bracelet, horn-ring, to keep my pack from fasting.*   4:4:596

Although speeches such as those of Launce and Autolycus are performed when there is no-one else onstage, I usually refer to them, not as soliloquies at all, but as regular speeches: speeches which happen to be addressed to the audience. 'A speech to the audience' is also how I regard Richard the Third's opening speech *(discussed above as a type of epilogue delivered 'in character': page 94).*

Another speech where the Intimate Mode of audience address will work is with the Gaoler's Daughter soliloquy quoted above *(page 200: 'Why should I love this gentleman?').*

Such a character as this young 'low-born' lady may certainly have an intimate relationship with her audience, but in her case it is a relationship that is not quite as 'needful' as is the case with Launce or Autolycus. Although she can, and should, address the audience in Intimate Mode, the young girl's objective is defined not, as with Launce and Autolycus, solely in terms of her relationship to her public. Her objective is defined in terms of her relationship to *herself,* and to the pressures of her own situation; she does not *need* the audience in order to have her objective. As is the case with characters in most soliloquies, this hapless young girl launches into her speech in a desperate attempt to 'get a handle on' her overpowering feelings and, ideally, to get to know what on earth might be done about them.

Launcelot Gobbo, from *The Merchant of Venice,* provides a further example of a soliloquiser with a rapport with the playgoers similar to that of the Gaoler's Daughter. Although this clown's speech is, to some extent again, an entertaining 'set piece', and one which can be delivered in Intimate Mode, it is not merely a description of something that has happened – a tale meant to elicit a particular response from the audience. As with the Gaoler's Daughter, it is Launcelot, himself, who needs the soliloquy in order 'to get a handle on' an issue which greatly troubles him. He is unable to make up his mind as to which of two conflicting inner-voices he should listen to: the voice of the Devil (*'the fiend'*) which urges him to flee his tyrannical master, Shylock – or the voice of his conscience which, equally persuasively, is pressing him to stay:

> **Launcelot:** *Certainly my conscience will serve me to run from this Jew my master. The fiend is at mine elbow and tempts me saying to me, 'Gobbo, Launcelot Gobbo', 'good Launcelot,' or 'good Gobbo,' or 'good Launcelot Gobbo, use your legs, take the start, run away'. My conscience says 'No; take heed, honest Launcelot; take heed, honest Gobbo…*   2:2:1

Addressing the audience – Formal Mode

It has been discussed how the more broadly comic characters can have a chummy style of relationship with the audience, even playing off individual members within it. They may want to win their sympathy or approbation, or need them simply to listen while they talk out and try to get a handle on a difficult situation. Such characters might be regarded as existing at one end of our sliding-scale of intimacy and need.

There are other characters who exist a bit further towards the 'Formal' end of the intimacy scale. To a certain extent, the degree of need these characters have of the audience is in indirect proportion to their degree of 'sophistication', or 'social standing'. Take the soliloquy of the high-ranking gentleman and officer, Benedick, from *Much Ado About Nothing (looked at in detail in the chapter on Prose, page 184)*. Benedick is outraged that his good and, heretofore, soldierly friend, Claudio, has succumbed to the foolishness of being in love:

> **Benedick:** *I do much wonder that one man, seeing how much another man is a fool when he dedicates his behaviours to love, will, after he hath laughed at such shallow follies in others, become the argument of his own scorn – by falling in love: and such a man is Claudio! … I have known when he would have walked ten mile a-foot to see a good armour; and now will he lie ten nights awake, carving the fashion of a new doublet.*   2:3:6

This is certainly a comic speech, but one representing a register of comedy 'higher' than the speeches of a Launcelot or Gaoler's Daughter. On the 'Intimacy/Formality' scale it would normally be played in a fashion somewhere between the insinuating relationship a clown may have with the audience, and the more formal relationship a Macbeth, Lear, or Angelo from *Measure for Measure* will have. To get a feel for a 'Benedick-type' relationship with the audience, you might entertain the assumption that all of the house shall kindly be there to be addressed, as and when he requires them to be. Thus, as is his natural right, he can take advantage of their presence to help him come to terms with whatever feelings presently are assailing him.

Although a 'higher' comedic speech such as Benedick's is usually indeed played primarily 'to the house', it will usually be played 'Open' style, i.e. with a wide-open focus on the audience 'as a whole' – moving one's eyes around (and up and down if there are galleries); and not while intimately eye-balling individual spectators. In many modern theatre settings this will have to be the way of it, in any case, since the actor, dazzled by the lights, will either not be able to see the audience at all, or be unable to distinguish individuals within it. In a more informal theatrical setting, however, say in a production performed open-air in a park, or in an open-air theatre such as Shakespeare's Globe in London, a more direct relationship with the house – eyeballing individuals etc. – can seem more acceptable.

Where on the 'scale of formality' a particular character's relationship with the audience should be placed, can depend, therefore, not only on their status, and the nature of their needs, it can depend also on the nature of the setting (formal, semi-formal or informal); and, indeed on the style of production.

A Helena speech from *A Midsummer Night's Dream* provides another example of a 'higher comedic' soliloquy which, again *primarily*, might successfully be addressed to the audience in the same 'Open' style as Benedick's speech. The young girl explains how unfair Fate seems to be in her decisions as to who will be happy in love, and who not (her beloved Demetrius loves not her, but her friend Hermia):

Helena: *How happy some o'er other some can be!*
Through Athens I am thought as fair as she.
But what of that? Demetrius thinks not so…   1:1:226

Helena has a strong need to explain her circumstance to the audience, and might, for example, appropriately address them as if they were trusted loving maids more than happy to listen, while a very well brought-up young lady lays out the horrid injustice of her situation. However she conceives of them, Helena's amusing youthfulness, and the lightness of the play's comedy generally, might allow her to talk to her audience with a somewhat greater intimacy and neediness than, say, a Benedick.

Non-personal addressees in soliloquies

I have so far only dealt with soliloquies which can be addressed primarily to the audience, either in Intimate or Semi-Formal mode. But there are a number of alternative addressees towards which soliloquies, or sections of soliloquies, are regularly played to, *apart* from the house. These I categorise as 'non-personal' addressees. Identifying the non-personal addressee at any given point in any speech or soliloquy, and playing the words actively and specifically towards this addressee, will produce a greatly clarifying and energising effect.

The first of these non-personal addressees I wish to look at are 'personified objects'.

Addressing non-personal addressees: Objects – Antony, Helena and Lear

Here again is the opening of Antony's speech from *Julius Caesar*:

Antony: *Oh, pardon me, thou bleeding piece of earth,*
That I am meek and gentle with these butchers.   *3:1:254*

When I ask who Antony is talking to when speaking these lines, I might receive the answer 'to himself'; or even 'to the audience'. A student might often have to say the line over and over before suddenly saying, 'Oh, of course! Yes.' He realises that Antony is addressing the *bleeding piece of earth* – the remains of his friend, Julius Caesar. He is 'personifying' an object – the piece of dead flesh – as if it could hear, absorb and respond to his words.

With this instance of personification, the actor must establish a felt connection with the 'piece of flesh' and 'speak to it' with the same energy and commitment as he would when addressing himself to a living person.

What I often see, however, is the actor, first of all, disconnecting himself, not just from the corpse, but from the scene. His eyes cloud over as he looks inward, digging for the source of the speech somewhere deep in his own insides. Only then does he begin the speech, seemingly drawing it up from within himself.

And it is no good establishing the connection with the addressee somewhere along the way. What will produce a much more living and watchable result is when a living channel is *firstly* opened between Antony and the corpse. *The connection must come first.* The lines can then be directed through this already opened channel of connection; they can be 'carried' by, can 'flow' through, and along, this channel.

So that you can experience for yourself what I'm talking about, I want you now to act Antony's lines. Before you do, or say, anything, fully imagine the bleeding corpse lying before you; or better still, have a co-operative partner lie and 'be' the corpse for you. Even if only imagined, really 'see' the body and take it in. Keeping fully open yourself, wait until you feel you are genuinely connected to the corpse. When you feel the channel between you and the body is open and strong, then, and only then, address the lines to it. Keep the channel open all the while you are saying the line. Do this a few times until you arrive at a true sense of being connected to an object and acting towards it:

Pardon me, thou bleeding piece of flesh,
That I am meek and gentle with these butchers.

Did you start to feel that? Playing the lines this way makes the line feel more real, by providing it with an active target, and a purpose.

In *All's Well That Ends Well*, young Helena calls from France all the way to Italy, where her beloved Bertram has gone to fight in the wars. She addresses herself very specifically to the bullets (*'leaden messengers'*) which she envisages flying towards her loved-one as he fights.

Act Helena's lines now. First of all, look out through the walls of the palace and *see* those bullets, all those hundreds of miles away in that Italian battlefield. Open a channel and connect to them. Only then address them. Act the lines as if your command might actually influence the flight of those bullets towards your cherished lord:

Helena: *… O, you leaden messengers,*
That ride upon the violent speed of fire,
Fly with false aim…
          … do not touch my lord!   3:2:108

I have been putting great emphasis on establishing, and feeling, a living channel of connection between the actor and the addressee; but it is important to point out that when actually performing, you can't stop the play with a long pause and patiently wait for the connection to manifest. In the flow of performance, opening such a channel need take almost no time at all. Once it has been established in rehearsal a few times, the channel can be opened in no more than it takes to flick one's eyes from one position to another. Nonetheless it must be opened and felt; and, very importantly, *maintained*.

Following are some further examples of addressing 'personified objects' from *King Lear*. The old king calls to a number of natural phenomena:

Lear: *Blow, winds, and crack your cheeks! rage! blow!*   3:2:1

Here, Lear is speaking to, is addressing the *'winds'*; his line is an order. As if they were 'persons', he is telling the winds what it is he wants them to do. The line, therefore, must be delivered directly and purposefully towards, the *'winds'*.

After *'winds'*, Lear goes on to address other natural phenomena: *'cataracts'* (raging floods), *'hurricanoes'*, and *'thunder'*.

This time, he not only tells them what he wants them to do; we learn why it is he wants them to do it. He is ordering the elements specifically to drown, then destroy the planet, and to kill off the seeds of all future life, so that no more ungrateful humans can come into being. If Lear is to have his way, he must, therefore, look out to where he senses these three 'addressees' to be (the *cataracts and hurricanoes*' and *'all-shaking thunder'*), and make abundantly clear what he is telling them to do.

Read the lines to be certain of their meaning;

> **Lear:** … *You cataracts and hurricanoes, spout*
> *Till you have drench'd our steeples, drown'd the cocks!* *
>
> …
>
> … *And thou, all-shaking thunder,*
> *Strike flat the thick rotundity o' the world!*
> *Crack nature's moulds, all germens** spill at once*
> *That make ungrateful man.*   3:2:2

* weather-cocks   **seeds, life-giving elements

Rather than simply committing to the active surface of such a poetic device ('Lear orders the winds to blow so hard that they break their cheeks' etc.), actors may decide, 'Oh, this is just about Lear sounding out the extremity of his rage'. The actor then simply rants and roars, splattering the line around in all directions, and with no more meaningful objective than something such as 'releasing anger'.

'General raging' is the churning around of energy within and around oneself for one's own benefit. This comes across as unpurposeful and indulgent. In a theatre (as in real life), people lose patience very quickly with characters who love endlessly to express their negative feelings, but who never take any purposeful action to relieve them. Playing the lines in order 'to express' something misses how such devices work. It also reduces the involvement of the audience.

The more specifically and committedly Lear plays the surface, grammatical level of the rhetorical device – the literal level of 'I am ordering the winds etc. to do specific things' – the more the power of the device is released. As he gives these specific and very terrible orders, the audience witness *the evidence* of the rage that is in the king; they witness his actions, and from them they can *deduce* his rage. The audience, thereby, become more active.

This, of course, does not mean that the king's anger will not inform his delivery. Lear will, and must, feel a monumental rage at how his daughters have treated him; and he may consequently want to roar his orders out at great volume. His emotion and the noise, however, must not overwhelm his ability to achieve his objective of conveying persuasively to the elements what he wants them to do for him. Not containing his rage sufficiently may result in him not achieving the precision and clarity appropriate to getting his instructions across, and therefore getting the desired job done.

Act Lear's lines a few times now. Each time, work to open up an even more solidly felt channel with the addressees; and make sure they understand precisely what you want them to do. You don't necessarily have to raise your voice; but if you do, make sure you don't shout in a way, or so much, that your addressees won't clearly hear and take your instruction:

Lear: ... *You cataracts and hurricanoes, spout*
Till you have drench'd our steeples, drown'd the cocks!

...

And thou, all-shaking thunder,
Strike flat the thick rotundity o' the world!
Crack nature's moulds, all germens spill at once
That make ungrateful man.

Non-personal addressees: Absent characters – Lady Macbeth

Another addressee to which lines may be directed is an 'absent character'. I include absent characters under 'non-personal addressees', as when an absent character is addressed, it is, strictly speaking, 'the idea of the person' that is addressed, rather than the actual person.

Lady Macbeth receives a letter from her husband, explaining that the witches have predicted he will be king: she urges her off-stage husband to hurry home, so she can galvanise him for the wicked deed she thinks they must now perform:

Lady Macbeth: ... *Hie thee hither*
That I may pour my spirit in thine ear...   1:5:25

The vital point with lines such as these (and indeed all lines played to *any* type of non-personal addressee) is that you don't glaze the eyes over and 'internalise' the line, i.e. that you don't direct the line 'back into yourself', as if you were talking to the 'idea of Macbeth' somewhere 'in there' in your own head, or in some other part of your body.

Obviously the Lady knows Macbeth is not going to hear her order, but her words must still be directed out towards her husband. One can imagine the future queen looking straight out in front of her, as if seeing through the thick castle walls and over the countryside beyond, to where she imagines Macbeth is galloping towards her.

Act the lines a few times in this manner. Open a channel of connection, then focus your eyes 'seeingly' (not de-focussed) out over the landscape, willing your words to reach the person you so much desire to be with you. Speak them until you have a real feeling of a contact over distance with the approaching Macbeth:

> ... *Hie thee hither*
> *That I may pour my spirit in thine ear...*

I'd like, now, to give you experience of a different 'mode' in which an address to an absent character might be played.

In this mode, you do *not* need to have your eyes focussed directly on the non-personal addressee (in this case, the distant galloping Macbeth). You can have them connected, *just as seeingly*, to some other point straight 'out there' in front of you, in your environment. You could even be doing this while having your back to the imagined audience. In this mode, although you are not looking in the direction of Macbeth's surmised approach, it is vital that, in your awareness, you still open, feel, and maintain, a strongly felt connection to your addressee, to the absent Macbeth; vital that, just as strongly as before, he remains the target of your order. Although not connected to him visually, if you feel truly connected to Macbeth in this way, then the audience will sense it, and the line will keep its purpose and direction.

Have a go. Eyes connected seemingly out towards somewhere other than your husband, but in your awareness, resolutely retaining him as the addressee of your utterance:

> ... *Hie thee hither*
> *That I may pour my spirit in thine ear...*

This same principle can apply to *any* non-personal addressee. For example, one can imagine Antony being unable to look directly at Caesar's body, so looking out over the Roman forum as he addresses the body. If his intention is still genuinely to communicate with the body, the audience will feel this connection, and the lines will be alive. If by not looking directly at it, Antony's connection to the body, and his intention towards it, cease, the audience will sense the disconnection, and the line, having no direction, will have reduced impact.

There will be greater clarification of this idea, as further examples of 'addressing non-personals' are examined.

Non-personal addressees: Gods and spirits – Edmund and Lady Macbeth
In the various worlds in which Shakespeare's plays are set, the existence of 'God', 'The Gods', 'spirits' and 'devils' is taken for granted.

Below is the opening line of Edmund's soliloquy from *King Lear.* Edmund declares that, as an illegitimate son, his loyalty is to the law of nature – as opposed to the law of custom and convention:

> **Edmund:** *Thou, Nature, art my goddess; to thy law*
> *My services are bound...*   *1:2:1*

I have found that actors approaching these lines may not direct them to anyone in particular, but speak them as a targetless expression of generalised discontent and bitterness. Acted in this fashion, the explanatory level of the line is missed, and the intended addressee is ignored.

Edmund's explanation asks, of course, to be addressed specifically towards 'the goddess of Nature'; or towards 'the personification of Nature' (abstract ideas, such as 'Nature' can also be personified and addressed). In whichever way Edmund is thought to conceive of *'Nature'*, if the line is actively directed to Her, it will feel much more substantial, both to the actor and to the audience.

As with addressing absent characters and objects, when talking to Gods (or personifications of abstractions) as Edmund is here, it is possible also to be connected to them, and actively address them, without having one's eyes connected to the point or points where one instinctively feels is 'where they reside': towards the heavens, for example. But, as with objects and absent characters, if his eyes are not directed to 'where Nature is', they must still be outwardly connected and directed 'seeingly' and intentionally out towards something in the environment. And, although 'not looking at Her', he must still act the line with a feeling of connection to Nature, and with the intention to have his order reach Her.

Shortly after addressing her absent husband, Lady Macbeth talks to some spirits:

> **Lady Macbeth:**   *... Come, you spirits,*
> *Who tend on mortal thoughts, unsex me here,*
> *And fill me from the crown to the toe, top-full*
> *Of direst cruelty...*   *1:5:40*

Again, the character must first connect, then persuasively speak to, the invisible spirits *'wherever* (they) *wait on nature's mischief'.* Grammatically speaking, Lady Macbeth is again 'ordering' – ordering the spirits to come and follow her very specific instructions. What one sometimes witnesses instead, however, is 'wafty-spooky acting', directed to nowhere in particular.

Before acting these words, I want you to imagine where Lady Macbeth would look in order to sense a connection to the spirits she hopes will help her? Might she cast her gaze out at horizon-level, or raise it to a point some way above it? Or might she more effectively lift her gaze up into the shadowed recesses of the vaulting rafters, above her? It always strikes me as remarkable how playing to non-personal addressees, at various possible eye-levels, can have such a different effect. There are eye-lines that feel and look 'right', and others that are simply not as effective and which look 'wrong'. If the eyes are lifted too high, for example, it can look somehow silly. But in a lofty, traditional theatre with three balconies, it might look natural for a Lady Macbeth to raise her eyes much higher than would be the case if she were playing in a low-ceilinged studio.

I would like you now to act Lady Macbeth's lines four times. On each occasion, have your eyes and your attention directed out specifically to connect to the invisible spirits you are addressing; but on each separate occasion I want you to focus them at a different level:

- first very high, almost straight above your own head
- then medium high
- then at a point just above the horizon line.
- then somewhere below your own natural eyeline:

… Come, you spirits,
Who tend on mortal thoughts, unsex me here,
And fill me from the crown to the toe, top-full
Of direst cruelty…

Which of the different points, or heights, gives you a better sense that your words might reach the spirits? I want you to remember this for the purposes of an exercise to come.

Before going on to look at any further 'non-personals', there are two other general and important aspects of acting to such addressees that I would like to cover. The first is 'the nature of the relationship with the addressee'. The second is, 'what is involved when switching from one addressee to another'.

Nature of the relationship with addressees

In drama, as in life, the particular relationship we have with any person we encounter feels different to the relationship with any other. Similarly, the relationship a character has with each of his or her 'non-personal' addressees needs to be different. With all non-personal addresses, the actor must not only open a fresh channel, he needs also to define, and feel the precise nature of, the relationship he has with each of them; just as he would if it were another person.

How differently does Lear feel when he addresses the *'wind'* as opposed to the *'thunder'*, and as opposed to the *'cataracts'*. Does Edmund feel his relationship with *'Nature'* as flippant, or as one of genuine respect? What is Lady Macbeth's relationship to the *'spirits'*? Does she, for instance, approach them with awe and trepidation, fearing they may refuse her requests? Or does she readily assume their co-operation? Does she have a history relating to these spirits, or other types of spirits, or is this her first time?

Sometimes it is simple to establish what relationship a character has with an impersonal addressee, and sometimes a little thought may be asked for. Different Helenas from *All's Well That Ends Well* might even feel a different relationship with the bullets (*'leaden messengers'*) flying towards her lord *(see above: page 212)*. One might feel that the bullets need to be addressed with a terrified respect, another with an unapologetic and imperious hatred. Having clarity about such relationships will signally effect how any lines are delivered; and this will give the audience information about the speaker.

Switching non-personal addresses – Lady Macbeth

If I am a character in a scene giving separate orders to a number of individuals, as I move from addressing one to addressing another, I will break my connection with one and open up a separate channel with the next. And so it is with the different addressees there may be within a soliloquy: a separate channel of connection must be opened and maintained with each one of them.

When Lear has finished ordering the *'winds'* to *'blow'*, then he must break that particular line of connection, and open up a fresh one with the *'cataracts and hurricanoes'*. He then calls to them through this fresh channel.

For the purpose of practice in this important aspect of addressing non-personals, you will find below, Lady Macbeth's *'Come you spirits…'* lines coupled with a few lines from further on in her speech. In the later lines, she is no longer addressing the *'spirits'*, she is addressing *'Night'*: ordering Her to cover herself in the darkest (*'dunnest'*) hell-smoke:

> *… Come, you spirits*
> *That tend on mortal thoughts, unsex me here…*
>
> …

> *… Come, thick Night,*
> *And pall thee in the dunnest smoke of Hell*
> *That my keen knife sees not the wound it makes…*   1:5:40

First of all, make a quick, functional decision about how Lady Macbeth feels about both the *'spirits'* and about *'Night'*, and, therefore how she will relate to each.

When you have done that, deliver the first set of lines with your eyes connected out, at whatever level felt most appropriate to you earlier for connecting to the spirits. Then, before you speak the second set of lines, move your eyes away from the spirits and reconnect them to where you feel your eyes should best connect in order to speak to *'Night'*. It is only when you feel you have connected with, and opened a channel with, *'Night'* that I want you to address her. This may feel slow, ponderous and over-elaborate, but don't worry about that for now. Putting yourself consciously and slowly through the process in this way will give you a solid experience of what I am talking about. In the end, switching fully from one addressee to another will feel effortless and need only take a fraction of a second. The important point is that it must happen; and that both you and the audience *feel* it happen.

Before practising this switch from the *'spirits'* to *'Night'*, there is one other vital thing I want you to bear in mind. *Do not* break the external connection of your eyes as you move from one point to the other. Often, when asked to transfer attention from one addressee to the next, an actor will drop the eyes to the floor, or for a moment or two 'switch the eyes off', momentarily going internal. Not a good thing.

I want you to practise transferring the connection of the eyes from the *'spirits'* to *'Night'* now – without dipping, or switching the eyes off, in between. Whilst keeping the eyes connected out, let them smoothly glide between the first outward point of focus to the new point of focus. When you feel you have established that fresh, and felt, connection to *'Night'*, then, and only then, say to Her what it is you want her to do. In performance, as I have said, this can happen in a flash; but it *must* happen. Practise this 'connected switching' a few times now:

> *Come, you spirits that tend on mortal thoughts,*
> *Unsex me here…*

> *… Come, thick Night,*
> *And pall thee in the dunnest smoke of hell…*

Can you feel how, by doing this, there is a sense that the ball has not dropped in between the two sets of lines? The line of connection with the outside world remains 'taut'. No energy has 'leaked'. There are numerous soliloquies which contain a variety of addressees, and this principle of 'connected switching' should be applied to every instance of moving from one to the other. The principle applies whether you are ordering or questioning or explaining something to the addressee. Disconnect from one. And without dropping or disconnecting the eyes in between, connect to the other; *then* speak.

Shifting from one addressee to another will usually entail the eyes breaking their connection to one area of the environment, and moving to connect with another as just described; and this works. But the rule to 'shift the point of connection' is not one that can *never* be broken. It can work to keep the eyes connected out to a single point as you direct yourself to one, then to a separate addressee. If this is something you occasionally decide to do, however, what remains essential, is that you *still open* (and fully experience the differing quality of) a new channel for each. When you do this, even without your changing eye-lines, the switch of channel will still be felt by the audience; as it must.

Non-personal addressees: Internal – Claudius

In *Hamlet*, a guilt-ridden Claudius is endeavouring to make himself kneel so as to beg God's forgiveness for having murdered his royal brother. This soliloquy throws up an interesting pair of addressees: what I call 'internal non-personals'. You will come across quite a few of these in Shakespeare. Claudius has no fewer than three different addressees in these three short lines below. Firstly, he talks to the *'angels'*; then he addresses his *'knees'*, urging them to *'bend'*; and finally he addresses his *'heart'*, ordering it to *'Be soft'*.

> **Claudius:** ... *Help, angels! Make assay.* *
> *Bow, stubborn knees; and heart with strings of steel,*
> *Be soft as sinews of the new-born babe!* 3:3:69

* Make an attempt.

Where to connect the eyes when speaking to the *'angels'* usually does not cause a problem: the same principles apply for angels as for 'gods and spirits'. I have, however, known the second and third of these addressees to cause some understandable confusion. If I am suggesting that an actor's eyes must always be connected to where the addressee is known, or sensed, to be, then where does Claudius look when addressing his own knees? Half-way down his legs? And does he try to penetrate his own rib-cage with his gaze, when instructing his own heart? And where should Richard the Third look at the end of his opening speech, when addressing his own *'thoughts'*?

> **Richard:** *Dive, thoughts, down to my soul, here Clarence comes.* 1:1:41

Or Lear talking to the hysterical choking-malady (*'Hysterica passio'*) he feels rising up within him?

> **Lear:** *Hysterica passio, down, thou climbing sorrow,*
> *Thy element's below!*
> 2:4:55

I don't quite know why, or how it does, but, in such cases, this is what works:

The eyes remain outwardly and seeingly connected to the environment. At the same time as really seeing whatever you connect to 'out there', you connect, in your awareness (or perhaps, more specifically, in your 'body-awareness') to the object addressed. You maintain each connection in a sort of taut balance. Then, you speak to the addresses (the knees, the heart, the thoughts, the malady etc.); but *not* by directing the words inwardly. It may seem like a contradiction, but although the words are addressed to the 'inner object', they must still be directed outwards into the channel you are maintaining between yourself and your environment. This is what works. Your outward focus may remain at one fixed point; or it could feel equally, or more, 'natural' to re-adjust where the eyes focus (perhaps only slightly), as you shift your awareness from one addressee to another. Expressed in words, what I am describing might seem dauntingly complex. I assure you that, in practice, it feels and looks quite simple and natural. You can only achieve an understanding of how it feels right for the actor (and works for the audience), by doing it.

Dream up a quick, provisional idea of how you think this guilt-ridden Claudius must feel about his *'stubborn knees'*; and about his steely *'heart'*. Then I want you to act the lines a number of times with your eyes connected straight out and seeingly to a point somewhere outside of yourself. (You can quickly learn the words before doing this.)

Remain aware of what your eyes are focussed on 'out there', and, at the same time, in your body-awareness, maintain a connection to your knees and hold it there. Then, directing your words outwards; tell your knees what you want them to do. Having done that, disconnect your awareness from your knees and transfer it to your heart. As you do so, move your eyes (without lowering or disengaging them) to another point of focus. Maintaining this new connection, tell your heart now what you want it to do. I'm asking quite a lot here, so it will help to slow things down to begin with. Take as much time as you need to allow, and to feel, the dis- and the re-connecting to happen. Take time to allow, and to feel, the slight shift, or re-arrangement, that occurs within you in response to this switching of addressee. When you are happy with your slowed-down version, you can act the lines then in a more relaxed, less self-conscious way; the trace of the exercise will be there to support you:

Bow, stubborn knees; and heart with strings of steel,
Be soft as sinews of the new-born babe!

By way of affording you a further opportunity to extend your skill in addressing 'non-personals', I want you to act Claudius' lines again. This time, maintain *the same* visual focus as you transfer your awareness from your knees to your heart. But still feel the dis- and the re-connection, from one to the other.

Non-personal addresses: The 'whole self' – Angelo

At one point in Angelo's soliloquy in *Measure for Measure*, he asks his 'whole self' if it could possibly be Isabella's goodness that has roused his forbidden desire for her:

Angelo: *What dost thou? Or what art thou, Angelo?*
Dost thou desire her foully, for those things
That make her good?   2:2:173

As did Claudius when speaking to his own knees, when you address your 'whole self' in a speech in this way, the eyes must not attempt to look and see back into yourself. You must keep them outwardly and seeingly engaged, while *at the same time*, holding a part of your awareness connected to what I can only describe as 'a sense of yourself in your own body'; your 'whole self'. Then maintaining both connections in balance, the lines (even though in a literal sense, 'self-addressed') must be directed purposefully out into the world.

Addressees apart from audience and non-personals

You are now aware that individual sections of soliloquies may be addressed, not only out to the audience, but towards a variety of 'non-personal' addressees: to an object, a personification, an absent person, to gods, spirits or angels etc. But there is yet one other type of addressee towards which soliloquies, or parts of soliloquies, may be addressed.

Twelfth Night's lowly steward, Malvolio, has a long, 'overheard soliloquy' in which he fantasises, 'much above his station', about the behaviour he could get away with if he were married to his mistress, the Countess Olivia. Below are a few lines I have extrapolated from his speech which will give you the sense of its tone:

Malvolio: *... Having been three months married to her, sitting in my state,*
calling my officers about me, in my branched* velvet gown; having come from a
day-bed, where I have left Olivia sleeping... I will be proud, I will read politic
authors, I will baffle** Sir Toby, I will wash off gross acquaintance...   2:5:44

* embroidered   ** publicly disagree

The vast bulk of this speech is not directed to any non-personal addressee. I have seen it performed directly to the audience almost wholly in Intimate Mode; on other occasions, delivered without any direct acknowledgement of the audience at all. Both have worked.

If I ask students to whom, or to what such a speech might be addressed, if not to a non-personal addressee, or to the audience, an answer I might expect is 'to himself'. I would fervently propose that to suggest a character is talking to his- or herself is never useful. The audience may indeed *receive*, or *interpret* the speaking of a soliloquy as the character 'talking to himself', or 'thinking out loud'; but it is better for the performer not to think of it in such a way.

When an actor thinks of a speech as 'talking to myself', what he often, and understandably, tends to do is turn his attention *inward*. When he does this, what one observes to happen is that the eyes cloud over and lose their brightness. He has cut himself off from his environment, from the living world of the play; and rather than this 'internalisation' *bringing the audience in* on his inner thoughts, he actually becomes opaque. Not a good thing. Even when a character addresses himself by name, (as does Angelo in the lines quoted above), his words must still be directed outwards.

I saw a production recently where the actor playing Richard the Second focused his eyes at a point about eighteen inches in front of his own nose, and kept them there, for the duration of his great soliloquy: *'I have been studying how I may compare / This prison where I live unto the world...'* (5:5:1). The effect was of the character temporarily removing himself from the play and retreating into a private cloud of his own. A player may imagine such a show of intense introspection will make him appear frightfully deep and interesting – and some of the audience may be initially beguiled by this 'show of depth'. A lot of the energy of the speech, however, will be lost, and its active journey obscured. And even the most initially seduced audience will eventually feel 'left out' and begin to drift, seeking sustenance in their programme or, as the performer, in their own inner world.

Sometimes when an actor senses that a soliloquy should, indeed, not be directed to the audience, he decides that the best thing to do then is to look at the floor. Avoid the floor! As someone famously said, 'If an actor looks at the floor the only thing he is likely to find there is the play.' Turning the attention either inwards, or towards the floor, immediately throws up a barrier between the actor and the audience.

So if Malvolio is not to address the floor, or turn his attention inwards and 'talk to himself', and since he is not speaking to any 'non-personal' addressees, or the audience, then who can he be talking to?

Non-personal Addressees: The universe – Malvolio and Angelo

Apart from the audience, and all the other non-personal addressees towards which lines can be directed, the addressee towards which a character might direct his or her self is, what can be referred to as, 'the environment'; 'the wide world'; or 'the universe'.

As Malvolio, connect your eyes out to your environment, to the universe. We know he is in Olivia's garden, so you might imagine his gaze directed out over some flower beds, through some trees and towards the horizon. In the theatre this will probably mean looking out over the heads of the audience towards an imagined horizon. Really see what's out there in front of you, then steadfastly maintaining this visual contact, put out, explain, the details of your fantasy life with Olivia; with just as much energy and clarity as you would if talking to another character:

> *... Having been three months married to her, sitting in my state, calling my officers about me, in my branched velvet gown; having come from a day-bed, where I have left Olivia sleeping... I will be proud, I will read politic authors, I will baffle Sir Toby, I will wash off gross acquaintance...*

Feel OK? Better than trying to 'talk back into yourself'. It will certainly come across more satisfactorily to the audience.

I have heard it argued that if an actor does not address all soliloquies primarily to the audience, then the audience will begin to feel excluded. I would agree that they will begin to feel excluded if the actor 'goes into his or her self', as I have been warning against. But in my experience, a single character's active exchange with his environment (or with any other non-personal addresses) can be just as involving as a scene in which two actors exchange their lines exclusively with one another, and similarly make no acknowledgment of the audience at any time.

Below are some exercises which will help you feel the difference between 'addressing the universe' and 'talking to yourself'; and help you to begin sensing the relative dramatic strength of the former.

The following are, again, the opening lines of the highly puritanical Angelo's soliloquy from *Measure for Measure*. He desperately asks who can be held accountable for the intense sexual desire he suddenly feels towards Isabella, a novitiate nun come to plead for the life of her brother:

Angelo: *What's this? What's this? Is this her fault or mine?*
The tempter or the tempted, who sins most? Ha? …   2:2:162

In these lines, Angelo is not speaking to any of our previous list of 'non-personal' addressees. If he is not to turn his attention inwards and 'talk to himself', should he not then deliver his speech to the audience? It is easy to see that if a character as serious as Angelo chatted to the audience in the needy Intimate Mode of a Launce or an Autolycus, that the dignity of his character, and the great depth of his disturbance, would be diminished. However, I can see his soliloquy being delivered to the audience in the more 'Open' style – at a point much further towards the 'Formal' end of the intimacy scale than, say, the speech of either Benedick or Helena from *A Midsummer's Night Dream (see above: pages 209 and 210)*. To connect his vision and his awareness outwards, not to the audience, but to the universe, definitely is another option for an Angelo. In most circumstances, this is the option that I would take. For the fantasy sections of his speech, Malvolio puts out 'explanations' to the universe. In the first lines of Angelo's speech, what he is putting out are 'questions'; and if he is putting his questions out to the universe, he must ask them with just as much clarity and intention as he would if he were putting them to an eminent theologian.

Act Angelo's lines now, and first of all think of them as a 'private' and 'internal' process; as an 'inner investigation' where the answers to the questions you ask lie 'within'. Connect your awareness to the inside of yourself; search 'in there' for the answer as you speak – as if there is no inspiration to be won from a cold and empty, surrounding universe. Deliver the lines this way until you feel you have fully 'got' that way of delivering them.

What's this? What's this? Is this her fault or mine?
The tempter or the tempted, who sins most? Ha? …

Having completed this, I want you to play Angelo's lines again. This time look straight out into the world, the same way you might look deep into the eyes of a trusted friend you are hoping might come back with the answers you so desperately need. Then, without breaking your connection to what you are seeing out there, put your questions to the universe. Really *ask*:

What's this? What's this? Is this her fault or mine?
The tempter or the tempted, who sins most? Ha? …

Feels very different, doesn't it? Better? This 'addressing the universe' mode can be employed in very many soliloquies, and perhaps, for certain sections, in all of them.

Alternating audience and universe as addressee – Viola

I'd like to take a closer look now at a section of Viola's 'ring soliloquy' touched on earlier (*'I left no ring with her; what means this lady?' Etc.*).

I would suggest that *overall*, Viola's speech is one that can successfully be addressed to the audience, in either 'Semi-Formal' Open style (or, in more informal theatrical conditions, in a slightly more Intimate Mode). I would suggest, also, that it could work for some of Viola's lines to be delivered, not directly to the audience, but openly to the universe. For example, she could say directly to the audience, *'I left no ring with her...'* and then address *'... what means this lady?'* to the universe. Have a go at that.

For the first half of the line, connect to the audience; then, before delivering the second half, disconnect from the audience and re-connect to the universe (this might, for example, mean lifting your gaze slightly above the audience's head and slightly to the side):

Viola: (To audience) *I left no ring with her:* (To universe) *What means this lady?*

To give you further experience of the possibilities I am drawing attention to, I would like you to deliver some further lines of Viola's, in a few different ways.

Firstly, open up a visual and felt connection with your imaginary audience, and deliver all five opening lines directly to them:

Viola: *I left no ring with her; what means this lady?*
Fortune forbid my outside hath not charmed her!
She made good view of me; indeed so much
Methought her eyes had lost her tongue
For she did speak in starts, distractedly...

Do this a few times till you have a solidly felt sense of performing the lines in the 'to the audience' mode.

Now, deliver the lines again: this time, you will be delivering certain lines to the audience, and certain others to the universe. **AU.** indicates 'to the audience'; and **U.** indicates that the line, or lines following, are to be delivered still outwardly, but to the universe.

To begin, it is important that you do this part of the exercise at least a few times, and that you practise it *slowly*. At any point where there is a change of addressee, take all the time you want to feel you are fully disconnecting from the previous addressee, and are strongly re-engaging with the new one; then, and only then, should you proceed to deliver the next line: and as you do speak this new line, consciously maintain that sense of connection with the new addressee:

AU. *I left no ring with her:* **U.** *What means this lady?*
AU. *Fortune forbid my outside hath not charmed her!*
U. *She made good view of me;* **AU.** *indeed so much*
Methought her eyes had lost her tongue
For she did speak in starts, distractedly…

When you have delivered the lines at least a few times in this extra-careful manner, perform them at a more natural pace (observing the same **U./AU.** scheme), and trusting that your practice with the slower version will serve you.

How does that feel?

Now do the lines differently. Deliver them whilst *reversing* the addressees, as indicated below:

U. *I left no ring with her;* **AU.** *What means this lady?*
U. *Fortune forbid my outside hath not charmed her!*
AU. *She made good view of me;* **U.** *indeed so much*
Methought her eyes had lost her tongue
For she did speak in starts, distractedly…

Which of the two schemes feels more 'natural' to you? Would you rather give all these opening lines to the audience? Open or Intimate Mode? Or would you rather perform them all to the universe and allow the audience to witness you do this? Or would you mix and match them, but in a combination different to the schemes offered above?

Two side notes on connecting the eyes out:

The eyes in auditions and examinations
If you are auditioning, or performing for examination, I strongly suggest NOT addressing the speech towards the auditioner(s), or the examiner(s), but towards the imagined addressee (imagined other character, personification, the universe or imagined audience). The examiners need to feel free to take a good look at you, without feeling the need to play their part as your imagined public. If you choose to do it to an imagined audience, in your mind's eye you can place the audience, for example, just to the right or left of the auditioners, or slightly over their heads.

Eyes and spontaneity
There is another general advantage to keeping one's eyes outwardly and actively engaged (be this with the audience, with another character, with the horizon or anything else): it takes one's awareness away from oneself, and (seemingly paradoxically) this allows the actor to connect less self-consciously with his or her truer self. Actions and reactions become less guarded or edited; more natural and spontaneous. A good thing.

Having dealt with what questions to ask about the beginning and the end of soliloquies, and having explored the issue of 'to whom or what am I talking', the questions which remain to be examined are those questions most useful to ask when considering the main 'body' of the soliloquy. By way of preparation for a discussion of these questions, however, it will be useful, firstly, to familiarise you with two most important and basic notions that I have not yet touched on. The first is: the notion of the universe 'feeding back'. The other is: the unique ways in which explanations function within soliloquies (as opposed to how they function in the context of exchanges amongst characters).

The universe feeding back

I have suggested that connecting 'seeingly' and 'feelingly' to the universe provides a channel through which the character's utterances may travel effectively out into the world. Consider now that this same channel of connection provides the conduit through which energy also can *return to*, and penetrate the speaker.

When a character opens to the outside world, so as to direct his or her energy out into that world, then he or she will, at the same time, automatically be open *to receive* from that world.

As well as his openness allowing energy freely to *flow out* of him, he becomes capable of freely *absorbing* energy, of *letting it in;* he is open to absorbing enlightenment, to receiving insight. It only takes one wall to separate two people; by the same token, it only takes one open channel to facilitate a two-way traffic between a character and the world. The more rich and alive this two-way flow of energy is, the more rich and alive the audience will experience a character to be. The universe is not just a vast and dead empty space outside of ourselves. It is alive. It is affected by, and responds to, any energy that is directed out into it; and it is from the external universe that any inspiration a character receives, or is seeking, will come.

I would suggest that it is very useful to think of there being an 'acting law' which states:

*To the extent that one puts energy **out into** the universe, one must in turn, allow energy to enter into one **from** the universe.*

Another axiom as applicable to 'good living' as much as to 'good acting'.

Living is an ongoing process of destructive consumption and re-creation. We take in, and consume, different types of 'fuel', convert (re-create) it, and deliver it back out into the world in its changed form. We are constantly feeding off the universe in the form of the animals or plants we destroy, consume and convert into the vital energy which helps sustain our very existence. A human is constantly breathing out and breathing in; drinking and urinating; eating and defecating; absorbing and releasing heat; speaking and listening; giving and receiving information; telling and laughing at jokes; consuming love and physical support from others, and (in 'the best of all possible worlds') feeding it, in turn, to others.

If these ongoing exchanges of energy between an individual and the environment cease; if, for example, we stop breathing, eating, or drinking, then, in a very short space of time, we will have no decision to make as whether *'to be or not to be.'* And we know that infants do not thrive when they are deprived of an ongoing exchange of 'feeling energy' in the form of the giving, and receiving, of human touch. It is the constant penetration of energy from without, from the universe, which nourishes, stimulates, motivates, inspires.

This cycle of perpetual destruction and creation governs, not alone all human activity, it is also the dynamic governing the animal world, the vegetable world, and the cosmological world: the process of perpetual, often violent, preying and consumption of one element of the universe on another, in order constantly to renew and invigorate itself; the law that the consumer today will be the consumed tomorrow. Entire planets, galaxies and stars continually arise, new-born, out of the destruction of other cosmological elements; and these galaxies, planets etc. will, in their turn, be destroyed to serve as food to feed, and keep alive – for a time – some other cosmic entity or phenomenon, which in turn etc. etc....

To get in touch with, and fully experience, these fundamental realities of our existence is, I believe, what, human beings most yearn for; and putting us in touch with these 'eternal verities' is what art can do. A writer impelled to create a play for genuinely artistic reasons will always be striving (consciously or unconsciously) to create an image, a model, a microcosm of the dynamic process which governs human life, and the universe as a whole. Writers who create a play merely as a vehicle to promote their opinions will not be using the apparatus of theatre for the purpose it is best designed to serve; they will be using it, not so much to 'hold a mirror up to nature' and the world, but more to provide a reflector of what, in their opinion, nature and the world should look like. No play considered great has ever survived merely on the strength of the opinions it expressed. Any few 'opinion' plays that survive, do so only because the writers, in spite of themselves, have achieved something of more artistic value than they intended. This is the case with a few powerful sections of some, otherwise didactic, plays by Brecht.

A successful, artistically conceived play can put us in touch with, not merely an intellectual 'idea' of the fundamental truths of our existence; it can put us in touch with a powerful, *felt sense* of them. It can afford an experience of intimacy between ourselves and our universe. It offers an experience of the truth that, at the deepest level, we are not all separate, isolated individual bystanders looking out from within ourselves at a universe operating independently from us; but that we are very much an *essential part* of the cyclic processes of the cosmos.

If the dynamic of the universe is one of a perpetual cycle of energy-exchanges, of destruction and re-creation, then at every layer of its architecture, a play is 'imitating' nature. At the heart of any play experienced as being satisfyingly coherent, there lies a single and central action and reaction between characters; a central exchange of energy. Similarly, what forms the heart of any of the scenes making up a play is always a single and central energy exchange between characters; and, in turn, (leaving soliloquies aside for a moment) what any scene consists of is, of course, an ongoing series of energy-exchanges between characters; mostly in the form of dialogue.

And now to relate this to the acting of soliloquies.

In the same way that a scene represents an ongoing pattern of exchanges between, or amongst, characters, so, in a soliloquy, there needs to be a sequence of exchanges of energy between the character and his or her addressees. The orders, questions etc. that they put out amount only to fifty-percent of the event any speech represents; the energy, the inspiration they take in from without represents the other, equally important, fifty-percent. (It can be useful to remember that the word is, '*in*-spiration', not '*ex*-piration'; or any other kind of '-piration'.)

When actors perform soliloquies in this way, as a series of ongoing exchanges twixt within and without, their characters come across as being engaged in an active journey of discovery towards a conclusion. It does not seem that they are merely regurgitating something that was already mouldering down somewhere inside themselves. Consequent on a sequence of exchanges with the universe, a character will be in a different place at the end of a soliloquy than the place from which they began. Something, therefore, will have '*happened*'; something new will have been created; the character and the play will have 'moved forward'.

And this is why performers are trained always to keep their body and vocal apparatus relaxed: so that not only can they allow their energy to flow freely from them in an outward direction, but so they, also, can freely allow energy from the surrounding environment to enter, to move, inspire and motivate them.

Moments of conception

The moment when the energy coming from without 'touches' the performer within, I often refer to as the 'moment of conception'; or as 'the moment of creation'. That is indeed what it is. The character is penetrated from without and a new energy, a new impulse springs up, is conceived within. This new energy is then extruded, is born out into the world, in the form of an action, or actions (usually a question, explanation or order). And if the performer is indeed allowing these 'moments of conception' to occur, the audience will 'get' it; they will feel this process of penetration, conception and birth 'happen'. They will bear witness to a process of continuing destruction and creation, and one which stands as a dynamic model, or image, of the ongoing process of destruction and creation in the universe in general.

You may find yourself resisting the notion that all human inspiration comes from without. The suggestion may sound like so much metaphysical ballyhoo. You may prefer holding to the notion that human impulses, and inspirations, spring up spontaneously from a deep, and possibly limitless, reservoir within each human being. If this is more how you understand things, worry not; you can still take fruitful advantage of the notion I am proposing here. Think of what I am suggesting merely as an image, a metaphor, and act *as if* it is truly what is going on. Regard it as in imaginative trick or technique which can be used to achieve a theatrical illusion: the impression of someone convincingly engaged in a process of discovery.

And now to apply what I have been discussing to some Shakespeare lines. At the opening of his soliloquy, Angelo puts out the question, *'Is this her fault or mine? / The tempter or the tempted, who sins most?'* Unless they are purely rhetorical, questions in the real world are put out in the hope, or expectation, of receiving an answer back; and it is similarly in the hope, or expectation, of an answer back that a character addresses a question to the universe. When Angelo puts his question to the universe, it is in the hope that it will receive and absorb the question, and that, in response, it will breathe its answer back into him. And, indeed, the universe does give him the answer. The answer he receives is: *'Not she; nor does she tempt: but it is I…'* And right in the moments Angelo is receiving this answer, he puts it out, he explains what it is.

You have had the opportunity with some passages above, to practise directing utterances out *into* the world; I would like now to offer you the experience of 'receiving from the universe'; of 'letting inspiration in.'

Receiving from the universe 1 – Angelo

Below you will find Angelo's opening few lines again. I want you to act these lines, again keeping your eyes and your attention seeingly connected to the horizon. Sense that the reason you need urgently to keep so open and outwardly focussed, is to keep in touch with the source of inspiration (the universe around you); and you do this in order, A) that you can put your questions to it, and, B) that in turn, the universe can send back into you the answers it wishes to give.

This time, when you put your questions out, I want you to wait; in silence. No matter how long it takes, keep your eyes and all your senses alert, and connected out. Wait until you sense energy enter and touch you within; until you feel it triggering in you the impulse to perform the next action in the speech; the impulse to give birth to, to give voice to, the first of the answers that have been conceived in you.

Then allow yourself to *respond* to this impulse and put your explanation out.

I'm sure you understand that, in performance, I am not suggesting you take a long lunch-break everywhere there is an exchange, and moment of conception. Leaving quite long pauses, as an exercise, however, can help you achieve a strong sense of where each exchange lies, and give a feel for its particular nature. Here are the lines:

Angelo: *What's this? What's this? Is this her fault or mine?*
The tempter or the tempted, who sins most? Ha? **(Wait)**
Not she: **(Wait)** *nor doth she tempt: but it is I…*

When you feel you have solidly experienced the process of 'waiting, receiving, then putting out', I want you to act Angelo's lines again. You will find that your sense of the answer coming from without can remain just as palpable, but that it can happen in much less time. You will definitely still need that moment after you finish your questions, where you wait for answers; but now allow that the universe offers the answers with readiness, and without too much delay. (Remain clear, however, that even though the moment of enlightenment may happen in the course of a single second, it must be *experienced*.)

Angelo: *What's this? What's this? Is this her fault or mine?*
The tempter or the tempted, who sins most? Ha?
Not she: nor doth she tempt: but it is I…

Explanations within soliloquies

Questions and orders in soliloquies function in much the same way as they do within the context of dialogue. The only difference is that questions and orders within scenes are addressed to another character on stage, while questions and orders in soliloquies are addressed to the audience, to the universe, or to some other non-personal addressee.

In prologues and epilogues, and in 'speeches to the audience' such as those of Launce and Autolycus *(see above: page 207 and page 208)*, explanations are delivered in order to convey information directly to the audience, and so function more or less as they do in regular scenes.

In what might be regarded as soliloquies 'proper', speeches where the speaker needs the experience of the speech primarily for his or her self, explanations will still need to be delivered with explanatory energy. In such speeches, however, the explanations will arise out of intentions quite different from those which motivate explanations in prologues and epilogues, or 'speeches to the audience'.

Laying out of already known facts

In the first half-line of her soliloquy, Viola explains, she 'lays out', an already known fact': *'I left no ring with her…'* Such 'laying out of already known facts' is what a lot of characters are doing in quite a lot of lines, in probably a majority of Shakespeare soliloquies. And the purpose behind such laying-out is usually to achieve clarity about, and 'to get a handle' on, a difficult situation, and the feelings that attend on it.

In his, *'Oh, that this too, too solid flesh would melt…'* speech Hamlet repeatedly lays out the facts of his mother's hasty and unseeming marriage to her late husband's brother. These already known facts are so unbearable, and so barely believable, that Hamlet has to keep putting them out to the world in the hope of receiving back some inspiration which will help him get some sort of purchase on them.

Hamlet: … *That it should come to this!*
But two months dead! Nay, not so much, not two…

…

Why she, even she… married with my uncle,
My father's brother; but no more like my father
Than I to Hercules. Within a month…!   *1:2:137*

So if you find yourself wondering why a character seems to be stating facts he is already aware of in a soliloquy, it is always a good idea to ask if they are doing it to provide a clear basis for an examination of the situation in which they find themselves; and this with a view to discovering how best to respond to said situation, once clarified.

But there is something else a character might be doing when putting out an explanation.

Realising

Realising is what Macbeth is doing in part of his, *'If it were done...'* speech; in the course of it, he too lays out a series of known facts but, given his murderous intentions towards the innocent King Duncan, he is now fully, and guiltily, realising *the new significance* of these facts:

Macbeth: ... *He's* here in double trust;*
First, as I am his kinsman and his subject,
Strong both against the deed; then, as his host,
Who should against his murderer shut the door,
Not bear the knife myself.   1:7:12

* the King

Explaining the realisation

There is an imperative point that needs to be made about 'realising'. To suggest that a character is 'realising' when they speak a certain line, or lines, is not to suggest that the actor look *inward* to observe the realisation bubbling up within them; it is not an excuse to go 'all pale and interesting'. 'Realising' is not an internal, or passive, process. Soliloquising characters have not carried an interesting realisation privately within themselves for some time previous, and are now explaining what that old realisation was. Characters in soliloquies do explain their realisations, but they explain fresh realisations, right *as they are occurring*. There must be little or no gap between the beginning of the realisation (the moment of conception) and the beginning of its being explained. You may have heard the acting axiom, 'the line is the thought'; by the same token when a character is realising something, 'the explanation *is* the realisation'.

The lines below from the middle of Macbeth's dagger speech offer another example of 'realising'; but 'realising' of a different character to that already discussed.

Receiving from the universe 2 – Macbeth
Macbeth is describing (explaining) what he sees as the evil pertaining in the hemisphere of the earth currently cowled in the darkness of night:

Macbeth: *... Now o'er the one half-world*
Nature seems dead, and wicked dreams abuse
The curtain'd sleep; witchcraft celebrates
Pale Hecate's* off'rings, and wither'd murder...
  ...towards his design
Moves like a ghost...   2:1:49

* Goddess of witchcraft

I have heard the content of Macbeth's speech delivered as if he is merely churning out knowledge about 'night' that has already been inside him, and which is familiar to him. On the face of it, it might seem that this section of the soliloquy does consist of a series of one-way 'puttings-out' on Macbeth's part; with no evidence of the universe feeding back, or any need on Macbeth's part for it to do so.

I would suggest that to perform this (or indeed any) speech as if this were the case, would result in the speech going 'dead'. For this passage to work as part of a living, creative process, Macbeth must actively draw his inspiration from the environment. He must remain bodily and visually open to the whole sense of the darkened hemisphere as it appears, as it feels, as he experiences it in that very moment. Whatever he explains vis-à-vis what is going on in the dark half-of-the-world, he must see it somewhere 'out there' in front of him where it is, not 'somewhere down there' inside of him where it is not. And it must seem that everything he is visually realising, is something he is 'seeing' for the very first time; or if he has dimly been aware of these things before this moment, that they are now entering him with a fresh and arresting clarity, and with a new and disturbing significance.

I want you to act Macbeth's lines now, and in such a way that you can begin to experience the lines as a series of exchanges, of actions and reactions between yourself and your environment. You might imagine Macbeth staring through a window into the depth of the darkness outside, explaining the series of images to the universe as they unfold to him. Or he could just as easily be imagined standing in a windowless room, looking out into the space around him 'seeing' the darkness of the night through and beyond the walls.

Keep the eyes connected out, and immediately after you complete the explanation of each image, wait (exactly as you did with the Angelo lines above); wait and experience the vacuum that has been left; sense an awareness of the next image, the next realisation, being conceived within you; and more or less simultaneously with sensing it, find and put out the words to describe it.

> *... Now o'er the one half-world*
> *Nature seems dead,* **Wait until you see** *and wicked dreams abuse*
> *The curtain'd sleep;* **Wait...** *witchcraft celebrates*
> *Pale Hecate's off'rings,* **Wait...** *and wither'd murder...*
> *...towards his design*
> *Moves like a ghost.*

Now you can act the lines again, just as connected out as before, but without the long waits; do still feel the 'empty moment' after you complete one explanation; but trust now that the universe will respond freely to what you have put out, and that it will inspire you with little or no delay:

> **Macbeth:** *... Now o'er the one half-world*
> *Nature seems dead, and wicked dreams abuse*
> *The curtain'd sleep; witchcraft celebrates*
> *Pale Hecate's off'rings, and wither'd murder...*
> *...towards his design*
> *Moves like a ghost...*

And now one final experience of a further, slightly different, form of 'receiving from the universe'.

Receiving from the universe 3 – Malvolio

With the 'fantasising' section of Malvolio's speech, it may again seem that his utterances do, in fact, constitute an unbroken string of 'outputs', with no space or need for any 'inputs' from the outside world. As with Macbeth's lines above, I would suggest again that played in this way, the speech will lose a lot of vitality.

I want you to connect the eyes out and act Malvolio's lines. The more joyously and openly the deluded man is connected to his environment, the more freely will the universe be inclined to inspire him. Feel Malvolio's highly charged need to be fed with ever more delicious details about his imagined life with his mistress. And after you have put out each delightful detail... wait... experience the emptiness until you feel the inspiration for the next stimulating detail entering and effecting a conception within you; and as soon as you feel this, explain it to the universe. Then wait again etc:

> **Malvolio:** *... Having been three months married to her, sitting in my state,*
> **wait** *calling my officers about me,* **wait** *in my branched (embroidered) velvet*
> *gown;* **wait** *having come from a day-bed, where I have left Olivia sleeping... I*
> *will be proud,* **wait** *I will read politic authors,* **wait** *I will baffle Sir Toby,* **wait** *I*
> *will wash off gross acquaintance...*

And now act the lines again, but at a more natural pace. Still experience the 'empty moments', but allow the inspirations to penetrate you more flowingly and readily; and still put your explanations out into the world just as you feel them arrive:

> **Malvolio:** … *Having been three months married to her, sitting in my state, calling my officers about me, in my branched velvet gown; having come from a day-bed, where I have left Olivia sleeping… I will be proud, I will read politic authors, I will baffle Sir Toby, I will wash off gross acquaintance…*

Armed with the notion of the universe feeding back, and with an understanding now of the functioning of explanations within soliloquies, we can go forward to look into the final key question to be asked when taking on a soliloquy:

> **Q.** *What, in the course of the speech, are the individual steps the character takes to bring them from their reaction to the 'triggering-event', through to the new feeling and understanding arrived at by the end of the speech?*

Instead of it being a series of actions and reactions amongst characters on the stage (as in a regular scene), the steps that carry a character through a soliloquy to its end, are a sequence of actions and reactions between him or her, and the external addressee, or addressees, to whom it is directed. Understanding that the steps of soliloquy are the same as the steps in a regular scene, actors and students feel they are on more solid and familiar ground.

In response to a chain of questions, explanations, or orders put out to the universe, audience or non-personal addressees, the character receives back a series of inspirations, each one of which is a step leading him or her towards the final conclusion of the speech.

To identify, and play, the various steps leading a character through a soliloquy, one simply needs to:

- A) separate out the various outwardly directed questions, orders and explanations (and occasional exclamation) that make it up;
- B) know to whom or what these are directed; and
- C) be aware that each and every one must be understood to be, and *experienced as*, a reaction to energy, to inspiration, entering from without.

Angelo put out his questions, received his answers, and then put out what answers he received.

As an opportunity to see the principles I have been discussing applied to a complete soliloquy, I will shortly be working through Viola's speech in its entirety. Before that, however, there are a few last general (and closely related) ideas I feel it would first be valuable to understand when it comes to playing 'the steps.'

The steps must produce a cumulative charge in the character. In any scene, each exchange must create, however subtly, an increase in the scene's emotional charge; it is this steadily increasing charge of feeling in a play which provides the fuel for further, and increasingly consequential, action. In the same way, each step in a soliloquy, each conception, must create a charge of feeling in the character, greater than the charge produced by the step before. By the end of any soliloquy, therefore, characters will not only be in a state of greater enlightenment, they will be in a state of greater emotional charge.

The actor, then, needs to identify exactly what feeling is created in the character as each individual step is taken, and become clear about the precise strength of this feeling. He can then allow that feeling to inform the delivery of the line (not, of course, to the extent that it diminishes its effectiveness in the world as a clearly articulated question, explanation, or order). If he does this, the audience will experience with him this build-up of feeling.

No leaking between steps

Another idea I find myself referring to, time and time again, when directing or teaching, is that, in the course of a soliloquy (as in the course of a scene), there must be no 'leaking' of energy. It is an idea that is implied by saying that an actor must sustain a cumulative emotional build when acting a soliloquy; but it is so basic and important I think it is of value to discuss it in isolation.

As the feeling builds in a soliloquy, one must continue to *contain* it, not leak one drop of it. The vessel, the balloon, must keep filling.

One might think of a soliloquy as a staircase one is climbing, where each exchange with the environment represents a step. With each step taken, there needs to be a sense of the character having arrived at a new place, and at a place of higher charge. This new place, however, is not an unloading-bay, a place where, having taken in the added charge, one takes a nice rest, lets go of the charge, and starts out again as a freshly emptied vessel. The new charge that has been achieved with each new step must *be added to* the charge you have carried inside yourself from the step below. Then, with an even greater motivation to get to the conclusion of the speech, you must resolutely plough on up to the next step, with all of the charge accumulated so far, still packed, 'unleaked', inside you. No leaking!

Flights and landings

If you do imagine a speech as a stairway you are climbing towards the top storey of a house, then you can imagine that as well as having steps, this stairway may also have 'landings', and that each landing is connected by a separate 'flight'.

In a speech, a 'landing' represents a smaller internal 'climax of enlightenment', a *key stage,* on the way towards the climactic enlightenment of the speech's conclusion.

In most soliloquies (or regular speeches), you will discover two, three or perhaps more such landings; identifying them is a means to get in touch with another aspect of a speech's architecture. (Other terms you may hear equivalent to a 'flight' in a speech are 'phrase' or 'beat'. A 'landing' then would be the equivalent of the end, or closing, of one of these beats or phrases.)

In Macbeth's, *'If it were done…'* speech, there are a number of (quite short, but evident) flights and internal landings. The lines below represent the landing led up to by the short 'flight' of preceding realisations about the consequences of such an evil act as killing a king. I have marked in bold the phrase which represents the 'climactic tip', as it were, of this landing:

> **Macbeth:** … *This even-handed justice*
> *Commends th'ingredients of our poison'd chalice*
> **To our own lips.** 1:7:10

Having stood on this climactic realisation, Macbeth then needs to use it as a launch-pad from which to kick off up towards the next landing, whilst (as with individual steps) keeping all the charge so far accumulated, 'unleaked'.

The next flight Macbeth starts to climb is a pair of realisations about his own relationship to Duncan as *'kinsman'* and *'host'*, which leads to his next landing (marked in bold):

> … *He's here in double trust:*
> *First as I am his kinsman and his subject,*
> *Strong both against the deed; then as his host,*
> **Who should against the murderer shut the door,**
> **Not bear the knife myself!** 1:7:12

Having firmly set his foot on the solidity of this new landing, Macbeth then begins to mount another flight: this time, a new set of realisations about Duncan's character and stainless record as king:

> … *Besides, this Duncan*
> *Hath borne his faculties so meek…*

And so on to his final climactic realisation.

(The idea of 'flights and landings' is similar to the notion of 'stanzas' within a speech, as discussed in the section dealing with 'Acting Shakespeare's Prose', page 179.)

Standing over the end of soliloquies and speeches

Having completed the last step of a soliloquy, a mistake often made is to 'bring the character down' to a place of calm neutrality; to regard the conclusion of the speech as a place at which the character releases the charge that has been built up. Releasing the accumulated charge at the end of a speech or soliloquy I call 'signing off'.

The charge achieved by the end of any speech must remain 'locked in'; the actor must continue to contain it when moving into whatever events in the play he or she goes on to participate in. This is known as 'standing over' the end of a speech. (The principle applies to speeches within scenes as much as soliloquies.) Standing over is a good thing. Signing off is not a good thing.

I would like to re-emphasise a point here, so as to anticipate a confusion often arising around this question of a character being in a state of higher charge at the conclusion of a speech. When I make this point about 'standing over' to an actor, he or she sometimes imagines that to follow such a guideline means the character must inevitably end up shouting and jumping about the stage in some form of extreme, high dudgeon. This, of course, is not what I am recommending. On a scale of ten, the build through any speech could be as dramatic as from one to nine or ten; but as I suggested in relation to the Hamlet and Benedick passages discussed earlier *(see pages 179 and 189)*, it may only be from one to three, or even two; but build there must be.

Also, a speech's final charge does not have to be simply *more* of the feeling with which the character started out. A speech could, for example, bring a character from a near-overwhelming mass of chaotic feeling caused by some event, through to a much clearer and calmer viewing of that event; many speeches do move from a blurred perception of a situation to a more focussed and calm view. But 'calm' need not, and must not, represent a deflation. It cannot be a calm resulting from a letting go of an accumulation of feeling. It must be a calm with a depth charge in it; a calm, for example, of grim resolve, or of despair; or of a quiet redoubled hatred. Whatever its quality, the built-up energy at the end of any soliloquy should vibrate with potential; it is energy likely to be called on to motivate future action in the story. Not hanging on to the charge, therefore, leaks energy, not only from the build of the character's overall journey through the play; it leaks energy from the build of the play as a whole. No signing off!

Anticipating

A classic 'no-no' in acting generally is for an actor to 'anticipate'. One pretty crude example of 'anticipating' in a scene, is if an actor glances towards a door a few seconds before someone is supposed unexpectedly to burst through it; in such a case, the illusion of surprise, and of reality, is somewhat diluted. Another example would be if, half-way through another character's speech, an actor gives a reaction which should only come as a result of something said later in the speech.

You can anticipate with a soliloquy 'as a whole'; and you can anticipate in particular instances *within* a soliloquy. Anticipating overall means you launch into the speech already experiencing the charge of feeling the speech is supposed to bring you to. Or you launch into it with an understanding which the character should be using the journey of the soliloquy to reach. A character shouldn't know where his 'dialogue with the world' will take him, any more than one should in a scene played out with another character. If he *does* know, then an entire soliloquy, which ought to seem *necessary* to the character, is now redundant.

Macbeth should not launch into his *'If it were done, when 'tis done...'* speech, having already decided that he is not going to go through with the plan to murder Duncan.

I have sometimes seen Hamlet's *'To be...'* speech played where it is pretty obvious the prince is already fully aware of what he knows and feels about the issue of *'self-slaughter'*. If Hamlet doesn't *need* the speech to get him to his conclusion, then his soliloquy effectively becomes a recitation.

'Not knowing' allows for two important things: it allows the speech to have a mounting and manifest effect on the character as it goes along, so the energy will continue growing from start to end; and it will create suspense in the minds of the audience, as they wonder where each new step in the speech is going to take the speaker.

Anticipating 'in a particular instance', as opposed to in an overall way, means you play a line, or section, of a speech, as if you are already aware of some individual discovery which should in fact represent a step or landing 'further up the stairway'. You shouldn't anticipate even to the extent of knowing what the very next inspiration or line is going to be, or where it is going to take you. A soliloquy should be a journey into the unknown.

Following, is a detailed breakdown of the 'journey of enlightenment' undertaken by Viola (dressed as a young man) in the course of her 'ring soliloquy'.

Steps, flights and landings in Viola's soliloquy

Step One: The 'energy from without' which gives rise to the first step of Viola's speech ('*I left no ring with her…* ') is Malvolio's action of 'returning' a ring which the young woman has never seen before.

Step Two: When Viola has put out this already known fact to the universe, the universe responds by triggering in her the need to know what Olivia's doing such a thing could possibly mean. And this results in her putting out the question: '*what means this lady?*'

Step Three: Having received this question into itself, the universe now responds by triggering in Viola the conception that Olivia might possibly have been beguiled by her, as a young man, i.e. by her 'outside' appearance, by her disguise. In response to this extraordinary possibility being conceived within her, Viola is impelled to put out her order: '*Fortune forbid my outside hath not charmed her!*'

Step Four: In response to her sending out her order, '*Fortune forbid my outside hath not charmed her…* ', the universe comes back to trigger in Viola a new way of understanding another already known fact; namely, an aspect of Olivia's behaviour: an aspect that Viola was aware of at the time, but which, up until this moment, she has not attached any particular significance to. She is moved to put out the explanation: '*She made good view of me…* '

Step Five: And having laid out that explanation, the space is created in her for a more refined, and even more significant, version of how Olivia behaved to come into her:

> *…indeed so much,*
> *That, sure, methought her eyes had lost her tongue,*
> *For she did speak in starts distractedly…*

Step Six: And now having laid out these 'already known facts', and viewed them in this startling new light, Viola is inspired to reach what is, at this point, a *fairly* convinced conclusion vis-à-vis the perplexing 'returning of the ring':

> '*She loves me sure…* '

Applying the notion of Viola's speech being a stairway, one should probably regard this as a first 'landing'; or perhaps as a 'mini-landing'. She could not have reached this fairly certain realisation without having put out all the questions and explanations etc. which went before.

More experienced actors may *feel*, and play, most of these types of exchanges in any soliloquy they approach, purely from instinct; without having painstakingly to pick through the text. But it is important *consciously* to know that these exchanges are the life-breath of a soliloquy and that they must be played. Even the most experienced performer can, with profit, fine-comb a speech for any exchanges they may be in danger of gliding over; more often than not, a number are unearthed by the process. With the repeated practice of fine-combing in this way, any actor will, indeed, find him- or herself sensing moments of conception, more and more, by instinct.

Before identifying Viola's next steps, I would like to look more closely at some important aspects of the steps identified so far.

The particular moment of conception between Step Four and Five offers itself as a good example of those which can easily be, and often are, overlooked.

Step 4: *She made good view of me* **Step 5:** *indeed so much*
That, sure, methought her eyes had lost her tongue,
For she did speak in starts distractedly.

When Viola begins the line: *'She made good view of me...'*, that is all she should have in her mind. She should not also have in her mind (should not anticipate) the follow-on thought: *'indeed so much etc.'* It should seem that she might well not have pressed any further with the first realisation (*'She made good view of me...'*); but that just as she has finished putting it out, she receives a new impulse: the inspiration to recall, with new significance, the already known fact of what, at the time, she herself had thought of Olivia's extraordinary ogling: *'...indeed so much / That, sure, methought her eyes had lost her tongue etc.'* Be on the look-out for such less obvious moments of conception, so you don't steam-roll through them.

In a similar vein, Viola's very first line, I think, is one likely to be regarded by some as representing not two steps, as I understand it, but only one:

I left no ring with her: what means this lady?

I don't believe to act the line as one step will bring the speech to ruin, but I'm sure you can see that played as two steps, there is simply more 'going on' in the line; it has more life. As a general rule, provided they are genuine and not manufactured, the more energy exchanges there are in any speech or line, the more energised and 'alive-seeming' that line or speech will be.

I have seen a Viola play that she knows *one-hundred-percent* that Olivia is in love with her, as early in the speech as when she says, *'Fortune forbid my outside hath not charmed her!'*

When this line is played in that way, then those which follow lose their purpose:

She made good view of me; indeed so much,
That, sure, methought her eyes had lost her tongue,
For she did speak in starts distractedly.
She loves me, sure...

The three lines cease to be absolutely *necessary* to bring Viola to her *nearing-certain* realisation, *'She loves me sure...'*; and so can only be played with a very generalised 'Oh, my God! Oh, my God!' type energy.

To ensure the words, *'She loves me sure...'* have their full impact, they must come as a genuine and troubling new truth to Viola; and all as a result, and *only as a result*, of the preceding sequence of steps. She only comes to this pretty convincing deduction that Olivia loves her, *right as she says it*. The line *is* the realisation.

Moving on now to look at the next steps in the speech.

When Viola says *'She loves me, sure...'* it must not be delivered with such total certainty that there isn't a little bit of need left for the next couple of steps which lead up to *'I am the man...'*:

Step 6: *She loves me, sure;* **Step 7:** *the cunning of her passion*
Invites me in this churlish messenger.

Step 8: *None of my lord's ring!* **Step 8:** *Why he sent her none;*

Step 10: FIRST PROPER LANDING *I am the man!*

It must only be as a result of laying out the 'ring-returning' evidence *again*, in steps 7, 8 and 9, that she achieves (right as she says the line, and not before) the now, not *fairly certain* realisation, but one-hundred-percent, jackpot, and *positively certain*, realisation: *'I am the man...'*

Here are the lines leading up to, what I regard as, Viola's next, and second landing. Read it over for meaning, then identify the various steps making up the flight; you may want to put a line between each of them:

I am the man! If it be so, as 'tis,
Poor lady, she were better love a dream.
Disguise, I see, thou art a wickedness,
Wherein the pregnant enemy does much.
How easy is it for the proper-false*
In women's waxen hearts to set their forms!
SECOND LANDING *Alas, our frailty is the cause, not we,*
For such as we are made of, such we be.

* handsome deceiver   ** weakness

How many steps did you decide on?

What follows is how I would talk myself through this section.

The highly disturbing conclusion that Olivia has fruitlessly fallen for her triggers in Viola a series of one-by-one realisations about life in general. The first is that *'Disguise'* is wicked: *,Disguise, I see, thou art a wickedness, / Wherein the pregnant enemy does much...'*. (It is probably better to regard *'Disguise'* here, as meaning 'the act of disguising' generally, as opposed to the disguising, male clothes Viola is wearing.) Having put out her realisation about the *'wickedness'* of her own false appearance, the next realisation conceived in Viola is 'how easily, *in general,* women can be taken in by what only appears to be real': *'How easy is it for the proper-false / In women's waxen hearts to set their forms!'* And as a result of putting out the explanation of this realisation, a further one is triggered, tendering a reason as to *why* women's hearts are so impressionable: *'Alas, our frailty is the cause, not we! / For such as we are made of, such we be.'* (A little piece of enlightenment representing Viola's second landing.)

Here is a mark-up reflecting this understanding of the steps making up this flight:

> *I am the man!* START OF SECOND FLIGHT 1: *If it be so,* 2: *as 'tis,*
> 3: *Poor lady, she were better love a dream.*
> 4: *Disguise, I see, thou art a wickedness,*
> *Wherein the pregnant enemy does much.*
> 5: *How easy is it for the proper-false*
> *In women's waxen hearts to set their forms!*
> 6: SECOND LANDING *Alas, our frailty is the cause, not we,*
> *For such as we are made of, such we be.*

Did you break it down differently? You may not wish to, but I would take, *'as 'tis',* in the first line, to be a parenthesis interrupting the main flow of Viola's explanation (albeit a relatively mannerly one): one which is unplanned, and occurs to her, only as she finishes saying, *'If it be so...'*. I grant it, therefore, its own moment of conception.

Below is the remainder of the speech. Again, read it over for meaning then, without reading on, mark up what you decide are the steps, flights and landings that it comprises:

How will this fadge?* My master loves her dearly;
And I, poor monster, fond as much on him;
And she, mistaken, seems to dote on me.
What will become of this? As I am man,
My state is desperate** for my master's love;
As I am woman, (now alas the day!)
What thriftless*** sighs shall poor Olivia breathe!
O time! thou must untangle this, not I;
It is too hard a knot for me t'untie!

*turn out   ** without hope   *** unfruitful

Following is how I would talk myself through this final section.

Viola now knows that Olivia is in love with her; and she knows that, central to this having happened, is the wickedness of her own disguising (combined with the generally impressionable nature of women). As a result of having put out all these realisations, the next thing she is inspired to do is to wonder how this intractable mess will work itself out; she is inspired to put out the question, *'How will this fadge?'* Consequent on putting this question out, the need is conceived in Viola to again lay out, to explain the facts of the situation in more detail, so that it might help her reach an answer as to how the situation, indeed, might possibly *'fadge'*:

START OF THIRD FLIGHT *1: How will this fadge?*
2: My master loves her dearly;
3: And I, poor monster, fond as much on him;
4: And she, mistaken, seems to dote on me.

And now that she has realised the knottedness of the situation with even more particular and devastating clarity than before, an *even greater* and more desperate need is conceived in her to know how it might be resolved. The question she then asks must come from a greater feeling of need, and carry a greater emotional charge than did the earlier question, *'How will this fadge?'* So, holding on to the energy built up within herself so far, and without leaking any of it, she asks:

5: What will become of this?

And having put this question out, the impulse is triggered in her to look again, but even *more deeply*, into what might be the full consequences of what has happened:

6: As I am man,
My state is desperate for my master's love;
7: As I am woman, 8: (Interjected exclamation) *now alas the day!*
(Explanation continued) *What thriftless sighs shall poor Olivia breathe!*

With these lines, Viola now understands fully, not only the facts of the situation she has helped to create; she understands now also the full and painful emotional implications for Olivia and herself. These lines I would regard as the third landing on the stairway of Viola's speech. All the lines following the second landing (*'For such as we are made of, such we be.'*) have been leading to, building up to, this new item of enlightenment.

This landing also represents the point of highest charge to which Viola has, so far, been brought within the speech. It is a moment of new dramatic potential, and one of great interest to the audience, being a moment when the play, and not only the speech, potentially could take off in a number of different directions. At this point the audience should be wondering what the character is going to do now, in response to having arrived at this place of 'new enlightenment and feeling'. And what does Viola do? It is as if she then makes a great leap from this third landing to her final landing: her conclusion as to what to do about this dreadful conundrum of a situation:

FOURTH LANDING *1: O Time! thou must untangle this, not I;*
2: It is too hard a knot for me t'untie!

Because she can see no means by which she might unscramble it herself, the action Viola takes is to hand the unravelling of the situation over to *'Time'*.

It would be tempting, to conclude that this final rhyming couplet provides an example of a character 'giving up' at the end of a speech, and so, indeed, throwing away all the charge she has accumulated, and 'doing nothing'. But Viola's handing responsibility over to *'Time'* is as much an action as is Macbeth's, when he decides, consequent on his *'If it were done…'* speech, not to follow through on the plan to murder Duncan. It is this action of Viola's that ensures that the remainder of the play's central action can take place. If she had, as a consequence of the experience of the speech, decided to remove her wicked disguise, and reveal her femininity to the world, then there wouldn't be any 'rest of Twelfth Night'; or there would be a very different one. It is the action she takes which allows her own suffering, and the play's many confusions to build exponentially. She does not resolve her situation, or free herself of tension, by handing the outcome over to *'Time'*; she remains completely 'filled up' with the consternation caused by her 'new understanding' of the hopeless triangle she has created. Her final couplet brings her to the speech's moment of highest charge; and she must make her exit with every drop of it still bottled up inside her, 'unleaked'; and go on to contain it within herself through the rest of the play; right up until the final, happy unravelling that the *'whirligig of Time'* eventually does bring in.

Here is Viola's entire speech marked up with all the possible moments of exchange (steps) that I identify; and with what I would regard as the four landings of the piece:

FIRST FLIGHT *1: I left no ring with her: 2: what means this lady?*
3: Fortune forbid my outside have not charm'd her!
4: She made good view of me; 5: indeed so much,
That, sure, methought her eyes had lost her tongue,
For she did speak in starts distractedly.
6: (Mini- or half-landing) *She loves me, sure 7. the cunning of her passion*
Invites me in this churlish messenger.
8: None of my lord's ring! 9: why, he sent her none.
10: FIRST PROPER LANDING *I am the man!* NEW FLIGHT *1: if it be*
so, 2: as 'tis,
3: Poor lady, she were better love a dream.
4: Disguise, I see, thou art a wickedness,
Wherein the pregnant enemy does much.
5: How easy is it for the proper-false
In women's waxen hearts to set their forms!
6: SECOND LANDING *Alas, our frailty is the cause, not we!*
For such as we are made of, such we be.
NEW FLIGHT *1: How will this fadge? 2: My master loves her dearly;*
3: And I, poor monster, fond as much on him;
4: And she, mistaken, seems to dote on me.
5: What will become of this? 6: THIRD LANDING *As I am man,*
My state is desperate for my master's love;
7: As I am woman, 8: (now alas the day!)
What thriftless sighs shall poor Olivia breathe!
FOURTH LANDING *1: O time! thou must untangle this, not I;*
2: It is too hard a knot for me t'untie!

Asides

An 'aside' is really a soliloquy (sometimes very short) delivered, not alone, but when another character or characters are on stage. It can be 'slipped in' between one's own lines, or those spoken by the other onstage character or characters. As with other soliloquies, it asks purposefully to be directed towards an external addressee.

Different rules for asides for different occasions

Asides can take place in different circumstances, and when it comes to acting them, there are slightly different conventions, or 'rules of the game', to be agreed with the audience. Helpfully, Shakespeare, usually makes it clear which 'game-rules' the actors are meant to be playing on any particular occasion.

For example, character A may deliver asides in reference to another onstage character who, at that moment, is unaware of character A's presence. The 'agreed game' with the audience, in such a case, is usually that the lines (the asides) that character A delivers, cannot be heard by the other onstage character.

While his uncle, Claudius, is kneeling rapt in prayer, Hamlet enters and delivers a soliloquy (or long aside), in which he considers killing Claudius:

> **Hamlet:** *Now might I do it pat, now he is praying;*
> *And now I'll do't. And so he goes to heaven;*
> *And so am I revenged...*   3:3:73

Obviously the convention here is that, even though Hamlet may be standing very close to his uncle, Claudius does not hear Hamlet's murderous musings as he prays. As to where Hamlet directs his lines: I reckon his words might quite appropriately be directed to the universe; even were he, for example, to keep his eyes on the back of the hated Claudius throughout. Or he might conceivably move between the universe and the audience. At one point, of course, he addresses himself to his own drawn sword:

> *Up, sword; and know thou a more horrid hent:**
> *When he is drunk asleep, or in his rage,*
> *Or in the incestuous pleasure of his bed;*   3:3:88

* grasp; 'know yourself grasped in circumstances when this man's death is likely to bring down on him the direst consequences'.

In the following example from *The Winter's Tale*, Old Shepherd and Clown (his son) are discussing what to do with the parcel (*'fardel'*) which contains evidence that it is they who raised King Leontes' lost daughter, Perdita. They are unaware that the rogue, Autolycus, is on stage with them, listening and commenting on what he hears. Until Autolycus addresses them directly, and no matter how loudly Autolycus chooses to deliver his lines up until then, the shepherds act as if they do not hear them:

> **Shepherd:** *Well, let us to the king: there is that in this fardel will make him scratch his beard.*

Autolycus: (Aside) *I know not what impediment this complaint may be to the flight of my master.*

Clown: *Pray heartily he be at' palace.*

Autolycus: (Aside) *Though I am not naturally honest, I am so sometimes by chance: let me pocket up my pedlar's excrement.* (Takes off his false beard) (To the Shepherd and Clown) *How now, rustics! whither are you bound?*

Shepherd: *To the palace, and it like your worship.*   *4:4:707*

Having such a robust relationship with the audience, any Autolycus will usually direct his asides straight out to the house. And the more unambiguously he does this, the more clearly the audience will understand the rules of the game that is being played, i.e. that the Shepherd and Clown cannot hear. In the know, the public will happily go along.

Macbeth tells King Duncan he will go ahead of him, to give happy warning to his wife that the king will stay that night in their castle. Before completing his exit, Macbeth (now Thane of Cawdor) delivers an aside in which he talks of the impediment to his becoming king represented by Duncan's eldest son, the Prince of Cumberland. Depending on which convention is being employed in any particular production, Macbeth's aside will be delivered either to the universe or to the audience;

Macbeth: … (to the King) *I'll be myself the harbinger, and make joyful*
The hearing of my wife with your approach;
So humbly take my leave.

Duncan: *My worthy Cawdor!*

Macbeth: (Aside) *The Prince of Cumberland! That is a step*
On which I must fall down, or else o'erleap,
For in my way it lies. Stars, hide your fires;
Let not light see my black and deep desires etc.   Exit   *1:4:45*

In this instance, the game played is that, as Macbeth speaks his lines, not only do the other characters not hear what he says, they are completely unaware that he has even stopped before exiting to have this aside – and begin an independent conversation (silent to the audience) on the subject of Macbeth's valour. As Macbeth finishes his aside and does exit, it is as if the volume then is turned up for the audience, on the king's ongoing conversation with the others:

Duncan: *True, worthy Banquo: he is full so valiant,*
And in his commendations I am fed…   *1:4:54*

The first two-and-a-half lines of Macbeth's aside (up until he addresses the 'Stars') you will, on occasion, see directed to the audience. I would prefer they constituted an exchange with the universe. If Macbeth is seeingly connected out to the universe, then the public will feel free of any responsibility towards him. They are left free to 'see' and 'look into' him, as he lays out for himself these now highly charged facts; just as they are left free of any responsibility towards him as they witness him address the remainder of his aside to the 'Stars'.

I remember seeing a production of *Macbeth* where the actor playing Macbeth stage-whispered this aside very, very softly, acting as if he was afraid the other characters on stage might hear him. To do 'ssssh acting' in such a case is an attempt to make this 'side-talking' device 'believable' to an audience, in a naturalistic way; this approach will have the opposite effect. If an audience is asked to interpret asides by the conventions of naturalism, then the asides will actually seem less real. An audience will think, for example, 'are Duncan and Banquo blind and deaf that they can't see Macbeth loudly whispering to himself over there?' The convention to be observed in such instances, and which the audience will accept, is that (within reason) no matter how loudly Macbeth speaks, the other characters need not seem to hear him, or acknowledge his continued presence on stage. Duncan and the other lords will be required to do 'continuing to have a conversation whilst totally unaware of Macbeth soliloquising quite near them' type acting; either in a 'relaxed freeze', or whilst remaining unobtrusively 'alive'.

A few scenes earlier, just after he has learned that the first of the witches' prophesies has come true (he is, indeed, now Thane of Cawdor), Macbeth has a longish aside while Banquo and other characters are present. He attempts to get a handle on the nature and implications of the witches' 'supernatural' predictions:

Macbeth: *This supernatural soliciting*
Cannot be ill; cannot be good
If ill, why hath it given me earnest of success,
Commencing in a truth? I am Thane of Cawdor…   1:3:130

In this instance, the rules are slightly different again. Here, what the public are asked to accept is that Banquo and the others can *see* Macbeth, but that they perceive him not as talking aloud (as he is, and needs to do, for the audience), but as being lost in his own thoughts:

Banquo: *Look, how our partner's rapt.*   1:3:143

This cannot be made to seem, nor should one try to make it seem, believable and 'real', by naturalistic standards.

Who or what is the Macbeth's addressee in this instance? For me, again, the universe, rather than the house (even if this is in 'Open' style); again so the audience will feel free to 'see' and 'look into' him, and witness the journey he takes in the aside.

At the top of a scene in *Twelfth Night*, Olivia enters with Maria and immediately has a three-and-half-line aside in which she wonders how best to receive her beloved Cesario (Viola disguised as a young man). It might be said to belong, not to the 'inaudible to others on stage' class of aside, but to a class that might be termed the '*potentially* audible' class. Olivia is concerned that she is perhaps talking so loudly that her speech may be overheard by Maria, and perhaps other members of her household in neighbouring rooms:

Olivia: *I have sent for him, he says he'll come:*
How shall I feast him? What bestow of him?
For Youth is bought more oft than begg'd or borrow'd.
I speak too loud.   3:4:1

Olivia's addressee? It could be the universe; but the audience might more appreciate Olivia's endearing fear of bungling her interview with Caesario, if she addresses them directly.

Asides in ongoing exchanges

Asides can occur in the course of an ongoing exchange between two or more characters.

While Rosalind, in *As You Like It*, reprimands Phebe for scorning the advances of a love-sick Silvius, Phebe (thinking the disguised Rosalind is a pretty young man) starts to make eyes at her. Rosalind observes this in an aside (highlighted in bold):

Rosalind: ... *Why do you look on me?*
I see no more in you than in the ordinary
Of nature's sale-work. * **Od's my little life!**
I think she means to tangle my eyes too.
No, faith, proud mistress, hope not after it...   3:5:41

* ready-made goods

When Rosalind says, '*Od's my little life! / I think she means to tangle my eyes too...*' she is no longer talking to Phebe: she is talking *about* her. She goes back to addressing her immediately after this line. This 'aside' line must be directed somewhere, and somewhere other than to Phebe.

Theoretically she could direct it to Silvius. More entertainingly, she might deliver it 'Open-style' to the house. Or if the style of the production and performance allows, even to an individual in the house. Either way could be fun and raise a laugh. Or Rosalind could address the line to the universe; and do this while, if she wants, still keeping her disbelieving eyes on Phebe. Whether played still looking at Phebe, or away from her towards the world, the line, of course, must still be delivered with a sense of a real connection outwards. What is not a good thing is for Rosalind to go 'internal', in an attempt to deliver the aside 'to herself'. If it is directed inwardly, it will be as if the character has temporarily stepped outside of the play.

As regards whether Rosalind's aside is to be regarded as 'audible' to the characters on stage: I think it could be played, either to the audience or to the universe, in a manner that suggests that what is spoken is private, and to be regarded as not to be heard by either Silvius or Phebe. But I would also regard such an aside as a potential representative of yet another, slightly different, convention to those examined so far. It can played in such a way that lets the audience know that, whoever she might be addressing, it is a matter of complete indifference to Rosalind whether she is overheard by any onstage characters or not.

In *Twelfth Night*, Sir Toby, Fabian and Sir Andrew, constantly interject their asides while Malvolio is fantasising about how he will treat Sir Toby once he has married the Lady Olivia. As with the short Olivia aside above, the trio's interjections here are 'potentially' audible. Even though the three will have to speak their asides loud enough to be audible to the entire audience (and often from a point behind Malvolio, so further from them), the game is that, if they speak *too* loudly, Malvolio might, indeed, hear their interjections. In order not to have their trickery exposed, Fabian, on a number of occasions, is made to work hard to ensure this does not happen:

Malvolio: *Seven of my people, with an obedient start, make out for him: I frown the while; and perchance wind up watch, or play with my – some rich jewel. Toby approaches; curtsies there to me –*

Sir Toby Belch: (aside) *Shall this fellow live?*

Fabian: (aside) *Though our silence be drawn from us with cars*, yet peace.*

Malvolio: *I extend my hand to him thus, quenching my familiar smile with an austere regard of control, –*

Sir Toby Belch: (aside) *And does not Toby take you a blow o' the lips then?*

Malvolio: *Saying, 'Cousin Toby, my fortunes having cast me on your niece, give me this prerogative of speech...'*

Sir Toby Belch: (aside) *What, what?*

Malvolio: *'You must amend your drunkenness.'*

Sir Toby Belch: (aside) *Out, scab!*

Fabian: (aside) *Nay, patience, or we break the sinews of** our plot!*

2:5:58

* chariots   ** destroy

In a farcical scene such as this, directors and actors will usually want to have some fun with the convention that Malvolio might possibly hear, and, on occasion, have him become aware that 'something is going on' behind him; particularly when Toby is driven to heights of outrage at one of Malvolio's more over-blown imaginings. Any time Malvolio turns to investigate, of course, the trio will, just in time, manage to find some means to conceal their presence.

SOLILOQUIES – Key points
– Overall thought: Approach a soliloquy, first and foremost, as a practical and active journey towards clarification and enlightenment, not as an exploration, or expression, of feeling.

MAIN QUESTIONS TO BE ASKED WHEN ACTING A SOLILOQUY
General question
Q. To whom or what is this soliloquy addressed? (Bear in mind that there may be a number of different addressees in the course of the speech: the audience, the universe, or a non-personal addressee such as an object or personification.)
Questions about the beginning of a soliloquy
Q. To what event is this speech a reaction?
Q. What feelings are stimulated, or re-enforced, in the character by this triggering event?
Q. What is the need – created in response to these feelings – which impels the character to launch into the speech? What does the character hope to achieve by working through this soliloquy? What is the overall and single objective of the speech?

Questions about the conclusion of a soliloquy

Q. What new **understanding** does the character come to, as a result of completing the soliloquy?

Q. What is the new **feeling** the character shifts into, as a result of completing the soliloquy?

Q. What will the character **do**, as a result of this new understanding and new feeling?

Questions about the 'body' of a soliloquy

Q. What, in the course of the speech, are the individual steps the character takes to bring him or her from their reaction to the 'triggering-event', through to the new feeling and understanding arrived at by the end of the speech?

Steps

—Every soliloquy moves forward in a sequence of steps.

—Each step will be an explanation, question or order.

— Identify these and be sure to play them as such.

—Be aware that every explanation, question or order must be understood to be, and **experienced as**, a reaction to energy, to inspiration, entering from without.

—Know to whom or to what, in the outside world, each explanation, question or order is addressed.

—Experience each as coming from a place of higher charge than the one previous; each must build on the experience of the one before; is only possible because of it.

OTHER GENERAL CONSIDERATIONS

Open separate channel of connection for each addressee:

Do not 'fuse' different addressees: separate out each individual addressee, and open a different connection for each. N.B. Don't drop or disconnect the eyes while transferring from one addressee to another.

Landings

— Check if there are any landings (subsidiary enlightenments) in the course of the speech.

— Be sure to feel a sense of arrival, indeed of 'landing', on these subsidiary enlightenments.

— And remember that every landing is not just a point of arrival, it is also the launch-pad from which to kick off up to the next or final landing.

Inspiration and 'moments of conception'
- All inspiration comes from without.
- Identify where every 'exchange' or 'moment of conception' takes place.
- The lines delivered should represent only fifty-percent of the actor's and the audience's experience of a speech; the energy that is taken in, and which inspires each question, order etc., represents the other fifty-percent.

Laying out of facts

The laying-out of already-known facts is always done with purpose; usually as a means of 'getting a handle on' some difficulty situation.

Realising

Explaining already-known facts may also represent the **realisation** of the new significance of such facts. Realisations are to be explained 'on the line', right as they are occurring. The explanation is the realization.

No internalising

Apart from occasions when a character is literally addressing his or her 'whole self' (often by name), it is never useful to conceive, or to suggest, that in a soliloquy, the characters are talking to themselves. Even when part of your awareness is connected to one's 'whole self', or to an aspect of oneself (such as one's thoughts, or a body part), the **lines themselves**, must still always be outwardly directed; never inwardly, back into one's own insides or mind.

Eyes always connected out

The eyes too must **always** be outwardly connected to one's environment, be that in the form of the audience, a non-personal addressee, or the universe; otherwise you will become opaque.

Don't anticipate

When launching into a soliloquy, a character must never know in advance to what enlightenments, or feelings, the experience of the soliloquy will bring them; either by its end, or at any point along the way.

Speech must have cumulative effect

A speech must produce a continuing cumulative charge of feeling in the character.

No leaking!

— You need to proceed from any one step in a soliloquy to the next, with all of the charge accumulated so far, still packed, 'unleaked', inside you.

— And you must keep the higher charge reached at the **conclusion** of the speech contained inside you; and keep it contained as you move into whatever action in the play you next become involved in. If you exit at the end of a speech, continue to contain the energy you have built up, and take it off with you without leaking a drop.

Asides

An 'aside' is a (sometimes very short) soliloquy delivered when another character or characters are on stage. They are often slipped in between lines you are addressing to said character or characters; or between lines which they are speaking, either to you, or to another.

— As with other soliloquies, asides mustn't 'float' like vapour somewhere in the air: they must be purposefully directed towards an external other, such as the audience, the universe, or a non-personal addressee.

— Asides can take place in different circumstances, and when it comes to acting them, there are slightly different rules, or conventions, to be agreed with the audience. These are primarily to do with whether the other characters might potentially hear the aside, or whether they are to be regarded categorically as **not** being able to hear. Shakespeare usually makes it quite clear which is which.

CHAPTER EIGHTEEN

CONNECTING THE EYES OUTWARDS
in speeches delivered to an onstage character or characters

Secondary addressees

In many 'regular' Shakespeare speeches, i.e. speeches directed to another character, you will frequently find addressees other than the character (or characters) towards whom the speeches are primarily directed. These I refer to as 'secondary addressees'.

The principles for directing lines to 'secondary' addressees in regular speeches are exactly the same as those for addressing different addressees in soliloquies. *(See 'Switching addressees': page 218.)*

In the course of one of his speeches directed primarily to Brutus, in *Julius Caesar*, Cassius disgustedly addresses, *'Age'* (the age he is living in), and *'Rome'*.

> **Cassius:**   *... Age, thou are shamed!*
> *Rome, thou hast lost the breed of noble blood.*   1:2:149

When Cassius speaks to *'Age'* his eyes should disconnect from Brutus and unambiguously look outwards, look deep into the sense of the shameful age which is everywhere around him. When he changes addressee and directs his words to *'Rome'*, he needs to open a new channel of connection with *'Rome'*, then speak to it. As with soliloquies, his eyes may shift from one external focus to another, as he switches addressee; or they could remain on one point 'out there' – provided he feels within himself, the disengagement from one, and the re-connection to the other. Or Cassius could continually move his eyes round and about himself while addressing both *'Age'* and *'Rome'* – as if to connect to, and take in, the totality of both.

Connecting the eyes to the universe in regular speeches

There are speeches in Shakespeare which are addressed entirely to a *single* addressee, but where, for certain sections of the speech, it might be more effective to connect the eyes, not to the character addressed, but to the universe. *(See 'Non-personal addresses – The universe': page 224.)*

When directly addressing another onstage character (or characters), one will, for the most part, direct one's gaze at him, her or them. But, for some of the speech, the actor could also decide to have his back turned to the character addressed, and even also to the audience. In such an instance, however, the eyes must *still* be connected actively, alertly, even hungrily, to something, or somewhere, in the outward environment: to the universe.

I sometimes ask students arbitrarily to connect the eyes out and away from the character addressed as they deliver a speech, simply to allow them the opportunity to claim the freedom to do this, and to become confident in doing it (at first it can feel uncomfortable and unnatural). Once they are comfortable, and commit to playing this way, the increase in the effectiveness and availability of the speech can be enormous.

One might think, 'What does it matter if my eyes are connected out, if neither the audience, nor the person addressed, can see them?' But I can assure you both will sense something missing: an 'aliveness' will be lacking. Keeping one's eye truly open to, and connected to, the environment keeps some other essential part of one's being open with it.

However, even though one is not directly looking at them, the *intention* of the utterance must still actively be connected to, and directed towards, the character or characters addressed. If as you speak, you are not maintaining the same intention to communicate with the addressee, as you would when looking straight at them, then the audience will sense this too. They will know if you have 'gone back into yourself', and their attention will become thinner, or drift away.

Drama, as human life, relies on an ongoing, and unbroken, circulation of energy between the outward environment and the person. In 'going into himself' the actor is instead attempting to circulate energy within his own being. Such 'inner-circulating' of one's own energy is non-creative; it tends towards victimhood; it tends ultimately towards atrophy and death.

I would thoroughly recommend completing these final, two short exercises, as it will offer you a taste of how much 'connecting the eyes out' can nourish regular speeches, and make them more available to the audience. It will also help you to feel comfortable 'connecting out' in the course of such speeches. Once you have gained a little confidence with this way of playing, the most effective occasions on which to use it will begin to occur to you quite naturally.

Connecting the eyes out 1 – Desdemona
Read these Desdemona lines from *Othello*:

Desdemona: ... *Oh, good Iago,*
What shall I do to win my Lord again?
Good friend, go to him...   4:2:150

Look straight at your Iago, or your imagined Iago, until you really know you are connected to him, and that you are truly *seeing* the man, fully sensing his presence. Then, while keeping him sharply in focus, directly address your question and order to him at least a few times – on each occasion consolidating your sense of connection.

When you have truly seen him and, honestly feel you are communicating with him, move some distance from Iago and turn your back on him. Look through a real or imaginary window, and through it see Othello storming across a large courtyard, roaring angrily at a group of his soldiers. As you say the lines again, keep your eyes connected to Othello as he storms about; but *at the same time*, remain just as strongly committed to your objective of getting through to Iago, as you were when you were looking directly at him. Act the lines a few times until you have a solid sense of how you can still be in full connection and communication with another character, without necessarily having your gaze connected to them:

     ... *Oh, good Iago,*
What shall I do to win my Lord again?
Good friend, go to him...

Connecting the eyes out 2 – Jaques

In *As You Like It*, the Duke (exiled in the Forest of Arden) has just witnessed the desperate plight of the starving Orlando. To the assembled lords he observes that Orlando's situation reminds them there are always those in the world whose suffering is worse than their own:

Duke: *Thou seest we are not all alone unhappy:*
This wide and universal theatre
Presents more woeful pageants than the scene
Wherein we play in.   2:7:136

And Jaques responds:

Jaques: ... *All the world's a stage,*
And all the men and women merely players:
They have their exits and their entrances;
And one man in his time plays many parts,
His acts being seven ages. At first the infant,
Mewling and puking in the nurse's arms.

Then, the whining school-boy with his satchel
And shining morning face, creeping like a snail
Unwillingly to school...   2:7:139

To begin with, say these opening lines of Jaques' speech whilst looking directly at the Duke; or fully imagining that you are looking at him. Do not remove your eyes from him, and (I needn't say it) explain yourself to him. Make the entire speech, not as some will make it, a soliloquy or 'set-piece', as if for a speech and drama competition. Make it what it is: an extended explanation, spoken in direct response to an observation by the Duke, and with the objective of enlightening him about the world. With the eyes so connected, you will sense that the speech has a specific and purposeful anchor; it is relieved of the potential 'speech and drama competition' trap.

If you don't know these lines by heart, you will need to lower then raise your eyes from the page from time to time. That is fine so long as, every time you raise your eyes, you don't continue the speech until you have freshly re-opened, and *felt* again, that living line of connection with your addressee. Allow space for the connection to the Duke to re-establish before continuing.

Having delivered the lines directly to the Duke, I want you to act them now in a different way. Deliver the first two lines with your eyes attached to him, exactly as before; then when you have completed them, detach the eyes from the Duke and, before you continue the speech, connect them outwards to the universe. You may want to gaze with an open focus through the trees of the Forest of Arden, deep into the imagined horizon, (not necessarily, but probably most effectively imagined as being somewhere out over the audience). Or your eyes may wish to focus on the fall of light on a far-distant tree, or a distant ploughman homeward wending his weary way (all aspects of the universe). As always, be sure you are not simply pointing your head in a particular direction with your eyes de-focussed, and your awareness turned inward. You need really *to see*; and the *awareness* of what you are seeing as you speak should not waver.

And to avoid any confusion: when I suggest that you may wish to focus on something specific in the surrounding universe, such as a particular tree or haystack (as opposed to looking out into the universe with an open-focus), I am not suggesting that you then should begin directing your words to that object. You will indeed be directing your words 'out', but you will be directing them out, still by way of communicating with your addressee (in Jaques' case, the Duke). For as long as you keep your gaze directed out to the universe (to a particular object, or objects, within it, or with an open focus) you must, at the same time, maintain the strength of the connection to your addressee(s), and the strength of your intention to get your points across to him, them or her.

The eyes do not have to remain trained on the same single point for the duration of the whole passage – although they may if it feels appropriate. They can move from one point to any other (within three hundred and sixty degrees, if you like) – so long as they *remain* unbrokenly connected out, even as they travel from one point to another. *(See 'Switching addressees': page 218.)*

The reason a character might connect out to the universe during a speech directed to another character is the same reason that, in real life, we sometimes take our eyes away from the person addressed, and connect them to the environment: it can allow us to be more finely receptive to the sequence of inspirations from without which is fuelling the questions, explanations etc. that we want to get across to the person we are talking to.

Delivering the third, and remainder, of Jaques' lines connected visually out in this way, you will feel that the inspirations needed to feed each new step (each explanation you want to get through to the Duke) can more readily flow into you. Try this now:

EYES WITH THE DUKE **Step 1:** ... *All the world's a stage,*
And all the men and women merely players:
TRANSFER EYES TO UNIVERSE **Step 2:** *They have their exits and their entrances;*
And one man in his time plays many parts,
His acts being seven ages. **3:** *At first the infant,*
Mewling and puking in the nurse's arms.
4: *Then, the whining school-boy with his satchel*
And shining morning face, creeping like a snail
Unwillingly to school...

CONNECTING THE EYES OUTWARDS
in speeches delivered to an onstage character or characters –
Key points

The principles for directing lines to 'secondary' addressees within regular speeches are exactly the same as those for addressing 'non-personal' addressees in soliloquies. **(See 'Addressing non-personal addressees: Objects': page 211)**

- There are speeches in Shakespeare which are addressed entirely to a single addressee, but where, for certain sections of the speech, it will be effective to disconnect the eyes from the addressee, and connect them 'seeingly' to the universe – focusing on a particular thing, or things within it (possibly moving from thing to thing), or with an open focus into the universe 'as a whole'. **(See 'Addressing non-personal addressees: The universe': page 224.)**

- Even though one is not directly looking at him, them or her, the **intention** of the utterance must still actively be connected to, and directed towards, the character or characters addressed.

- The reason we may connect out to the universe during a speech directed to another character, is that it can allow us to be more finely receptive to the inspirations from without which are fuelling the explanations, questions, etc. that we want to get across.

LAST WORDS

I said in the introduction that most of what I would speak about in this book, I had learnt through my work with students and actors over the years. In the course of the slow, difficult, but ultimately rewarding, process of then organising this knowledge into the subsequent chapters and sub-sections etc., I have, however, learnt a great deal more. I have become more fully convinced about certain ideas, have refined or rejected others, and have come to realise that there are areas about which I remain undecided, and which I need to look into more deeply. I sincerely hope that by reading the book, you, the reader, have learned something with me. I hope you have come to know that acting Shakespeare's language indeed benefits from the gaining and applying of a certain amount of know-how, but that this know-how is, by no means, atomic physics; that it is easily learnable by anyone. I hope that you now understand that there are certain *mechanical* aspects to playing Shakespeare's language, and that the specific and practical *purposes* of the language are what you must 'act'; that you have grasped that when you do align your efforts with these mechanical aspects, and play the practical purposes which motivate the words, you create the structure, the solid conduit, through which the life and soul encrypted in the language can be revealed to, and shared with, the audience.

And a quick word to remind you that there are very few, if any, of the principles explored here which cannot be applied to more 'naturalistic' texts, to all acting. Once you have provided yourself with a felt sense of these principles in the context of Shakespeare's language, I invite you to bear them in mind when approaching texts apart from Shakespeare, and know that you will find it productive to apply them.

'Issue' productions

Before signing off, I would like to say a few words about one other matter which did not find a natural place in any preceding section. This is a particular circumstance which often results in the language of a classic play (Shakespearean, Greek, Jacobean etc.) being less than well-served.

As well as encountering the many 'opinion plays' to which I refer in an earlier chapter *(see page 229)*, one regularly comes across stagings of classic plays which I would regard as 'opinion *productions*'. These are 'interpretations' which can neuter the truth of a play by subjugating it to some opinion, or ideology, of the director; where a play is used as a wall on which to scratch slogans. In such cases, the staging often represents no more than a labour-intensive, often expensive, form of foot-stamping about some contemporary (and, in the great scheme of things, usually temporary) 'issue'. Staging the play becomes an act of attempted control ('I want to make you think this about that'); as opposed to its being an act of service; an act where one's intention is to honour the text in such a way as to deepen the felt contact between the audience and their own souls; between the audience and their universe. 'Issue' productions direct the spectators to disapprove of, or even hate, something which the director disapproves of, or hates; this is divisive and less than wholly human. In the face of such enterprises, it can feel as if one is being told, 'No need to attend to the specifics of the play's language; more important is that you notice all the ways I, the director, have found to *use* the play, in order to impose judgement on certain sections of humanity. Please leave the theatre feeling righteous and condemning these people.' Not a good thing.

I believe the challenge of artists and interpreters is to delve deep into our own consciousness, deep enough to reach a level beneath our individual 'beliefs and convictions'; 'beliefs and convictions' we may cling to so dearly as to imagine they define 'who we are'; 'beliefs and convictions' which, on the surface, may convince as being 'only right and just', but which ultimately serve to separate us from an awareness of what unites us as humans. Our endeavour must be to tap down into the clear waters of the more *universal* truths which run somewhere deep in all of us, which flow somewhere below the personal ranklings and dysfunctions which we all have, and which can so blind us to the greater realities of existence; realities which while being physically invisible, can be viscerally felt, and which are so much more meaningful, unifying, and nourishing to our souls than our 'beliefs and convictions'.

Shakespeare was an artist who, with apparent effortlessness, tapped deeply into these rich waters; over and over again. He does not use his writing to wag the finger from a position of superiority to his characters or his audience. Nor need we use his words to do this. To make manifest to an audience the humanising truths on which Shakespeare's plays draw, the task of the actor is to identify and serve, selflessly, and moment to moment, the structures and purposes of his language.

My final wish is that what I have striven to share with you in these pages may, in some way, assist you towards that end.

INDEX OF EXERCISES

EXPLANATIONS, QUESTIONS AND ORDERS

Playing explanations, questions and orders 1 – Romeo, Beatrice 7
Playing rhetorical questions 1 – Rosalind 9
Playing rhetorical questions 2 – Paulina 10
Playing explanations, questions and orders 2 – Helena, Antony 11
Playing explanations within orders – Antony, Lady Anne 13
Playing explanations within questions – Edmund 16

OPPOSITIONS

'Exaggerate then ease off' exercise – Rosalind et al. 19
Playing shared oppositions – Helena and Hermia 20
Playing multiple oppositions within speeches – Richard III 21

IMAGERY AND POETIC LANGUAGE

Play the concrete surface of the image – Romeo 24
'Addressing a child' exercise – Duchess of Gloucester 25
Playing imagistic language – Oberon, Hamlet 26
Playing abstract, or 'idea', images – Portia 28

ALLITERATION, ASSONANCE AND ONOMATOPOEIA

Playing assonance and alliteration – Benedick 31
Playing assonance, alliteration and onomatopoeia – Edward IV 32
Connecting to the feeling in alliteration – Paulina 35

ACTING SHAKESPEARE'S VERSE – Part 1

Introductory scanning practice – Puck, Lady Macbeth, Richard III 65
Identifying syllables to be 'restored' as strong – Antonio, Macbeth, Brutus 67
Restoring dropped beats in multi-syllable words – King, Macbeth 69
Flashing the strong beats 71

ACTING SHAKESPEARE'S VERSE – Part 2

Irregularities	74
Comparing alternative scannings 1 – Helena	81
Comparing alternative scannings 2 – Hamlet	84

ACTING SHAKESPEARE'S VERSE – Part 3

Line-endings and beginnings	88
Playing line-endings and beginnings – Romeo, Antipholus	90
Playing pivotal sense-breaks – Duchess of Gloucester et al.	92
Swing-boating – Phebe	96
Playing off-centre sense-breaks – Cassius, Orsino	97
Pivotal breaks: Interjecting questions – Hamlet	98
Playing caesurae: Interjecting thought bubbles – Macbeth	104
Enjambements and caesurae embodying inner conflict – Shylock	106
Self-interruptions – Leontes	107

RHYME

Playing rhyme 1 – Helena and Hermia	116

PRONUNCIATION

Pronouncing the 'e' in past tense words – Richard III et al.	125
Pronouncing words with apostrophes – Lady Macbeth et al.	126

PLAYING SENSE-BREAKS IN PROSE and PLAYING PARENTHESES

Swing-boating; clapping and stamping – Hamlet	131
Experiencing the emptiness – Shylock	133
Playing the spine of the sentence – Antony and Calpurnia	135
Playing multiple parentheses – Titania	136

ADJECTIVES AND ADVERBS

Omitting the adjectives etc. – Henry V et al.	142

SHORT LINES

Playing shared lines – Juliet et al.	148

BREATHING THE VERSE

Practice with breathing the verse 1 – Antipholus	155
Practice with breathing the verse 2 – Prince Hal	157
Breathing irregular lines 1 – Lady Macbeth et al.	160
Breathing irregular lines 2 – Edmund	162
Breathing irregular lines 3 – Hamlet	164

ACTING SHAKESPEARE'S PROSE

Identifying poetic devices in prose – Hamlet   174
Speaking out the structural units – Hamlet   182
Playing stanzas, headlines, see-saws etc. – Benedick   184

SOLO SPEECHES

Addressing non-personal addressees:
Objects – Antony, Helena, Lear   211
Absent characters – Lady Macbeth   214
Gods and spirits – Edmund, Lady Macbeth   216
Switching non-personal addressees – Lady Macbeth   218
Addressing non-personal addressees:
Internal – Claudius   220
The 'whole self' – Angelo   222
The universe – Malvolio and Angelo   224
Alternating audience and universe as addressee – Viola   226
Receiving from the universe 1 – Angelo   232
Receiving from the universe 2 – Macbeth   234
Receiving from the universe 3 – Malvolio   236

CONNECTING THE EYES OUTWARDS

in speeches delivered to an onstage character or characters

Connecting the eyes out 1 – Desdemona   259
Connecting the eyes out 2 – Jaques   260

ACKNOWLEDGEMENTS

My gratitude to Dave Carr, Emer Casey, Colm Hefferon and Rosemary O'Loughlin who painstakingly read through the manuscript, providing numerous detailed and insightful comments. And many thanks to my editor, Melina Theocharidou, for her encouragement and care.

Andy Hinds

DIRECTING

For ten years Artistic Director of Classic Stage Ireland. Directed: Abbey, Gate, Druid, Glyndebourne, Wexford Opera, Scottish Opera, King's Head, Bristol Old Vic. Productions include: *The Bacchae, Macbeth, As You Like It, The Winter's Tale, Fidelio, La Cenerentola, Mother Courage, The Revenger's Tragedy, All's Well That Ends Well, Twelfth Night, Julius Caesar, Midsummer Night's Dream, As You Like It, Iphigenia in Aulis, Agamemnon, Oedipus the King.*

TEACHING

Acting: RADA, Gaiety School of Acting, Trinity College, Shakespeare's Globe, Classic Stage Ireland Acting Studio. **Directing:** National Theatre of Canada. **Academic:** University College Dublin (lectured on Masters Degree in European Theatre).

PLAYS

October Song, Sea Lavender (both Carysfort Press), *Morning and Afternoon* (Oberon Books), *Crystal's House, Bloodties* and *First of the Day* for RTE Radio.

ACTING

Hinds made his debut as an actor in his own play, *Morning and Afternoon* at Project Arts Centre, Dublin, and as part of the Edinburgh Fringe Festival in 2013 ('A triumph' The Scotsman).

BOOKS

Acting Shakespeare's Language, Oberon Books (2015)

The Fall of the House of Atreus, verse translations of Euripides' *Iphigenia in Aulis* and Aeschylus' *Oresteia* trilogy in one volume, Oberon Books (2015)

COACHING, COURSES, WORKSHOPS AND MASTERCLASSES

The author conducts individual coaching sessions (in person or online), group workshops, and masterclasses.

Contact: ahnomdeplume@gmail.com